Reinventing Critical Pedagogy

Reinventing Critical Pedagogy

Edited by
César Augusto Rossatto,
Ricky Lee Allen, and Marc Pruyn

ROWMAN & LITTLEFIELD PUBLISHERS, INC.
Lanham • Boulder • New York • Toronto • Plymouth, UK

ROWMAN & LITTLEFIELD PUBLISHERS, INC.

Published in the United States of America
by Rowman & Littlefield Publishers, Inc.
A wholly owned subsidiary of The Rowman & Littlefield Publishing Group, Inc.
4501 Forbes Boulevard, Suite 200, Lanham, Maryland 20706
www.rowmanlittlefield.com

Estover Road
Plymouth PL6 7PY
United Kingdom

British Library Cataloguing in Publication Information Available

Library of Congress Cataloging-in-Publication Data

Reinventing critical pedagogy : widening the circle of anti-oppression
    education / edited by César Augusto Rossatto, Ricky Lee Allen,
    and Marc Pruyn.
        p. cm.
    Includes bibliographical references and index.
    ISBN-13: 978-0-7425-3887-0 (cloth : alk. paper)
    ISBN-10: 0-7425-3887-7 (cloth : alk. paper)
    ISBN-13: 978-0-7425-3888-7 (pbk. : alk. paper)
    ISBN-10: 0-7425-3888-5 (pbk. : alk. paper)
    1. Critical pedagogy.   I. Rossatto, César Augusto, 1961–   .
    II. Allen, Ricky Lee, 1963–   . III. Pruyn, Marc.
    LC196.R44 2006
    370.115—dc22   2006014827

Printed in the United States of America

♾™ The paper used in this publication meets the minimum requirements of
American National Standard for Information Sciences—Permanence of Paper
for Printed Library Materials, ANSI/NISO Z39.48-1992.

César Augusto Rossatto would like to dedicate this book to all of the conference coorganizers who worked tirelessly to create a space for true intellectual exchange and human interaction. Among them were Maria Teresa Montero Mendoza, Laura Patricia Gonzalez Campos, Dora Maria Aguilar Saldivar, Kathy Staudt, Ken Ducre, Marc Pruyn, Gerardo Ochoa Meza, John Marquez, Elaine Hampton, Susan Ripperberger, Ricky Lee Allen, Nancy Tafoya, and the staff at the University of Texas at El Paso (UTEP) University Relations Office. He would also like to thank the staff at the UTEP College of Education for their assistance with the index. A special thank you goes to all of the participants, who made the event a profound expression of our collective commitment to education, students, social justice, and social transformation.

Ricky Lee Allen would like to dedicate this book to all of those critical educators, scholars, and activists who work in harsh economic or psychosocial conditions. Their experiences remind us that social justice is, among other things, a struggle for wholeness, healthy forms of interconnectedness, and humanization.

Marc Pruyn would like to dedicate this book to Jessica Benton, Silvia Chávez Baray, Jeannie Elliott, Jeannie Gonsier-Gerden, Kaitlin Langston, Amy M. Lam, Hannah Michels Tellez, Tallulah Moore, Jacquie Valencia, and especially Debbie Michels, women who continually motivate him as impassioned and determined, organic intellectuals driven to struggle for social justice through critical activism and creativity.

Contents

Introduction

Reinventing Critical Pedagogy: Widening the Circle of Anti-Oppression Education is the fruit born of the Second International Conference on Education, Labor, and Emancipation (SICELE), held in October 2004 in El Paso, Texas, and Ciudad Juárez, Mexico. The title of this book served as the conference theme. The SICELE grew out of the roots put down by the First International Conference on Education, Labor, and Emancipation held in October 2000 at Florida International University in Miami, Florida.

At the SICELE, there prevailed a genuine spirit of solidarity among an international group of educators who shared their concerns and insights about the impact of oppression on students' well-being, material realities, and dreams for the future. The participants' postconference evaluations revealed their general satisfaction with the event; some even mentioned that they sensed a feeling of love in the air. Perhaps this was the meaning that Paulo Freire was trying to convey in his writings, where a deep sense of dedication to social justice and its viability emanated from a loving spirit of praxis. Perhaps the multicultural and bilingual aspect of the gathering, rather than hindering, provided participants with a space to feel whole, to feel humanized. People were able, literally, to cross borders as the conference moved from the United States, where it was held on the first day, to Mexico for the second day of events. In this kind of humanizing spirit, a sort of radical liminal space, it felt as though it were possible, at least for a brief weekend, to move beyond the visible and invisible barriers that often divide people.

Yet, within this embrace of community, tension also existed. The conference proposed no small task, and it was by no means an achieved utopia of unity in diversity. The SICELE challenged participants to *reinvent* critical pedagogy, to push into areas where dialogue becomes difficult and a sense of unity in diversity becomes a question mark. For, in order to reinvent, one must critically reflect upon one's own praxis, as well as the praxis of the community as a whole. In particular, the SICELE set out to expand or redraw the boundaries of critical pedagogy's historical limitations of examining mainly capitalist relations and cultural hegemony in the classroom. Even though critical pedagogy has indeed addressed other forms of oppression, the objective of the SICELE was to make more central forms of critical analysis that engage white supremacy, patriarchy, and ethnocentrism, while renewing and deepening the field's more established critique of global capitalism and the exploitation of labor. This inclusive approach addresses how these multiple hegemonic systems work both separately and synergistically to establish relative power and privilege between hierarchically arranged oppressor-oppressed groups.

A traditional, or orthodox, Marxist approach, generally speaking, deemphasizes the importance of *relative* power and privilege and the structures that create it, such as white supremacy and patriarchy, opting instead for the alleged clarity of class consciousness and "classes." But, in the direction we are taking, radical agents must intervene in their relative race, gender, and class power so as to create a more cohesive counterhegemonic movement, bonded one to another in authentic, realistic, and loving ways. In other words, neither Marxism nor critical pedagogy has adequately or completely addressed the reasons why variously oppressed people have remained fractured, subject to the divide-and-conquer strategies of the agents of white supremacist, capitalist patriarchy, although the critical and "revolutionary" pedagogy of the last decade has made strides in this direction. This book is an effort toward drawing the field's attention to the relations between relatively oppressed groups as they are constructed through the realities of labor and property within larger oppressive totalities.

Therefore, *Reinventing Critical Pedagogy* humbly and boldly seeks to take critical pedagogy in new directions for a new generation. One of our goals is to provide a text that builds upon past accomplishments in critical pedagogy while it also critiques and transforms those elements that contradict the radically democratic orientation of the field. We believe that critical pedagogy needs to be a form of praxis truly welcoming of a wider representational and ideological array of those who are the oppressed and that it should do so in a way that makes the field more of a counterhegemonic force. Once again, this is no small task, one that we can only begin to address within these pages. Therefore, we selected for this book conference papers from the SICELE that either revisit established notions in the field or take on new areas of contestation.

The book is divided into three parts: "Race, Ethnicity, and Critical Pedagogy," "Theoretical Concerns," and "Applications, Extensions, and Empirical Studies." The first part, "Race, Ethnicity, and Critical Pedagogy," addresses an area that has only received cursory attention from most critical pedagogy scholars. In "The Race Problem in the Critical Pedagogy Community," Ricky Lee Allen questions why there are not more Black and Indigenous people who participate in and contribute to the critical pedagogy movement. He argues that critical pedagogy's lack of focus on white supremacy as a totalizing structure has alienated Black and Indigenous people in the United States. In "Racism without Racists: 'Killing Me Softly' with Color Blindness," Eduardo Bonilla-Silva and David Embrick show, through empirical data, how color-blind racism operates through white people's race talk. They expose the ways in which whites employ various discursive moves in an attempt to appear nonracist at the same time as they demonstrate their underlying belief in white superiority. Violet Jones's "Violence, Discourse, and Dixieland: A Critical Reflection on an Incident Involving Violence against Black Youth" examines whiteness as a position of power and privilege that terrorizes people of color and diminishes agency among border people. She critically invokes Michel Foucault's *panopticon* to show how surveillance, power, and racial oppression gave shape to an act of violence against a group of her students. In "Latino Youths at the Crossroads of Sameness and Difference: Engaging Border Theory to Create Critical Epistemologies on Border Identity," Cynthia Bejarano examines the divisions among youths of Mexican descent whose identities are located along a wide continuum of Mexicanness. Her ethnographic study suggests that problems arise when participants practice only one identity as either Mexicana/o or Chicana/o. In "Education as a State of Exception: Unraveling the Heart of the School-to-Prison Pipeline," Tyson Lewis and Elizabeth Vázquez Solórzano describe the overdetermined relationship that exists between schools, prisons, and the economy, where the *school as camp* becomes the pedagogical space of late capitalism's attack on the poor, creating the preconditions for sustaining an ever-expanding Black and Brown prison workforce.

The second part, "Theoretical Concerns," comprises chapters that critically rethink premises and concepts already established in critical pedagogy in order to shed new light on or deepen our understanding of them. In "Some Reflections on Critical Pedagogy in an Age of Global Empire," Peter McLaren works through a series of reflections to fashion a critical pedagogy aimed at the capitalist imperialism of the Bush administration. He elucidates the urgent need to move beyond distorted understandings of Marxist theory and recover its contributions in order to develop a philosophy of praxis that will serve as the engine of revolutionary critical pedagogy. Benjamin Frymer's chapter, "Youth Alienation in Everyday Life: The Promise of Critical Pedagogy," analyzes the problem of alienation and its conceptualization, while encouraging critical pedagogists to interrogate and intervene in current forms of youth objectification, passivity, and disengagement. In "Is Religion Still the Opiate of the People? Critical Pedagogy, Liberation Theology, and the Commitment to Social Transformation," César Rossatto questions whether critical pedagogy adequately examines the association between religion and schooling to see the alienation process that affects our world today, where organized religion can become the opiate (i.e., an alienating mechanism) of the people if it does not guide them to spirituality or critical consciousness. Seehwa Cho's "On Language of Possibility: Revisiting Critical Pedagogy" examines three major shifts in mainstream Anglo-American critical pedagogy: cultural politics, identity politics, and moralized individual politics. By linking these shifts to political climates and the politics of theory, she problematizes the notion of a "language of possibility" and argues that, at best, critical pedagogy will modernize rather than transform the system. The last contribution to this section is "Social Justice Requires a Revolution of Everyday Life" by E. Wayne Ross and Kevin Vinson, who argue that social justice requires resisting the factories of collective illusion, such as schools that offer students little more than alienation, spectacle, surveillance, and training for consumption, or a corporate media that offers fear and perpetual war.

The last part, "Applications, Extensions, and Empirical Studies," is an important and exciting section because these authors help to expand our definition of critical pedagogy by looking at areas that are undertheorized and underrepresented as major critical pedagogical concerns. Also, it builds upon our inclusion of empirical studies in this book, which we began in the first part. In "Mathematical Power: Exploring Critical Pedagogy in Mathematics and Statistics," Lawrence Lesser and Sally Blake discuss how critical pedagogy in mathematics can engage students in learning and nurture their spirit of critical inquiry, while empowering them to understand meaningful situations through "ethnomathematics." David Goodin's "Teaching Ecocide: Junk Science and the Myth of Premature Extinction in Environmental Science Textbooks" is a case study of how the term *premature extinction*, a recent trend in pseudoscience, has made its way into environmental textbooks, thus the classroom. In particular, he looks at how the notion of premature extinction diverts our attention away from the mass extinction of germlines currently going on around us (and because of us). "Hooters Pedagogy: Gender in Late Capitalism" by Nathalia Jaramillo is an ethnographic study of women working in one Hooters restaurant that links gender to the social relations of capitalism, specifically, at the level of production. YiShan Lea argues in "The Matrix of Freirean Pedagogy, Time, and Cultural Literacies" that there is a global literary tradition that depicts evil as the act of rendering invisible another human consciousness. In contrast, she looks at the use of Chinese fables and metaphors in a cross-cultural context as an example of how to bridge the worlds, thus the consciousnesses, of storytellers and listeners, cultural workers, and students. Finally, in "Generating Hope, Creating Change, Searching for Community: Stories of Resistance against Globalization at the U.S.-Mexico Border," Michelle Téllez testifies to how the people of Maclovio Rojas collectively challenged the "empire," putting an end to their repressive conditions and courageously creating an alternative for themselves to raise their families safely within a "globalization of resistance."

We hope that the talented authors contained in this collection provoke your thoughts as much as they did ours. Yet, humility requires us to ask ourselves, Might a true reinvention of critical pedagogy sprout from the thoughts within this text? This we don't know. But we do know that it will take a movement of committed and loving students, scholars, intellectuals, and community workers to widen the circle of anti-oppression alliances in critical pedagogy to make the field more vital and to prepare it for the struggles ahead. In the meantime, *Reinventing Critical Pedagogy* offers an opportunity for folks to read, discuss, and debate, that is, to teach one another about how to read the world more critically. Maybe, out of these dialogues, what can germinate is the desire for emancipation from the oppressive forces that fragment those who cannot afford to be fragmented.

—Ricky Lee Allen,
César Augusto Rossatto,
Marc Pruyn

I

RACE, ETHNICITY, AND CRITICAL PEDAGOGY

1

The Race Problem in the Critical Pedagogy Community

Ricky Lee Allen

In *Teaching Community*, bell hooks (2003b) argues that fear and anxiety are enemies of education as the practice of freedom. People engaged in critical dialogue often respond to their fear and anxiety with silence, defensiveness, aggressiveness, or detachment. These behaviors create the opposite of authentic dialogue, that is, inauthentic dialogue, since they prevent participants from being fully present in the moment. Inauthentic dialogue constructs a feigned notion of community where common sense is fashioned through the consensual denial of a group's complicity in oppression. Those wishing to create an authentic dialogue must understand that fear and anxiety can neither be ignored nor simply wished away. If authentic dialogue is ever to be achieved and truly create communities that are humanizing, anti-oppressive, and hopeful, then spaces must be opened for participants to share what makes them fearful and anxious in group discussions and how they behaviorally and emotionally respond to these feelings. I have tried doing this a few times in the classes that I teach and have been overwhelmed by how much fear and anxiety students say that they wrestle with when dialoging. It seems to me that my willingness to spend time exploring the role of emotions and their relationship to dialogical behaviors has made my classes warmer, yet more open and critical.

I would like to experience in my writing the same kind of freedom that I am beginning to find in the classroom. But freedom doesn't come easy. Writing this chapter on the "race problem" in critical pedagogy makes me nervous because I fear what might happen when powerful critical pedagogy figures read it. As an assistant professor soon to be going up for tenure, I understand the importance of having influential allies; being a radical in academia can be very tricky business. Also, I have learned a lot from these powerful figures. Some I

3

consider mentors and friends. It makes me anxious to think about how this chapter might upset some of them and spark a feud.

Yet, I know that I must say what I am going to say anyway. If critical pedagogy is to become a stronger movement, we in the critical pedagogy community must be willing to embrace the possibilities that can come from airing our dirty laundry. And the race problem in critical pedagogy is like that grungy pile of laundry that's been sitting in the corner of your closet for weeks. You know it's there because you can smell it and the door will barely shut. But rather than dealing with it, bringing it out into the light of day, you try not to look at it because seeing it only reminds you of how you have avoided the work that needs to be done. My race critique of the critical pedagogy community is rooted in my ten-year experience as a white male member with working-class roots. Although I understand the shortcomings of anecdotal experience, I also understand how the common sense of a community can negate the claims of its critics, even when the critics are doing little more than stating the obvious.

THE ELEPHANT IN THE ROOM: ANTI-BLACK POLITICS IN THE CRITICAL PEDAGOGY COMMUNITY

I have noticed over the years that critical pedagogy events (e.g., conferences, conference panels, courses), along with published scholarship, are primarily white and non-Black Latino affairs. But, if I go to events that focus on critical discussions of race, whether focused on critical pedagogy or not, I see much higher percentages of people of color, most notably Black and Indigenous people. So, it appears to me that Black and Indigenous people aren't attracted, in general, to what critical pedagogy has to offer as evidenced by their choice not to participate in the critical pedagogy community. After all, we vote with our feet and our pens. Some critical pedagogists simply dismiss this glaring reality, for reasons that I discuss later on, and they seem perfectly content with an audience that comprises mostly whites and non-Black Latinos. This troubles me deeply. How can the critical pedagogy community claim to be on the side of the oppressed when the members of the two most historically oppressed groups in the United States (and throughout the Americas), Blacks and Indians, don't show up to our events or have a strong, leading presence in critical pedagogy scholarship (bell hooks, aside)? The Reinventing Critical Pedagogy Conference, the conference that produced this book, didn't fare any better than most critical pedagogy events I've attended. Once again, the participants were mostly whites or non-Black Latinos. This raises some serious questions. Why don't we talk more about this racialization of the critical pedagogy community? Is critical pedagogy anti-Black and/or anti-Indigenous in its assumptions and effects?[1] From what I have witnessed and read, my answer would have to be yes. At some point, intentions have to match results. If we say we want more solidarity with Blacks and Indians, and over time we have little to show for it, then there's a problem. In fact, beyond those whom we normally think of as Blacks and Indians, I would say that critical pedagogists, consciously or not, have been somewhat dismissive of all of those groups that Eduardo Bonilla-Silva defines as the "collective Black,"[2] or those who are treated as if they were Black, which includes Filipinos, Vietnamese, Hmong, Laotians, dark-skinned Latinos, Blacks, New West Indian and African immigrants, and reservation-bound Native Americans (2003a, 278).

I have been a witness to the racist talk of white and non-Black Latino critical pedagogists. Much of it is aimed at Blacks. Of course, this isn't new to leftist circles (Bonilla-Silva 2001). Across all disciplines, white marxists[3] and their supporters have had a history of scrutinizing the contradictions of Blacks much more harshly than those of non-Blacks. For instance, there's a tradition in U.S. Marxism that sees Blacks as insufficiently anticapitalist—as if somehow whites are more critical. Are we to believe that the group made the most poor by capitalism, while making the most money for capitalists, is the least aware of capitalism's damaging effects? This is interesting in light of observations such as the following by bell hooks: "Often, African Americans are among those students that I teach from poor and working-class backgrounds who are the most vocal about issues of class" (2003a, 145). While it is true that many of the white students I teach are often vocal about class, they are usually most vocal about class when I bring up the issue of whiteness. The exception to this are those whites who are committed to a critique of capitalism and do not simply become Marxist all of a sudden in order to distance themselves from race critique; they are vocal about class all of the time. For this group, there is instead a tendency to minimize or ignore the role that white supremacy plays within white-oriented anticapitalist movements. For example, many white marxists and their allies point to the lack of unionization among the Black population as alleged evidence of their "less radical" orientation (see Bonacich 1980), even though U.S. unionism was designed for the explicit protection of working-class white status and has functioned as an institutionalized form of white supremacy (Bonilla-Silva 2001; Roediger 1999). Or, they point to videos of rappers living ghetto-fabulous lifestyles as evidence of Black people's wholesale embrace of individualism and "bling." All of this, despite the fact that Blacks are one of the few groups who have organized themselves to stand up against mass murder and extreme forms of oppression (e.g., the Haitian revolution and the civil rights movement). The same can be said of Indigenous people. It is the arrogance of many white marxists that precipitates the need for corrective statements like the following by Ward Churchill in his edited book *Marxism and Native Americans*:

> Let Marxism explain its utility to its hosts [i.e., Indigenous people]. Let it dif-
> ferentiate itself clearly from synthetic reality. And let the hosts for the first time
> take an active role in assisting in this process, denying what is false, supporting
> what is true. (1983, iix)

It's obvious to me that significant distortions about Blacks, as well as about the collective Black, still thrive. And these distortions influence not only who attends critical pedagogy events or values our cultural products but also who become the main movers and shakers of our community. If you ask those who consider themselves to be critical pedagogists to name the leaders in the field, the chances are great that most of the names will belong to whites or non-Black Latinos—bell hooks might be the one exception. The point is that Blacks aren't the primary leaders of the field; thus, they aren't the major source of intellectual and political inspiration. But this situation shouldn't surprise us. Just consider for a moment the questions not being asked in the field of critical pedagogy. I can't recall anyone in the community seriously asking, Why aren't there more Blacks, Native Americans, and dark-skinned people of color leading the field of critical pedagogy? We should also be asking, On whose terms does one become a leader? Are these terms racialized? How did it get that way? Whose interests does it serve? The current situation seems like a glaring hypocrisy given Paulo Freire's admonition (1993) that the oppressors—and I would add suboppressors—can't lead the struggle for humanization.

Yet, this isn't a contradiction when one understands the racist mythologies that permeate the logic of the field (see Allen 2004). I saw all of this play out one day at a regional meeting for critical educators. The meeting was organized to consider how to create a more unified critical pedagogy community in the major metropolitan area where I was living at the time. In the opening session, one of the participants expressed concern that there were no Blacks in attendance. The facilitator of the dialogue, a light-skinned Latino who was also the main organizer of the meeting, responded angrily by saying, "I'm not playing that numbers game!" In the discussion that followed, it was made clear that the facilitator firmly believed that if an educator or scholar were "sufficiently" critical, he or she would have been at the meeting. Given that the entire discussion was about why Blacks weren't present, the obvious implication of the facilitator's comments was that Black educators and scholars, at least in this particular city, weren't sufficiently critical, and their absence proved it. It was therefore perfectly okay with this person that the attendees were mostly whites and non-Black Latinos because they were sufficiently critical in the facilitator's eyes; their presence supposedly proved it. I was furious at this response, but I didn't say anything when it happened. And that made me angry with myself. I kicked myself for participating in a group that simply fell in line with the facilitator's anti-Black comment. Since that time, I have wondered whether the other attendees also believed that Blacks were insufficiently critical or whether they, like me, were just too afraid to speak out.

I have also been a perpetrator of anti-Black racism. Through books, conferences, classroom dialogues, and personal interactions, the hidden curriculum of critical pedagogy taught me that a person of color isn't sufficiently critical unless that person demonstrates, consciously or not, that he or she thinks of capitalism as the larger totality that encompasses race, class, and gender. Certainly, there are those who are the exceptions to this rule, but they are usually not seen as the megastars and power brokers of the field. In addition, I learned that the extent to which a person of color is accepted into the critical pedagogy community, as well as the level of visibility that person can reach, hinges upon whether he or she is willing not to talk about, or not to see, the fundamental race problem within. Who can we name who has become one of the vanguard of U.S. critical pedagogy who talks about racial issues within the U.S. critical pedagogy community? Initially, I went along with the pervasive assumption that Blacks weren't as critical of capitalism as other groups, namely Latinos, and therefore weren't sufficiently critical. This is the commonsense explanation, normative to the field, for why there are so few Blacks in the field. Though I believed at that time that race and racism were vital areas of study, I had internalized the assumption that too many Blacks overemphasize the importance of race and many more Latinos, particularly those who are lighter skinned, put race in the proper context, that is, subordinate to a critique of capitalism, or "class-dominant analysis."

I can hear my critics asking, What about hegemony? Sure, hegemony affects Black people as it does all groups (though not in the same way). Why then do so many non-Blacks believe that Blacks are the least aware of the influence of capitalism? Hegemony alone doesn't explain the low numbers of Black participation in critical pedagogy. Besides, there are plenty of educational and scholarly communities that attract a larger percentage of Blacks than critical pedagogy. Anyway, I used to be one of those non-Blacks who held this kind of anti-Black belief, and it is anti-Black in its assumption of Black intellectual and political inferiority. It is impossible to mount a challenge to white supremacy if those most affected are not at the table. But this is why it's clear to me that white supremacy is not a major focus of critical pedagogy. How could a group focused on white supremacy not be concerned with the absence of the collective Black at the table? The simple answer is that critical pedagogy is not really that concerned with white supremacy (see Allen 2004). So, there is no contradiction in the absence of Blacks.[4]

My beliefs began to change as I engaged the literature on whiteness. I began to see that white supremacy is at least the equal of capitalism (Allen 2001; Mills 1997). And, I learned to see how racism in Latin America (see Graham 1990; Twine 1997; Wade 1997) parallels the institutionalized racism within the critical pedagogy community. Few people in the United States are aware of the racial caste systems found in Latin American countries, where whites are on top, mestizos occupy a middle buffer group, and Blacks, Indigenous people, and dark-skinned mestizos make up the bulk of the bottom strata. If we look at their actual practices and not their rhetoric, it's clear that the Latin American Left, led mostly by white Latinos, has long ignored its own pro-white, anti-Black, and anti-Indigenous tendencies (Adams 2001).[5] In the alliance between white and lighter-skinned mestizo leftists, the racial strategy, whether exercised consciously or not, is to divert attention from white supremacy and toward the capitalist class so that when revolutions occur, the problem of racial struggle is overlooked and the darker masses still have a lower status. Such is the case with Afro-Cubans. My critics might argue that, at least in places like Cuba, the economic differences between lighter and darker people are much smaller than in other places. While that's an important point not to be dismissed, that's not the issue. The issue is who's in charge and who's plotting the course for whom? How can so-called revolutionaries from the oppressor group (e.g., whites or mestizos) love the oppressed if they don't trust the leadership of groups like Afro-Cubans that have arguably been most oppressed and are relegated to the lowest social status? And when I say leadership, I don't mean just a few key or token individuals. I mean broad-based leadership.

Critical race theory (CRT) has received significant attention over the last few years. Numerous educational scholars (e.g., Allen 2001, 2004; Ladson-Billings and Tate 1995; Leonardo 2002, 2004; Lynn 1999, 2004; Parker, Deyhle, and Villenas 1999; Parker and Lynn 2002; Parker and Stovall 2004; Solorzano and Delgado Bernal 2001; Solorzano and Yosso 2002; Tate 1997) with academic links to critical pedagogy have drawn from and added to the CRT discourse. In fact, I think it's fair to assume that these scholars, many of whom are second-generation critical pedagogists, grew tired of critical pedagogy's failure to address white supremacy adequately and found in CRT a more vital and empowering project. CRT has yet to receive much attention from more traditional critical pedagogy scholars. While no critical pedagogy scholars to my knowledge have conducted extended critiques of CRT, some have critiqued versions of race theory that don't situate class analysis as the bottom line (see Darder and Torres 2003; McLaren 2003; Scatamburlo-D'Annibale and McLaren 2005). At this point, it remains to be seen whether critical pedagogists will react to CRT by substantively transforming the racial politics of the field, erecting barriers to exclude critical race theorists from the critical pedagogy community, or marginally including critical race theorists so as to not appear contradictory to outsiders.

Historically, critical pedagogy has been a class-focused paradigm that has never seriously considered white supremacy a significant force with its own community (Allen 2001, 2002, 2004). It isn't surprising then that critical pedagogy has never sufficiently addressed the productive and iterative relationships between white supremacy, labor, property, and ideology. Nor is it surprising that those who are the most targeted by white supremacy often find critical pedagogy, as it is currently configured, to be a limited and unsatisfying approach to transformative educational practices that seek to undo poverty. Nevertheless, many of these same folks gravitate to critical pedagogy because they see it as better than the other available choices.

I don't think that our focus should be on merely bridging the emergent rift between CRT- and Marxist-oriented critical pedagogists by concocting some sort of synthesis. I won't do this because I believe that this rift marks a historic and much needed shift in the racialized plate tectonics of critical pedagogy. Though there may be (at least) two sides to the debate, the two sides aren't equal in terms of power. A younger generation of critical pedagogists is breaking through. This second generation is not monolithic, so I can't speak for all of the emerging camps. I can say that one group of scholars employs an epistemological framework that differs largely from that of the older vanguard, a group that's mostly white or close to it. In many ways, those who have promoted critical pedagogy over the last few decades have done a good job of opening gates for radical and progressive people of color. But this older vanguard seems to not realize how central the experience of white domination is not just to the CRT-oriented critical pedagogists but also to the collective Black all over the world who struggle against white supremacy and its associated economies. And while some have addressed whiteness in their scholarship, these writings have not led to a substantive retheorization of critical pedagogy or an evaluation of how this inattention to whiteness has impacted the racial politics, thus the community demographics of and ideological representation within, critical pedagogy itself (Allen 2004). In addition, they have for the most part failed to realize how some radical and progressive whites, such as myself, are committed to abolishing both capitalism and white supremacy (as well as other systems of oppression). This type of commitment calls for more than having written an article or two about whiteness when it was fashionable to do so (i.e., late 1990s).

MIS/UNDERSTANDING CRITICAL RACE THEORY

Some critical pedagogists whom I have talked to haven't yet studied the CRT discourse. They are often skeptical about the notion of placing so much emphasis on race. Moreover, I get the feeling from them that they don't think CRT is "critical." Critical pedagogists have long argued, and rightfully so, that all struggles over meaning are political. The struggle over the term *critical* is no exception. The term *critical* has long been a point of contention among those who wish to call themselves critical but don't agree at an ideological level about the root(s) of oppression and the strategies for changing it. The purpose of this section is to clarify the "critical" elements of CRT, especially for those who might not be familiar with the foundational readings of this field. It's very easy to build straw man arguments against CRT since it's a discourse not embraced by the relatively powerful white Left. Therefore, before engaging in criticism of CRT, I urge critical pedagogy scholars to suspend judgment at least long enough to learn more about the transdisciplinary presuppositions of CRT. A reactionary rush to judgment may mean missing an important opportunity for critical self-reflexivity and more authentic forms of political solidarity across racial lines.

Much of the CRT scholarship in education has emphasized narrative and counterstorytelling (e.g., Solorzano and Yosso 2002) and educational policy (e.g., Taylor 1999). As CRT continues to grow, the depths of the structural nature of white supremacy, which I discuss below, will be explored much more deeply by educational scholars. In fact, scholars need to take on the task of applying CRT not just to the theorizing of research methodology or educational policy, *but also to every realm of educational theory.* It needs to be understood that CRT is only at the emergent stage in education. In the meantime, those wishing to learn more about CRT need to read beyond the field of education in order to see the broader scope of CRT scholarship. My fear is that without understanding the structural and determining nature of the white supremacist totality—a problem at the heart of most CRT scholarship—the reader or critic may dis/miss some of the more empowering and liberating aspects of CRT.

CRT is premised upon the idea of *racial realism,* which is to say that while white supremacy is a social construction, it is nevertheless quite real, deeply entrenched, and highly predictable. It determines relations of power, the re/production of labor divisions and property, the construction of social status, and the context and script of race struggles. White supremacy isn't just a local phenomenon; it's functional to the normative operations of states, nation-states, and international organizations, as well as their associated social institutions. As a social institution, public schooling should be understood as a site where the reproduction of (and resistance to) the white supremacist totality is played out. Therefore, the CRT educational scholar doesn't begin an inquiry by asking, *Does* racism/white supremacy construct inequality and power differences through schooling? Instead, the CRT scholar asks, *How* does racism/white supremacy construct inequality and power differences through schooling?

It seems as though many CRT articles in education begin with a list of the basic premises of CRT. But, one common problem with these lists is that they sometimes conflate "race" and "culture," as if they are synonyms. Another problem is that they sometimes list assumptions that aren't necessarily particular to CRT, thus allowing some readers to believe that that they are also critical race theorists, even though their beliefs are more consistent with ethnicity-based forms of multiculturalism or liberal notions of constructivism and not with CRT. In an attempt to move beyond these shortcomings, I have devised a list of assumptions from my reading of CRT literature. This list emphasizes the premises of CRT in direct, race-focused terms, much as the literature from legal studies and sociology does.

1. Racism is structural, determining, and predictable, not an aberration or irregular event.
2. Racism is really about white supremacy, which is the central organizing principle of society and not a fringe element of white culture. Struggles over sexuality, gender, ethnicity, and class are both mediated through, and reproduced by, a white supremacist totality.
3. CRT works for racial justice and the elimination of white power and privilege at both the material and ideological levels.
4. White supremacy exists and interrelates at multiple geographical levels: local, state, national, international, and global.
5. CRT is primarily a "left intervention into race discourse and a race intervention into left discourse" (Crenshaw et al. 1995, xix).
6. CRT challenges the ways in which notions such as objectivity, neutrality, meritocracy, and color blindness are used to construct white supremacy.
7. Theories of antiracist agency must consider the history of how whites have agreed to the civil rights demands of people of color only when they saw how their interests could ultimately be served. Moments of racial progress have been followed by periods of racial regress (such as our current era) because white power was affected and reshaped but not eliminated.
8. The root assumptions of CRT are predicated upon the knowledge and wisdom gained by people of color through their historical and contemporary experience with white supremacy.
9. Since white supremacy is a hegemonic system, meaning that it is perpetuated in part through the complicity of those it oppresses, some of the knowledge and beliefs of people of color conform to white supremacy. Also, *no group conforms to white hegemony more than whites themselves.*
10. CRT methodology seeks to construct knowledge of the workings of white supremacy by juxtaposing the resistance narratives of people of color against the dominant, hegemonic narratives of whites.

To address what makes CRT critical more directly, let's take a closer look at item 5 from the list. A "left intervention into race discourse" means to deconstruct hegemonic racial discourses for their inability to see the structural nature of white racism. It calls attention to the ways in which various race discourses totally miss the ideological and material dimensions of white supremacy. For example, one primary target of CRT is color-blind ideology. Color-blind ideology, which is the dominant post–civil rights white supremacist ideology, publicly denounces the use of race to explain persistent, if not seemingly "permanent," imbalances of power while at the same time diverting attention from the daily maintenance of racialized social mechanisms (e.g., tracking) and the unjust accumulation of white capital (Bell, 1992; Bonilla-Silva 2001, 2003b; Tatum 2003). Color-blind ideology defines racism as overt acts of racial bigotry or hatred. It depicts white racism as the actions of the cold-hearted, greedy, or mentally ill, thus as an abhorrent behavior since most whites are supposedly nonracist people. Life in the United States after the end of Jim Crow is depicted as fundamentally fair and mostly free of racism, so success and opportunity is cast as being open to all who choose to work hard and play by the rules. Given the wide-scale investment in this white supremacist myth, it should be no surprise that white people now feel entitled to say that the "racists" are those who claim that systemic racism still exists.

A "race intervention into left discourse" means that leftist discourse, which is largely shaped by a Marxist, class-dominant analysis, needs to be deconstructed for its complicity with white identity politics. Class-dominant analysis has a very difficult time answering—if it even attempts to answer—certain crucial questions pertaining to the links between race and class. For example, why do working-class whites tend to blame people of color rather than more economically advantaged whites for their situation? Why do people of color make up the majority of the world's poor? Why do whites seem to fear some nonwhite races more than others? Why are race-radical people of color, particularly those of the collective Black, often reluctant to join leftist movements led by whites? Class-dominant analysis is usually dismissive of white supremacy, if it even acknowledges its existence, which is rarely the case. Even those who do argue that white racism is a significant problem (e.g., MacLeod 1995) often depict it as an irrational behavior that blinds whites, especially working-class whites, to the alleged "truth" of class consciousness; that is, white racism prevents the white working class from allying with workers of color. While I agree that this is in fact the case, this view misses the fact that white supremacy establishes a system whereby it's quite rational for whites to participate in a form of racial identity politics that maintains white power and privilege (Bobo and Smith 1998). Even poor whites comply with the agendas of more powerful whites because they understand that they receive "the public and psychological wages of whiteness" (DuBois 1935). In other words, they understand at some level that it's better, in general, to be white than to be a person of color in this society. (Those who don't believe me should try asking a group of working-class whites, or whites of any class, if they would like to have the white race trade places with another race.) Thus, working-class whites are making a "reasoned," but immoral, choice given their assessment of their situation within capitalistic white supremacy. As Cheryl Harris (1995) has argued, whiteness itself is a form of property that society and the legal system protect with iron fists. Class-dominant discourses have done little, if anything, to shed light on this aspect of property and material life, which is upheld by the vast majority of working-class whites. Thus, these types of leftist discourses have operated as a kind of suboppressor ideology, policing the privilege of white marxists who claim to be on the side of the oppressed. For the exploitation of labor to cease and the existence of bourgeois property and surplus value to be abolished, working-class whites must be convinced to commit race suicide.

THE IDEALISM OF CLASS-BASED APPROACHES TO RACE

In this section, I critique two chapters in *The Critical Pedagogy Reader* (2003). These chapters are significant in that they are written by major critical pedagogy figures and are grounded in a class-dominant approach to race. If I had read these two chapters ten years ago, they would have been very satisfying to me. As a working-class white male with an Appalachian background, but without a critical race consciousness, they would have affirmed my belief that people of color who promote a more race-radical discourse don't know what is best for themselves, let alone for others. For years, this allegedly commonsense approach to race in critical pedagogy supported my belief in non-Black superiority and Black inferiority, at the same time that I denounced racism and economic exploitation of any form. So, it's my contention that both of the chapters I discuss promote a type of anti-Black politics (that affects Blacks in particular, and the collective Black generally), despite the best intentions of the authors. Plus, their approaches are idealist in the sense that they avoid dealing in any meaningful way with the everyday realities of white identity politics in the field they helped to shape.

I find "Shattering the 'Race' Lens: Toward a Critical Theory of Race" by Antonia Darder and Rodolfo Torres (2003) troubling on numerous levels, but I only have space in this chapter to address one major concern. It is clear that Darder and Torres have an axe to grind with scholars who use white supremacy as a context for studying racism. They argue that "white supremacy can only have any real meaning within populations whose exploitation and domination is essentialized based on skin color" (256). They go on to say that there are groups who have been racialized but not as a result of white supremacy. For example, they state, "White supremacy cannot be employed to analyze . . . the racialization of Jews in Germany in the 1930s, or Gypsy populations in Eastern Europe, or the Tutsi population in the Congo [*sic*]" (256). They say that the typical "white supremacy" discourse operates through a "Black/white" paradigm that makes skin color, thus Black people, the primary object of racism. The implication is that Blacks who operate through a white supremacy analysis are unable to see the racism that affects other groups.

> There is little room [in a white supremacy analysis] to link, with equal legiti-macy, the continuing struggles against racism of Jews, Gypsies, the Irish, im-migrant workers, refugees, and other racialized populations of the world (in-cluding Africans racialized by Africans) to the struggle of African Americans in the United States. (255)

In other words, they argue that Black scholars in the United States who work within an analysis of white supremacy segregate themselves from po-tential allies around the world because they are too focused on the experi-ence of phenotypic racialization at the hands of whites, an experience that Darder and Torres suggest is not universal to all of the groups that experi-ence racism.

The major flaw with their argument is that they fail to understand the complexities and nuances of the racialization of bodies within global white supremacy. One of these complexities is that white supremacy affects all groups, not just Blacks. For example, their argument that the murder of Jews by Nazis had nothing to do with white supremacy is just absurd. As stu-dents of whiteness know, membership in the white group is not a given; a group's membership can be revoked or new groups can be included de-pending on the political pressures placed upon whites (e.g., the Irish). There is no question that the Nazis did not include Jews in their construc-tion of whiteness, thus decided to kill them, along with anyone else whom they did not see as white. If this isn't white supremacy, then I'm not sure what white supremacy is. This leads to another complexity that Darder and Torres fail to address: white supremacy creates racial hierarchies that are closely linked to the politicization of phenotypic constructs. While Jews were not whites to the Nazis, other whites did see them as white, or at least as very close to white, and were outraged and horrified by the Holocaust. However, many of these more sympathetic whites were not as outraged by Germany's slaughter of Blacks in the Congo, or, for that matter, by the whites' slaughter of people of color around the world in the centuries lead-ing up to World War II. In other words, whites in general deal more sensi-tively with the Holocaust than they do with the slaughter and enslavement of people of color because Jews are seen as white, or at least close to it

(Churchill 1997; Mills 1997). In Rwanda, the German, then Belgian, colonizers constructed a racial hierarchy by delineating between Tutsis and Hutus, assigning the Tutsis more privilege than Hutus because they were perceived to have more European features (e.g., lighter skin and narrower noses). Whether real or not, these constructed differences were cemented into a very real white supremacist nation-state structure with whites on top, Tutsis in the middle, and Hutus on the bottom. Inhabitants learned to discern one another's race by sight (though these differences may not be discernable to outsiders), and thus seemingly arbitrary features were reified and made politically real. So, despite the claims of Darder and Torres, Hutus and Tutsis did not racialize one another outside of a context of white supremacy. It was the white racism of Germans and Belgians that drove their racialization.

Racial hierarchies also exist in the Americas, where the collective Black occupy the bottom rung of the social ladder, and those who are closer to white receive a little more relative status and privilege from those whites at the top, especially if they avoid calling attention to this racialized social system. It should come as no surprise then that those at the bottom of racial hierarchies will want to call attention to the determinate nature of colorism and phenotype and those who occupy higher strata will tend to dismiss these claims because their color and phenotype offers them more relative privilege. Darder and Torres reject the effects of skin politics without first exploring the ways in which people like themselves are or are not privileged by having lighter skin. If they had instead given evidence that people of color with lighter skin have no greater privilege or status than the collective Black, then their argumentation would be more aligned with their assertion about the inadequacy of white supremacy analysis. But they don't do this. Instead, their knee-jerk rejection of analysis that focuses on white supremacy demonstrates to me a form of anti-Black politics that suggests that all oppressed groups suffer equally from racism. With this move, they shield themselves, as well as Anglo whites, from exploring their own race privilege. It is as if they are saying that many Blacks perpetrate some sort of reverse racism against non-Blacks by playing the "skin color card," much as whites talk about people of color playing the "race card."

Darder and Torres are correct in critiquing notions of white supremacy that only see whites as perpetrators and Blacks as victims. However, they are wrong in suggesting that this is a position held by bell hooks. Few critical scholars of color are as supportive of white antiracist work as hooks (see hooks 2003b). Furthermore, most CRT scholars agree with hooks in that they see a role for white antiracists. As a white antiracist person, I am thoroughly troubled by Darder and Torres's apologia for white people. Theirs is the kind of scholarship that lets us white people off the hook all too easily because they seem to be telling us whites that we can just tell Blacks to stop complaining about white supremacy because "the Irish had it bad, too." In the end, they have merely repackaged the old Marxist view of "race as false ideology" to try to convince us that race relations don't matter in struggles against racism. But, how can we struggle against racism if we repress the fact that some groups of color have more racial privilege than others? How can we struggle against racism if those of us who have more relative racial privilege are unwilling to be accountable for our investment in our skin privilege? Darder and Torres would have us believe that we should just ignore this problem. In fact, their argument implies that we should attack (or at least dismiss) those who take these questions seriously. It is my contention that their criticism of hooks, as well as of others, is not only flawed but also demonstrates that they seem to have a particular axe to grind with Black scholars and their supporters who dare assume that white supremacy is real and impacts all of us.

Peter McLaren's "Revolutionary Pedagogy in Post-Revolutionary Times" (2003) is a more subtle critique of race-based approaches to racial inequality, which in many ways makes it all the more patronizing. He isn't as dismissive of the use of race in social analysis as Darder and Torres are. He seemingly validates struggles of all sorts when he says, "A critical pedagogy *based on class struggle* [emphasis added] that does not confront racism, sexism, and homophobia will not be able to eliminate the destructive proliferation of capital" (170). So, although he supports a variety of struggles, he assumes that these struggles must be working toward anticapitalist ends. He makes this crystal clear when he says, "The struggle against capital is, after all, the main game" (175). I agree that some forms of identity politics "keep workers and subaltern groups divided against each other" (168). I don't agree, however, that all identity politics are the same. Some are the identity politics of the oppressed. Some are the identity politics of the oppressor. And some are the identity politics of suboppressors. For example, white identity politics is the kind that seeks to perpetuate white wealth and domination. But, McLaren erroneously conflates counterhegemonic identity politics, such as those supported by CRT scholars, with all kinds of identity politics; he devotes little or no space to discerning among them. In the end, McLaren is trying to pull off the tried and true Marxist critique of race, but in a sugarcoated way, by using "identity politics" as a code for those groups that have a race focus, which, by implication, are groups that have succumbed to alleged illusions of race promoted by the capitalist class ideology. Like Darder and Torres, he diverts attention away from the analytical importance of the vested interests that whites and non-Blacks have in their racial group formations, in other words, away from white supremacy. Thus, by default, he is critiquing white supremacy analysis, even though he does not mention white supremacy or white supremacy analysis directly.

CONCLUSION

I care deeply about critical pedagogy. It has in many ways been my intellectual and spiritual home for the last decade or so, and I don't want to leave
it. Most of the people I know who make up this community are vibrant, caring, loving, and committed people, including those I critique in this chapter. However, sometimes that's not enough. My hope in writing this chapter
is that the critical pedagogy community will begin to take seriously its own
race problem. We need to hear more, read more, and write more about what
it means to be a white critical pedagogist versus a critical pedagogist of
color. We need to explore what the differences and similarities are for Black
and non-Black, lighter- and darker-skinned, critical pedagogists. We need to
have more authentic dialogues about our fears and anxieties around talking
about our own racial demographics and ideologies. And, ultimately, the
complexion of the community, both figuratively and literally, needs to
change, as does what counts as valid critical pedagogy ideology. I will close
by saying that my discussion about racial inclusion isn't about some kind
of liberal "numbers game." It's about whether we are living up to our own
ideals. And let us be judged not merely by our intentions but by our results.

NOTES

1. A person, group, or institution doesn't have to discriminate consciously
against Blacks and Indians in order to be anti-Black or anti-Indian. Instead, the person, group, or institution need only support those ideas and practices that disprivi-
lege Blacks and Indians relative to non-Blacks and non-Indians.

2. In this chapter, I will use the terms *Black* and *collective Black* in context. When
I mean to refer mostly to U.S. Blacks or African Americans, I use the term *Black*.
When I mean to include all of those groups who are treated most like Blacks, I invoke the term *collective Black*. There are certainly occasions where either term could
be used and the sentence would still hold true. Also, unlike Bonilla-Silva, I capital-
ize the word "Black" in "collective Black" to be consistent with how Black is capi-
talized in this chapter.

3. In this chapter, I will use the term *white marxists* to deal with the issue that
there are competing camps among the white Left, such as orthodox Marxists, Marxist humanists, libertarian socialists, anarchist socialists, communists, and neo-
Marxists. While I'm not a student of the debates each has with the others, I do
know that they generally agree with many of the basic assertions Marx made about
capitalism and its importance as a political target. Additionally, they share a general suspicion, if not outright rejection, of race analyses that situate white supremacy as a totality. Therefore, rather than capitalizing "Marxist" as if it were the
proper name of a group, I will use a lowercase letter to indicate a broader group
that includes those who may or may not consider themselves to be Marxists, since
they have been heavily influenced by Marxist thought. Also, I do this because there

is a tendency for white marxists to deflect criticism about the whiteness of their politics by distancing themselves from what they see as a narrow, or straw-man, notion of Marxism. Instead, they say that they are socialists, Marxist humanists, or something of that nature, and not Marxists in the traditional sense. However, these kinds of distinctions mean very little to the argument I make in this chapter since none of these camps, at least in the United States, are known for having been created and led by the collective Black.

4. I want to make it clear that there are certainly other systems of oppression besides white supremacy that impact Blacks, Indians, and the collective Black. However, this chapter focuses on the race problem in critical pedagogy and thus requires a sustained focus on race.

5. Of course, there are notable exceptions, such as in the movement in Xiapas.

REFERENCES

Adams, H. 2001. Race and the formation of Cuban national and cultural identity. In *Global multiculturalism: Comparative perspectives on ethnicity, race, and nation,* ed. G. Cornwell and E. W. Stoddard, 193–211. Lanham, MD: Rowman & Littlefield.

Allen, R. L. 2001. The globalization of white supremacy: Toward a critical discourse on the racialization of the world. *Educational Theory* 51 (4): 467–85.

———. 2002. Wake up, Neo: White consciousness, hegemony, and identity in *The Matrix*. In *The Freirean legacy: Educating for social justice,* ed. J. Slater, S. Fain, and C. Rossatto, 104–25. New York: Peter Lang Publishers.

———. 2004. Whiteness and critical pedagogy. *Educational Philosophy and Theory* 36 (2): 121–36.

Bell, D. 1992. *Faces at the bottom of the well: The permanence of racism.* New York: BasicBooks.

Bobo, L., and R. Smith. 1998. From Jim Crow racism to laissez-faire racism. In *Beyond pluralism: The conception of groups and group identities in America,* ed. W. Katkin, N. Landsman, and A. Tyree, 182–220. Urbana: University of Illinois Press.

Bonacich, E. 1980. Advanced capitalism and Black/white relations in the United States: A split labor market interpretation. In *The sociology of race relations,* ed. T. Pettigrew, 341–62. New York: Free Press.

Bonilla-Silva, E. 1996. Rethinking racism: Toward a structural interpretation. *American Sociological Review* 62 (June): 465–80.

———. 2001. *White supremacy and racism in the post–civil rights era.* Boulder, CO: Lynne Rienner Publishers.

———. 2003a. "New racism," color-blind racism, and the future of whiteness in America. In *White out: The continuing significance of racism,* ed. A. Doane and E. Bonilla-Silva, 271–87. New York: Routledge.

———. 2003b. *Racism without racists.* Lanham, MD: Rowman & Littlefield.

Churchill, W., ed. 1983. *Marxism and Native Americans.* Boston: South End Press.

———. 1997. *A little matter of genocide: Holocaust and denial in the Americas, 1492 to the present.* San Francisco: City Lights Books.

Crenshaw, K., N. Gotanda, G. Peller, and K. Thomas. 1995. Introduction. In *Critical race theory: The key writings that formed the movement*, ed. K. Crenshaw, N. Gotanda, G. Peller, and K. Thomas, xiii–xxxii. New York: New Press.

Darder, A., and R. Torres. 2003. Shattering the "race" lens: Toward a critical theory of racism. In *The critical pedagogy reader*, ed. A. Darder, M. Baltodano, and R. Torres, 245–61. New York: Routledge Falmer.

DuBois, W. E. B. 1935. *Black reconstruction in America*. New York: Simon and Schuster.

Freire, P. 1993. *Pedagogy of the oppressed*, trans. M. B. Ramos. Rev. ed. New York: Continuum.

Graham, R., ed. 1990. *The idea of race in Latin America, 1870–1940*. Austin: University of Texas Press.

Harris, C. 1995. Whiteness as property. In *Critical race theory: The key writings that formed the movement*, ed. K. Crenshaw, N. Gotanda, G. Peller, and K. Thomas, 276–91. New York: New Press.

hooks, b. 2003a. Confronting class in the classroom. In *The critical pedagogy reader*, ed. A. Darder, M. Baltodano, and R. Torres, 142–50. New York: Routledge Falmer.

———. 2003b. *Teaching community: A pedagogy of hope*. New York: Routledge.

Ladson-Billings, G., and W. Tate. 1995. Toward a critical race theory of education. *Teachers College Record* 97 (1): 47–68.

Leonardo, Z. 2002. The souls of white folk: Critical pedagogy, whiteness studies, and globalization discourse. *Race, Ethnicity and Education* 5 (1): 29–50.

———. 2004. The color of supremacy: Beyond the discourse of "white privilege." *Educational Philosophy and Theory* 36 (2): 137–52.

Lynn, M. 1999. Toward a critical race pedagogy: A research note. *Urban Education* 33 (5): 606–26.

———. 2004. Inserting the "race" into critical pedagogy: An analysis of "race-based epistemologies." *Educational Philosophy and Theory* 36 (2): 153–66.

McLaren, P. 2003. Revolutionary pedagogy in post-revolutionary times: Rethinking the political economy of critical education. In *The critical pedagogy reader*, ed. A. Darder, M. Baltodano, and R. Torres, 151–84. New York: Routledge Falmer.

MacLeod, J. 1995. *Ain't no makin' it: Aspirations and attainment in a low-income neighborhood*. 2nd ed. Boulder, CO: Westview Press.

Mills, C. 1997. *The racial contract*. Ithaca, NY: Cornell University Press.

Parker, L., D. Deyhle, and S. Villenas, eds. 1999. *Race is . . . race isn't: Critical race theory and qualitative studies in education*. Boulder, CO: Westview Press.

Parker, L., and M. Lynn. 2002. What's race got to do with it? Critical race theory's conflicts with and connections to qualitative research methodology and epistemology. *Qualitative Inquiry* 8 (1): 7–22.

Parker, L., and D. Stovall. 2004. Actions following words: Critical race theory connects to critical pedagogy. *Educational Philosophy and Theory* 36 (2): 167–82.

Roediger, D. 1999. *Wages of whiteness: Race and the making of the American working class*. Rev. ed. London: Verso.

Scatamburlo-D'Annibale, V., and P. McLaren. 2005. Class dismissed? Historical materialism and the politics of "difference." In *Critical pedagogy and race*, ed. Z. Leonardo, 141–57. Malden, MA: Blackwell Publishing.

Solorzano, D., and D. Delgado Bernal. 2001. Examining transformational resistance through a critical race and latcrit theory framework: Chicana and Chicano students in an urban context. *Urban Education* 36 (3): 308–42.

Solorzano, D., and T. Yosso. 2002. Critical race methodology: Counter-storytelling as an analytical framework for education research. *Qualitative Inquiry* 8 (1): 23–44.

Tate, W. F. 1997. Critical race theory in education: History, theory, and implications. In *Review of research in education*, ed. M. Apple, Vol. 22, 195–250. Washington, DC: American Educational Research Association.

Tatum, B. D. 2003. *"Why are all the Black kids sitting together in the cafeteria?" and other conversations about race.* 5th ed. New York: BasicBooks.

Taylor, E. 1999. Critical race theory and interest convergence in the desegregation of higher education. In *Race is . . . race isn't: Critical race theory and qualitative studies in education*, ed. L. Parker, D. Deyhle, and S. Villenas, 181–204. Boulder, CO: Westview Press.

Twine, F. W. 1997. *Racism in a racial democracy.* New Brunswick, NJ: Rutgers University Press.

Wade, P. 1997. *Race and ethnicity in Latin America.* London: Pluto Press.

2

Racism without Racists: "Killing Me Softly" with Color Blindness

Eduardo Bonilla-Silva and David G. Embrick

In the post–civil rights era, nothing seems "racist" in the traditional sense of the word. Even David Duke, Tom Metzger, and most members of the Ku Klux Klan and other old-fashioned white supremacist organizations claim they are not racist, just pro-white. Moreover, the "white street"[1] asserts that whites "don't see any color, just people." They assume that although the ugly face of discrimination is still around, it is no longer the central factor determining minorities' life chances. Finally, they claim to aspire, much like Dr. Martin Luther King Jr., to live in a society where "people are judged by the content of their character, not by the color of their skin."

However, regardless of whites' "sincere fictions" (Feagin et al. 1995; Feagin and Sikes 1994), racial considerations shade almost everything in America. Blacks and dark-skinned minorities lag well behind whites in virtually every area of social life; they are about three times more likely to be poor than whites, earn about 40 percent less than whites, and have about one-tenth of the net worth of whites. They also receive an inferior education compared to whites, even when they attend so-called integrated (at best, desegregated) schools (for details on all these statistics, see ch. 4 in Bonilla-Silva 2001).

How is it possible to have this tremendous degree of racial inequality in a country where most whites claim that racism is "a thing of the past"? More importantly, how do whites explain the apparent contradiction between their professed color blindness and the United States' color-coded inequality? Eduardo Bonilla-Silva refers to this as the strange enigma of "racism without racists." In his 2003 book, *Racism without Racists*, he attempts to solve this enigma by arguing that "whites," as a social collectivity, have developed a new, powerful, and effective racial ideology to account for contemporary racial matters, which he labels color-blind racism. Whereas Jim Crow racism explained minorities' standing mainly as the result of their imputed biological and moral inferiority, color-blind racism avoids such facile arguments. Instead, whites rationalize minorities' status as the product of market dynamics, naturally occurring phenomena, and their presumed cultural deficiencies. Despite its apparent "racism-lite" character, this ideology is as deadly as the one it replaces.

Before we attempt to deconstruct color-blind racism, let us explain why a new racial ideology is at play in the first place. Color-blind racism acquired cohesiveness and dominance in the late 1960s as the mechanisms and practices for keeping blacks and other racial minorities "at the bottom of the well" changed. We argue that contemporary racial inequality is reproduced through "new racism" practices that are predominantly subtle, institutional, and apparently nonracial (see Bonilla-Silva 2001, ch. 4). In contrast to the Jim Crow era, where racial inequality was enforced through overt means (e.g., signs saying "No Negroes Welcomed Here" or shotgun diplomacy at the voting booth), systemic white privilege is maintained nowadays in a "now you see it, now you don't" fashion. For example, residential segregation, which is almost as high today as it was in the past, is no longer accomplished through overtly discriminatory practices (e.g., bombs and housing covenants) (see Massey and Denton 1993). Instead, covert behaviors, such as not showing all the available units, steering minorities and whites into certain neighborhoods, quoting higher rents or prices to minority applicants, the racializing of credit scores, or not advertising units at all are the weapons of choice to maintain separate communities. New racism practices have been documented in a variety of venues: schools, jobs, banks, restaurants, and stores. Hence, as we will illustrate, the contours of color-blind racism fit quite well with the way racial inequality is reproduced these days.

METHODOLOGY

The data we use to make our case comes from two similarly structured projects: the 1997 Survey of Social Attitudes of College Students and the 1998 Detroit Area Study on White Racial Ideology. The Survey of Social Attitudes of College Students is based on a convenient sample of 627 students (of which 451 of the respondents were white) from large universities in the South and Midwest and a mid-size university on the West Coast. Of the white students who provided contact information (about 90 percent), 10 percent were randomly selected for interviews (forty-one students altogether, of which seventeen were men and twenty-four women and of which thirty-one were from middle- and upper-middle-class backgrounds and ten were from working-class backgrounds).

The 1998 Detroit Area Study is a probabilistic survey based on a representative sample of 400 black and white Detroit metropolitan area residents (323 white residents and 67 black residents). The response rate to the survey was 67.5 percent. In addition, 84 respondents (67 whites and 17 blacks) were randomly selected for in-depth interviews. The hour-long interviews were race matched, followed a structured protocol, and were conducted in the subjects' homes (for details, see Bonilla-Silva 2003).

Since ideologies are discursive, we use mostly interview data to document the major components of color-blind racism. By racial ideology, we mean *the racially based frameworks actors use to justify/oppose the racial status quo*. We operationalize the notion of racial ideology as an interpretive repertoire made up of *frames*, *style*, and *racial stories*. The *frames* of any dominant[2] racial ideology are *set paths for interpreting information* and *operate as cul-de-sacs* because they explain racial phenomena in a predictable manner, as if those who invoke them are getting on a one-way street without exits. Frames are not false consciousness as they provide the intellectual and moral road map whites use to navigate the always-rocky road of domination and derail non-whites from their track to freedom and equality.[3] The four central frames of color-blind racism are abstract liberalism, naturalization, cultural racism, and minimization of racism, and we illustrate each one separately in subsequent sections.

Abstract Liberalism: Unmasking Reasonable Racism

This frame incorporates tenets associated with political and economic liberalism in an abstract and decontextualized manner. By framing race-related issues in the language of liberalism, whites can appear "reasonable" and even "moral," while opposing all practical approaches to deal with de facto racial inequality. For instance, by using the tenets of the free market ideology in the abstract, they can oppose affirmative action as a violation of the norm of equal opportunity. The following example illustrates how whites use this frame. Jim, a thirty-year-old computer software salesperson from a privileged background, explained his opposition to affirmative action as follows:

> I think it's unfair top to bottom on everybody and the whole process. It often, you know, discrimination itself is a bad word, right? But you discriminate every day. You wanna buy a beer at the store and there are six kinda beers you can get, from Natural Light to Sam Adams, right? And you look at the price and you look at the kind of beer, and you . . . *it's a choice*. And a lot of that you have laid out in front of you, which one you get? Now, should the government sponsor Sam Adams and make it cheaper than Natural Light because it's brewed by someone in Boston? That doesn't make much sense, right? Why would we want that or make Sam Adams eight times as expensive because we want people to buy Natural Light?

And it's the same thing about getting into school or getting into some place. And universities, it's easy, and universities is a hot topic now, and I could bug you, you know, Midwestern University I don't think has a lot of racism in the admissions process. And I think Midwestern University would, would agree with that pretty strongly. So why not just pick people that are going to do well at Midwestern University, pick people by their merit? I think we should stop the whole idea of choosing people based on their color.

Since Jim assumes hiring decisions are like market choices (e.g., choosing between competing brands of beer), he embraces a laissez-faire position on hiring. The problem with Jim's view is that labor-market discrimination is alive and well (e.g., it affects black and Latino job applicants 30 to 50 percent), and most jobs (as much as 80 percent) are obtained through informal networks (Braddock and McPartland 1987; Royster 2003). Jim's abstract position is further cushioned by his belief that although blacks "perceive or feel" like there is a lot of discrimination, he does not see much discrimination out there.

Hence, by upholding a strict laissez-faire view on hiring and, at the same time, ignoring the significant impact of discrimination in the labor market, Jim can safely voice his opposition to affirmative action in an apparently race-neutral way. This abstract liberal frame allows whites to be unconcerned about school and residential segregation, oppose almost any kind of government intervention to ameliorate the effects of past and contemporary discrimination, and even to support their preferences for whites as partners/ friends as a matter of choice.

Naturalization: Decoding the Meaning of "That's the Way It Is"

A frame that has not yet been brought to the fore by social analysts is the naturalization of race-related matters. The word "natural" and the phrase "that's the way it is" are often interjected to normalize events or actions that could otherwise be interpreted as racially motivated (residential segregation) or racist (preference for whites as friends and partners). But, as social scientists know quite well, these are not natural but socially produced outcomes. An example of how whites use this frame is Bill, a manufacturing firm manager in his fifties, who explained the limited level of school integration as follows:

I don't think it's anybody's fault. Because people tend to group with their own people. Whether it's white or black or upper-middle class or lower class or, you know, Asians. People tend to group with their own. Doesn't mean if a black person moves into your neighborhood, they shouldn't go to your school. They should and you should mix and welcome them and everything else, but you can't force people together. If people want to be together, they should intermix more.

[Interviewer: Okay. So the lack of mixing is really just kind of an individual lack of desire?]

Well, individuals, it's just the way it is. You know, people group together for lots of different reasons: social, religious. Just as animals in the wild, you know. Elephants group together, cheetahs group together. You bus a cheetah into an elephant herd because they should mix? You can't force that [laughs].

Although most respondents were not as crude as Bill, they still used this frame to justify the racial status quo.

Cultural Racism: "They Don't Have It Altogether"

Pierre Andre Taguieff (2001) has argued that modern racial ideology does not portray minorities as inferior biological beings. Instead, it *biologizes* their presumed cultural practices (i.e., present them as fixed features) and uses that as the rationale for justifying racial inequality (he labels this "differentialist racism"). This cultural racism is very well established in the United States.[4] The newness of this frame resides in the centrality it has acquired in whites' contemporary justifications of minorities' standing. The essence of the frame, as William Ryan (1976) pointed out a long time ago, is "blaming the victim" by arguing that minorities' status is the product of their lack of effort, loose family organization, inappropriate values, or some combination thereof. An example of how whites use this frame is Kim, a student at Midwestern University. When asked "Many whites explain the status of blacks in this country as a result of blacks lacking motivation, not having the proper work ethic, or being lazy. What do you think?" Kim responded,

Yeah, I totally agree with that. I don't think, you know, they're all like that, but, I mean, it's just that if it wasn't that way, why would there be so many blacks living in the projects? You know, why would there be so many poor blacks? If they worked hard, they could make it just as high as anyone else could. You know, I just think that's just, you know, they're raised that way and they see that parents are, so they assume that's the way it should be. And they just follow the roles their parents had for them and don't go anywhere.

Although not all whites were as crude as this student, most subscribed to this belief, whether in its nastiest, most direct versions or in a "compassionate conservative" manner.

Minimization of Racism: Whites' Declining Significance of Race Thesis

Most whites do not believe that the predicament of minorities today is the product of discrimination. Instead, they believe that it's because of their "culture," "class," "legacies from slavery," "Mexican/Puerto Rican backward culture," "culture of segregation," "lack of social capital," "poverty," and so on and so forth. It's "anything but racism!" An example of how whites use this frame is Sandra, a retail salesperson in her early forties, who explained her view on discrimination as follows:

> I think if you are looking for discrimination, I think it's there to be *found*. But if you make the best of any situation, and if *you don't use it as an excuse.* I think sometimes it's an excuse because people felt they deserved a job, whatever! I think if things didn't go their way, I know a lot of people have a tendency to use prejudice or racism or whatever as an *excuse.* I think in some ways, yes, there is [*sic*] people who are prejudiced. It's not only blacks, it's about Spanish, or women. In a lot of ways there [is] a lot of *reverse* discrimination. It's just what you wanna make of it.

This needs very little comment. Since most whites, like Sandra, believe discrimination has all but disappeared, they regard minorities' claims of discrimination as excuses or as minorities playing the infamous "race card."

THE STYLE OF COLOR BLINDNESS: HOW TO TALK NASTY ABOUT BLACKS WITHOUT SOUNDING "RACIST"

Ideologies are not just about ideas. In order for the frames of an ideology to work effectively, those who invoke them need rhetorical devices to weave arguments in all kinds of situations. In the case of color-blind racism, given the post–civil rights normative context, whites need these devices to save face and still be able to articulate their racial views. Hence, we define the *style* of a racial ideology as its peculiar *linguistic manners and rhetorical strategies* (or *race talk*), that is, the technical tools that allow users to articulate its frames and racial stories. Since a full discursive analysis of the five stylistic components of color blindness is beyond the scope of this chapter, we only illustrate three: semantic moves, projection, and rhetorical incoherence.

Semantic Moves

Semantic moves, such as phrases that protect users' moral standpoint (e.g., "I am not a racist, but . . ."), allow whites to express their racial views in a coded and safe way—safe because they can always go back to the safety of the disclaimers ("I didn't mean that because *I am not a racist*" and "Some of my best friends are black"). However, since moves like "I am not a racist" or "Some of my best friends are black" have become cliché and are therefore less effective, whites have developed new moves to accomplish the same goals.[5]

One such rhetorical move for stating racial views without opening yourself to the charge of racism is taking apparently all sides on an issue. We label this as the "Yes and no, but . . ."move. Sandra, the retail person in her forties cited above, answered the question "Are you for or against affirmative action?" in the following apparently cryptic manner:

> Yes and no. I feel someone should be able to have *something*, education, job, whatever, because they've earned it, they deserve it, they have the ability to do it. You don't want to put a six-year-old as a *rocket scientist*. They don't have the ability. It doesn't matter if the kid's black or white. As far as letting one have the job over another one just because of their race or their gender, I don't believe in that.

Sandra's "yes and no" stand on affirmative action is truly a strong "no" since she does not find any reason whatsoever for affirmative action programs to be in place.

It Wasn't Me! The Role of Projection in Color-Blind Racism

Psychologists know that projection is part of our normal equipment to defend the "self." It is also an essential tool in the creation of a corporate identity ("us" versus "them"). More significantly, projection helps us "escape from guilt and responsibility and affix blame elsewhere." Thus, it was not surprising to find that whites projected racism or racial motivations onto blacks as a way of avoiding responsibility and feeling good about themselves.

The following example illustrates how whites project racial motivations onto blacks. In her answer to the interracial marriage question, Janet, a student at Southern University, projected onto people who marry across the color line:

> I would feel that in most situations they're not really thinking of the, the child. I mean, they might not really think anything of it, *but* in reality I think most of the time when the child is growing up, he's going to be picked on because he has parents from different races and it's gonna ultimately affect the child and, and the end result is they're only thinking of them. Both their own happiness, not the happiness of, of the kid.

By projecting selfishness onto those who intermarry, Janet was able to voice her otherwise problematic opposition to these marriages safely.

Rhetorical Incoherence

Finally, we want to provide one example of rhetorical incoherence. Although incoherence (e.g., grammatical mistakes, lengthy pauses, or repetition) is part of all natural speech, the level of incoherence increases noticeably when people discuss sensitive subjects. And because the new racial climate in America forbids the open expression of racially based feelings, views, and positions, when whites discuss issues that make them feel uncomfortable, they become almost incomprehensible.

For example, Ray, a Midwestern University student and a respondent who was very articulate throughout the interview, became almost incomprehensible when answering the question about whether he had been involved with minorities while in college.

> Um so to answer that question, no. But I would not, I mean, I would not ever preclude a black woman from being my girlfriend on the basis that she was black. Ya' know, I mean, ya' know what I mean? If you're looking about it from, ya' know, the standpoint of just attraction, I mean, I think that, ya' know, I think, ya' know, I think, ya' know, all women are, I mean, all women have a sort of different type of beauty, if you will. And I think that, ya' know, for black women, it's somewhat different than white women. But I don't think it's, ya know, I mean, it's, it's, it's nothing that would ever stop me from like, I mean, I don't know, I mean, I don't if that's, I mean, that's just sort of been my impression. I mean, it's not like I would ever say, "No, I'll never have a black girlfriend," but it just seems to me like I'm not as attracted to black women as I am to white women, for whatever reason. It's not about prejudice, it's just sort of like, ya' know, whatever. Just sort of the way, way like I see white women as compared to black women, ya' know?

The interviewer followed up Ray's answer with the question, "Do you have any idea why that would be?" Ray replied: "I, I, I [sighs] don't really know. It's just sort of hard to describe. It's just like, ya' know, who you're more drawn to, ya' know, for whatever reason, ya' know?" Ray's answer suggests that he is not attracted to black women and has serious problems explaining why.

RACIAL STORIES

The last component of color-blind racism is racial stories. In this chapter we examine two kinds of racial stories. First are *story lines, or socially shared tales that are fablelike and incorporate a common scheme and wording.* Story lines are fablelike because they are often based on impersonal, generic arguments with little narrative content. Second are *testimonies, or accounts where the narrator is a central participant in the story or is close to the characters in the story.* Testimonies provide the aura of authenticity and emotionality that only "firsthand" narratives can furnish.

The major[6] story lines of color-blind racism are "The past is the past," "I didn't own any slaves," "If Jews, Italians, and the Irish have made it, how come blacks have not?" and "I did not get a job (or a promotion or admitted to a college) because of a minority." Since most people are somewhat familiar with these stories, we will just provide one example. Roland, an electrical engineer in his forties, combined the story lines of "The past is the past" and "I didn't own any slaves" to oppose the idea of reparations:

> I think they've gotten enough. I don't think we need to pay them anything or I think as long as they are afforded opportunities and avail themselves to the opportunities like everybody else. I, I don't know why we should give them any reparation for something that happened, you know . . . I can't, I *can't* help what happened in the 1400s, the 1500s, or the 1600s, when the blacks were brought over here and put into slavery. I mean, I had no control over that, neither did you, so I don't think we should do anything as far as reparations are concerned.

Of interest here is that although the question dealt with the effects of past (slavery and Jim Crow) and contemporary discrimination, Roland, like most whites, translated the issue to slavery as if racism were a matter in our remote past.

RACIAL TESTIMONIES

Testimonies are the second kind of racial story. In this section, we discuss three types of testimonies: stories of disclosure of knowledge of someone close who is racist, stories of interactions with blacks (positive and negative), and *sui generis* personal stories. Testimonies are very important in the color-blind drama as almost every respondent interjected one or more into his or her answers. We will discuss just one example each of positive and negative stories of interactions with blacks. The example of positive interaction with blacks is Mary, a student at Southern University, who said in response to a question on so-called black self-segregation that her family is racist. In this context, she told this story:

> My floor actually, the year I had a black roommate, happened to be predominantly African American and so those became some of my best friends, the people I was around. And we would actually sit around and talk about stereotypes and prejudices and I learned so much just about the hair texture, you know? What it means for a black person to get a perm versus me, you know. I learned *a lot*. And it really, I think, for me, broke down a lot of barriers and ended a lot of stereotypes I may still had. Because, like I said, I mean, those really became some of my best friends. And even still we don't really keep in touch, but if I see any of 'em on campus, still, you know, we always talk with each other and everything.

Mary's story rings with self-presentation from start to finish. Yet, because Mary's delivery is close to paternalistic Southern racial parlance, the story does not help her that much. For instance, she uses the word "those" when referring to African Americans twice and points out twice that they became "some of my best friends." Furthermore, her claim of having learned a lot from this interaction seems superficial since she only talks about hair texture and perms. Finally, these nameless "best friends" became only casual acquaintances after a year of rooming with her.

An example of a negative story of interaction with blacks is Bill, a retired schoolteacher in his eighties, who narrated a story to explain why he thinks blacks and whites are different. After pointing out that blacks "seem to be very religious" and that they bought a church in his neighborhood, he claimed they forced a restaurant out of business and explained it as follows:

> They like to eat. They *pile their* dishes just loaded with that stuff and I actually didn't see it, but I saw one lady come in with a full plate of chicken. I didn't pay much attention, but the next thing I know, they are leaving. Now I know she didn't eat all that chicken. She probably put it in her purse and walked out with it. I didn't see that. Lot of them are doing that, how can they make any money? And seeing that they are all *heavy people*, it seems like they do a lot of eating. *So* I don't know what to say about something like that.

Although this story is based on Bill's racist interpretation of events, the fact remains that he used it to validate his belief that blacks "like to eat," are cheap, and steal.

CONCLUSION

In this chapter, we suggested there is a new dominant racial ideology in town: color-blind racism. This ideology is suave but deadly, hence the line from the song by Roberta Flack, "killing me softly," in the title of our chapter. *But let's not forget that a soft, color-blind approach to racial death still leads to death!* Whites need not call minorities niggers, spics, or chinks to keep them in their new, but still subordinated, place.

Yet, at the heart of color blindness lies a myth: the idea that race has all but disappeared as a factor shaping the life chances of people in the United States. This myth is the central column supporting the house of color blindness. Remove this column from the house's foundation, and the house collapses. Removing this column, however, will not be an easy task because whites' racial views are not mere erroneous ideas to be battled in the field of rational discourse. They constitute, as we argued in this chapter, a racial ideology, that is, a loosely organized set of frames, phrases, and stories that help whites justify contemporary racial inequality. These views, then, are symbolic expressions of whites' dominance and cannot just be eradicated with "facts" because racial facts are highly contested. In the eyes of whites, evidence of racial disparity in income, wealth, and education is evidence that there is something wrong with minorities; evidence of blacks' overrepresentation in the criminal justice system or on death row is proof of blacks' criminal tendencies.

Let us now conclude by suggesting concrete things we can do to fight color-blind racism. First, we need to nurture a large cohort of antiracist whites to begin challenging color-blind nonsense from within (Feagin and O'Brien 2003). Whites' collective denial about the true nature of race relations may help them feel good, but it is also one of the greatest obstacles to doing the right thing. In racial matters, as in therapy, the admission of denial is the preamble for the beginning of recovery. Are we suggesting that all whites are color-blind racists? The answer is no. We classified 10 to 15 percent of the white respondents as "racial progressives."[7] However, the identity of these respondents may surprise some of you: young working-class women. Why would this section of the white population be more likely to be racially progressive? We suggest that it is because they experience the double-whammy (being women and workers) and can empathize with minorities' plight. It is equally important that they are more likely to share intimate social spaces (e.g., neighborhoods, jobs, schools) with minorities, which, combined with their low status, produces the kind of race contact that Gordon Allport (1958) believed would produce better race relations.

Second, researchers need to provide counterideological arguments to each of the frames of color-blind racism. We need to counter whites' abstract liberalism with concrete liberal positions based on a realistic understanding of racial matters and a concern with achieving real racial equality. Are blacks color-blind, too? The answer is that color-blind racism has a small direct, and a larger indirect, effect on them that blunts the potential all-out character of their oppositional ideology. This means that color-blind racism is a dominant ideology as it makes happy, happy, happy those at the top of the racial order and confuses those at the bottom; that is, it has become a hegemonic ideology (similar to capitalism, patriarchy, and the like).

Third, we need to undress whites' claims of color blindness. We must show in creative ways the myriad facets of contemporary whiteness: whites living in white neighborhoods, sending their kids to white schools, associating primarily with whites, and having their primary relationships with whites. And because of the subtle character of modern white supremacy, new research strategies, such as audits (e.g., Housing and Urban Development audits), mixed research designs (surveys and interviews), and racial treason (Ignatiev and Garvey 1996), will be required to unveil the mask of whiteness. Given the new demography of the United States, why the focus on the black-white dyad? To this, our answer is twofold: 1. A new research project by Bonilla-Silva and Michael Emerson is being conducted to assess the parameters of the new racial stratification order (the Latin Americanization of race relations) and can offer arguments and preliminary data on how other groups might fit into the ideological constellation. In this project, they are positing that a new racial order is emerging in the United States, characterized by a tri-racial, rather than a bi-racial, division and the increasing salience of skin tone as a stratification element (see Bonilla-Silva 2004). 2. Despite the new racial demography, we believe, like Joe Feagin (2000) and others, that the black-white paradigm still ordains the macro racial issues in the country; it is still through this prism that newcomers are assessed (close to whiteness or blackness).

Fourth, modern white supremacy must be challenged wherever it exists—in churches, neighborhoods, schools, our places of work, and even in academic organizations such as the American Educational Research Association and the American Sociological Association. Those committed to racial equality must develop a personal practice to challenge white supremacy. Is this a racial ideology or a general post–civil rights ideology? In this chapter, we described the racial ideological aspects of the larger ideological ensemble, which always includes a plurality of subjects of domination (e.g., gender, race, class). At least one analyst makes the case that post–civil rights ideology is characterized by "muted hostility"[8] (Jackman 1994).

Finally, the most important strategy for fighting "new racism" practices and the ideology of color blindness is to recreate a civil rights movement. Changes in systems of domination and their accompanying ideologies are never accomplished by racial dialogues, "Can't we all just get along?" "workshops on racism," education, or "moral reform" alone. Moral, counterideological, and educational appeals always need a social movement, in our case, a new civil rights movement that demands equality of results now! Only by demanding what seems impossible now will we be able to make genuine racial equality possible in the future.

NOTES

1. We are using the notion of "white street" to refer to how "average" whites think and talk about race. The idea is similar to the way that American commentators talk and write about the "Arab street."

2. In this chapter, we only examine the dominant racial ideology. However, we would be remiss if we did not point out that not all whites spout this ideology. In fact, we document the views of white racial progressives, who make up about 10 percent of the white respondents in these samples in chapter 6 of Bonilla-Silva 2003.

3. Here, we are using the notion of ideology in the Althusserian sense, that is, of ideology as a practice that allows users to accomplish tasks.

4. Although some analysts believe that the idea of the "culture of poverty," as elaborated by Oscar Lewis in the 1960s, was the foundation of a racialized view on poverty, historians have documented the long history of this belief in America. See, for example, Michael A. Katz's *In the Shadow of the Poorhouse* (1986).

5. These moves have not disappeared completely as many respondents still used them. However, because ideologies are always in process, in construction, new and more refined moves have emerged.

6. We are not arguing that these are the only story lines out there. Our point is that they are the most salient at this historical juncture.

7. We classify as racial progressives respondents who support affirmative action and interracial marriage and who recognize the significance of discrimination in the United States.

8. In her book *The Velvet Glove*, Jackman (1994) argues that in the post–civil rights era, gender, class, and race ideology has shifted from overt to covert, or "muted," hostility. Thus, in Jackman's estimation, men, capitalists, and whites are less likely to employ the "nasty" tropes of the past, and hit women, workers, and minorities with a "velvet glove."

REFERENCES

Allport, Gordon W. 1958. *The nature of prejudice.* New York: Doubleday/Anchor Books.

Bell, Derrick. 1992. *Race, racism, and American law.* Boston, MA: Little, Brown, and Company.

Bonilla-Silva, Eduardo. 1997. Rethinking racism: Toward a structural interpretation. *American Sociological Review* 62 (3): 465–80.

———. 2001. *White supremacy and racism in the post–civil rights era.* Boulder, CO: Lynne Rienner Publishers.

———. 2003. *Racism without racists: Color-blind racism and the persistence of racial inequality in the USA.* Boulder, CO: Rowman & Littlefield.

———. 2004. From bi-racial to tri-racial: Towards new system of racial stratification in the USA. *Racial and Ethnic Studies* 27 (6) (November): 1–20.

Bonilla-Silva, Eduardo, and Amanda E. Lewis. 1999. The "new racism": Toward an analysis of the U.S. racial structure, 1960–1990s. In *Race, Nation, and Citizenship,* ed. Paul Wong, 100–50. Boulder, CO: Westview.

Braddock, Jomills, and James McPartland. 1987. How minorities continue to be excluded from equal employment opportunities: Research on labor market and institutional barriers. *Journal of Social Issues* 43 (1): 5–39.

Feagin, Joe R. 2000. *Racist America: Roots, realities, and future reparations.* New York: Routledge.

Feagin, Joe R., and Eileen O'Brian. 2003. *White men on race: Power, privilege, and the shaping of cultural consciousness.* Boston, MA: Beacon Press.

Feagin, Joe R., and Melvin Sikes. 1994. *Living with racism: The black middle class experience.* Boston: Beacon.

Feagin, Joe R., Hernan Vera, and Nikitah Imani. 1995. *The agony of education: Black students at white colleges and universities.* New York: Routledge.

Firebaugh, Glenn, and Kenneth E. Davis. 1988. Trends in antiblack prejudice, 1972–1984: Region and cohort effects. *American Journal of Sociology* 94 (2) (September): 251–72.

Ignatiev, Joel, and John Garvey. 1996. *Race traitor.* New York: Routledge.

Jackman, Mary R. 1994. *Velvet glove: Paternalism and conflict in gender, class, and race relations.* Berkeley: University of California Press.

Katz, Michael A. 1986. *In the shadow of the poorhouse: A social history of welfare in America.* New York: Basic Books.

Lewis, Oscar. 1966. The culture of poverty. *Scientific American* 215 (4): 19–25.

Massey, Douglas S., and Nancy A. Denton. 1993. *American apartheid: Segregation and the making of the underclass.* Cambridge, MA: Harvard University Press.

Royster, Deirdre A. 2003. *Race and the invisible hand: How white networks exclude black men from blue-collar jobs.* Berkeley: University of California Press.

Ryan, William. 1976. *Blaming the victim.* New York: Vintage Books.

Schuman, Howard, Charlotte Steeh, Lawrence Bobo, and Maria Krysan. 1997. *Racial attitudes in America: Trends and interpretations.* Cambridge, MA: Harvard University Press.

Sniderman, Paul M., and Thomas Piazza. 1993. *The scar of race.* Cambridge, MA: Harvard University Press.

Taguieff, Pierre-Andre. 2001. *The force of prejudice: Racism and its doubles.* Minneapolis: University of Minnesota Press.

3

Violence, Discourse, and Dixieland: A Critical Reflection on an Incident Involving Violence against Black Youth

Violet Jones

Border studies examines the critical issues encountered by peoples who straddle the physical and psychic divide between the United States and Mexico. Within border studies, we also examine whiteness as a position of power and privilege and how that privilege diminishes agency among border people. There are several dynamics working within *La frontera* (Anzaldúa 1999). This study focuses on three of these: the panopticon as an apparatus of surveillance, power, and oppression; and two dynamics facilitated by the panopticon, the gaze and the focus on the Other (Foucault [1977]1995; Spivak 1993).

As an African American woman who has worked in both the borderlands of the southwestern United States and what I call the "microborders" in this country's interior, I realize that several issues have emerged regarding the way "borders" are currently theorized within the United States. One problem with border studies is the way theorists and researchers sometimes create distance between themselves and the oppressed by couching the latter in theories disconnected from the actual lives of border people. In other words, those of us who study border people tend to assume this spectral absence in terms of our own subjectivity, a distance that dehumanizes the very people we seek to (re)present and that allows us to speak of them in ways that diminish the importance of their agency toward realizing *conscientização* (Freire 2000; Villenas 1996).

The other problem deals with borders as a figuration that generally applies to the southwestern United States, the areas that border Mexico between the Gulf of Mexico and Baja California. This border functions as a physical geographic Othering tool that one can easily see (Rella 1994). Theorizing and examining borders and border people using this familiar context limits the critique available about what borders do to people within the United States. Although the U.S.-Mexico border and the experiences of people who populate it magnify the historical racism (both linguistic and ethnic), economic exploitation, and subjugation sanctioned by people and governments in the United States, a closer examination of this nation's interiors reveals that many other borders exist and have for centuries. Furthermore, these invisible borders, which I refer to as microborders, exhibit practices against people similar to those executed along the U.S.-Mexico border.

In November 1997, five high school students whom I was supervising on an overnight field trip experienced violence at the hands of white people who unofficially reinforced a microborder in a large city in the southeastern United States. The high school academic team members who were shot at included one sixteen-year-old male (Josh), three fifteen-year-old females (Stephanie, Michelle, and Rosanne), and one fourteen-year-old male (Amari). In 2003 and 2004, I conducted a qualitative interview study to examine how the subjectivities of three of these young people had changed because of the violent racial event.

After completing the study, I moved to El Paso, Texas, a city that epitomizes all that is both good and bad about living on the border. After reading about this particular border, observing the way some of my undergraduate and graduate students experienced the gaze and Othering in this panoptic space (Foucault [1977]1995), and examining the discourses that border situations generate, I realized that the black young adults I had taught and coached experienced similar events in the microborder they violated in 1997.

As a part of my original study, I also examined my own subjectivity and how it affected the ability of these young adults to resist the subjugating efforts of white supremacists. Specifically, I examined how participants use Eurocentric and Africanist discourses (Asante 1998; Baldwin [1963]1993; Daniel and Smitherman 1976; Diop [1960]1987) to resist or capitulate to racialized Othering. I found that although participants were effective at using both discourses, their discursive choices and the consequences of these choices are directly related to their subjective position and the way they perceive power operating around them (Foucault [1972]1980). Likewise, the discourse I used when teaching these young people often contributed to their inability to find tools of resistance to the shooting and its effects (Dillard 2000; hooks 1992, 1994; Howard-Hamilton 2000).

Americans of color are bound and endangered by assumptions. We assume we are safe based on the chimera of U.S. military might and so-called homeland security. We often buy into the dominant discourse that assumes a spectral enemy far away and fails to see the enemy within our own borders. This enemy is neither a person of Middle Eastern origin nor a brown man or woman. Instead, the enemy that we fail to detect may be young or old; he or she is often white and poses as the authority we assume will protect us.

I hope this chapter serves as a method of resistance, or what Michel Foucault ([1976]1990) calls "an incitement to discourse" (105–6), against the enemy of good people who have been violated. I also seek to engage the reader with our everyday habitat and to bring attention to the apparatuses operating within the borderlands that seek to monitor and control the reader's behavior. The panoptic borderlands in the United States comprise myriad discourses (Anzaldúa 1999; Bhabha 1997; Foucault and Miskowiec [1984]1986). I will examine, according to the poststructural question, what those discourses do and what events they cause (Derrida and Dufourmantelle 2000; Foucault 1977; Lyotard [1979]1984).

RAGE WITHIN THE MICROBORDERS OF DIXIELAND

As I stated earlier, this study was precipitated by an Event[1]—something Jacques Derrida describes as "falling on you" (E. St. Pierre, personal communication, 2002)—a catastrophe, a crisis, a cataclysmic occurrence one does not expect because one is busy living (or dying) in the nomadic journey that is life. Although no one was physically injured during the 1997 shooting Event, my research reveals that these young people sustained numerous psychic injuries.

The shooting occurred on Friday, November 17, 1997, at around nine o'-clock in the evening during an overnight trip to an academic team tournament in the southeastern United States. A parent chaperone (identified as Carolyn in this study), the students, and I attended a national tournament at a large, private, predominately white university. The site of the Event was a nicely appointed major-chain hotel located in an affluent area. We departed our home school on Friday morning, stayed overnight at the hotel, and returned to our home school the following day.

This Event happened in an area not usually evoked when one thinks of borderlands. This site comprises a border that, as Gloria Anzaldúa (1999) suggests, is "not particular to the Southwest," but is "physically present wherever two or more cultures edge each other, where people of different races occupy the same territory, where . . . lower, middle and upper classes touch, where the space between two individuals shrinks with intimacy"(19). This is a space where men and women of color are profiled to keep them on their side of this invisible microborder (Aguirre 2004; Meehan and Ponder 2002).

The borders I describe delineate neighborhoods where the affluent *insiders* can live *safely*, in other words, where they can reside with little expectation of encountering *Others* like us (Abrams 2002; Braidotti 2001; Crittenden

2002; Cruz 2001). As the guard who shot at these young African American students reminded me, this was a race-based border, one where, according to the guard, "whenever [he] saw a group of black kids [he] assumed they were doing something illegal like drugs" (Jones 2004, 6).

The microborder violated by my students and me during the 1997 shooting Event were the same microborders of the inland United States where Mexicana/o people are now becoming increasingly profiled. Vigilantes, who often function under the intentionally misdirected gaze of official authorities, patrol them. In the case of Mexicana/o people, both along the U.S.-Mexico border and within microborders, organizations have sprung up that proudly vaunt their intention to monitor people of Mexican origin in an effort to capture those who have transgressed borders (e.g., the Minutemen Civil Defense Corps and Americans for Legal Immigration). Similarly, white supremacists are savvy and well-organized regarding their official efforts to keep any Other outside spaces unofficially designated for white occupation and recreation (e.g., Stormfront.org and Military Order of the Stars and Bars). Although these microborders are not juridically sanctioned, they are enforced through unofficially approved acts of control, surveillance, subjugation, and violence. This violence occurs when the Other violates racial, ethnic, sexual, economic, and linguistic borders.

BORDERS, THE GAZE, AND THE PANOPTICON: THEORIZING DISCIPLINARY APPARATUSES

The figuration of the border operates for those who wish to observe and control the Other through a set of focused apparatuses. Foucault, in *Discipline and Punish: The Birth of the Prison*, explains that three apparatuses, "the gaze, the eye of power, and the Benthamite Panopticon" (Foucault [1977]1995, 171; Goldstein 1994, 109), were erected during the nineteenth century to monitor and control aberrant behavior among undesirables.

The first of these apparatuses, the gaze, occurs when one person or group focuses on another. At the same time, we often focus the gaze on those who are like us. For instance, many border patrol members who are of Mexican origin gaze upon Mexicanos/as with suspicion. African Americans, regardless of status, face the gaze from both within and outside our communities. Michelle and Stephanie, by expressing their trepidation at my finding out about the shooting, revealed their awareness that I had focused my gaze on them.

Even though the gaze and the eye of power are used in border situations like the ones described above, they are also affected by other law-enforcement members, gatekeepers who police entry into elite public and private institutions. Similar to my own gaze identified earlier, educators also use the gaze in their own panopticon (i.e., the school campus).

EUROCENTRISM AND THE PANOPTICON

Foucault ([1997]2003) credits racist discourses to a "declining aristocracy," an aristocracy with "great mythical impulses, and with the ardor of the revenge of the people" (57). Similarly, organizations like the Minutemen, the Military Order of the Stars and Bars, and Stormfront.org credit their mission to the myth of an America created, built, and ideologically grounded by white people of European descent. Although the Minutemen carefully avoid using racist discourse in their publicity, the latter two organizations are proudly white supremacist.

White supremacists should not be confused with Eurocentrists; the former refers to Eurocentrists who are violently fanatical about racial purity (Futrell and Simi 2004), while the latter includes people of all ethnicities who believe in the primacy of epistemologies, philosophical ideas, and discourses originating in Europe (Asante 1998; Diop [1960]1987; Gordon 2000). Even though many people of color are Eurocentrists, I believe that, by definition, all Eurocentrists racialize the Other (Akintunde 1999; Allen 1994; Anderson 1995).

FORGETTING *SANKOFA*[2]

I forgot to remember. This mistake created an environment where young people whom I loved were placed in danger. I forgot *Sankofa*, the West African Adinkra message that translates "never forget the past."

Notes from my journal, November 18, 1997, approximately 1 a.m.:

After everyone received their keys and unpacked in their rooms, we reunited in the room that Carolyn and I shared. The girls asked if I would call the desk and request an iron. Two young white men, one dressed in the uniform of a security guard and another dressed in the shirt and tie uniform of a hotel representative, delivered the iron.

It is dark, about 10 in the evening. Carolyn and I have settled into our beds. We are startled by a telephone call from the front desk. They need me to come to the lobby immediately. As I exit the elevator, I see teary-eyed Michelle and Stephanie sitting on a bench. I ask the clerk what has happened. He says the security guard saw "them" acting suspicious and arrested "them."

Michelle: Yeah. I said, "What did we do?" He was like, "You all were loitering. And I had to make sure you all weren't drug dealers."

Stephanie: And he walking and I'm thinkin'. So he walks us around the corner and he tells us to kneel down. Michelle said, "I'm not 'bout to kneel down there. It's water down there!" He was like, "Yes you are." So he knelt me down on that. He just pushed me by my shoulders. He's like, "are ya'll guests at this hotel?" We was like, "Yes." He said, "I need to see your ID." We like, "We don't have any ID. We just came outside to talk." He was like, "Who are you here with?" We told him. I was like, "Are you gonna arrest us?" He was like, "I need to know that you all are [hotel guests] here." I think I said something like, "Are you gon' put those [handcuffs] on us?" He was like, "don't act like you not used to wearing them." He took us back through the parking lot, like a display basically. *Like we were his booty of war.* He said, "Who ya'll here with?" And we were like, "No. The rooms aren't in our names. Check under Carolyn Chastain." He checked, and we said, "Check under Violet Jones."

VJ: Why didn't you give him my name first?

Stephanie: Because we didn't want to get into trouble. And we were like, "The other people probably made it safe upstairs. Nobody knows what's goin' on." We didn't want to get everybody in trouble. . . . *Have you mad at us* while we were on this away trip. Because it was like competitive to go. And we were selected to go . . . and we didn't want to mess it up.

RUNNING FROM THE MASTER'S GAZE

I witnessed firsthand what happens to young African Americans when they begin to mirror the master's view of themselves.

The guard told me that he had fired his pistol over their heads to scare them into stopping and that he fired blanks. He then took out the pistol and proudly showed it to me. I asked him again why he shot at them. Again he said that he "saw a group of black kids who looked suspicious," so he tried to sneak up on "them." He said to me that usually when "we" [in my naiveté, I wonder, who the hell is "we"?] see a group of black kids huddled in a group we assume they are trying to sell drugs or something else illegal.

The guard's words could serve as the slogan for white supremacy, patriarchy, and neocolonialism. We could have been in post-Apartheid South Africa, along the Rio Grande, or in Palestine. I believe the racist discourse he used when speaking to me about his violent acts is used in various countries, cities, neighborhoods, schools, prisons, hospitals, and other public places across this nation. I also do not make the naive assumption that all speakers of the patriarchal discourse of white supremacy are of European descent for I have read and heard the castrating, nullifying, rapacious voice of white supremacy, patriarchy, and neocolonialism spoken and written by brown and black people.[3]

CONCERTED AFRICANNESS

While these young people were targeted because of their African ancestry, Africanist epistemologies also gave them the weapons to resist the effects of this event. One Africanism that facilitated their resistance was the solidarity among them. In African communities, there is a saying that "there is no I without a we." When they recall this Event, these young black people identify as one—one consciousness, one victim, one collective spirit, communally interdependent and interconnected (Delpit and White-Bradley 2003; Mbiti 1990). Notice how Michelle and Stephanie speak of themselves in the collective:

Michelle: He gets up on us and I'm like, "Ok. Michelle. We got to stop." So we slow down. He had the gun at my head. And I was just thinking about . . . you know, "are they gonna take me to the hospital? If I died, what's gonna happen to my family . . . to my sisters?"

Changing Attitudes about Race: How the Event Changed Them

Although Stephanie and Michelle have worked through their animosity, Amari has handled his differently. In order to analyze the resistance of these three young adults, I must first explain how I came to apply Africanist and Eurocentric notions in analyzing the discourses they use for resistance. M. K. Asante (1998) suggests three themes salient to Africanist discourse, "human relations, human relationship to the supernatural, and human relationship to their own being" (184).

Given these Africanist perspectives about race, I believe that both females utilized an Africanist (and Freirean) view in their approach toward white people after the Event. Even though both Stephanie and Michelle were angry toward white people for a short time after the Event, both eventually came to understand that not all white people were like the ones who criminalized them.

VJ: What kind of things did you feel and do different when you got back home?

Michelle: I grew up playing softball with all white people. I no longer wanted to play softball with the [white] people who I grew up with because I had resentment for all white people. I was like, "How could one race do this to another race and think nothing of it?"

VJ: Did you have any white friends?

Michelle: Yeah. I [became] very distant with them, too. My brother's marriage [to a woman of European descent] is what really brought me to. Finally I realized that it's not every white person that has that attitude, it's just a few just like it's not every black person who is racist against white people, it's just a few. I can't hold what happened to me against the whole race.

Stephanie also resolved her initial resentment toward white people.

VJ: How did it affect your attitude toward white people?

Stephanie: Immediately following that, I was rather distant toward . . . you know . . . [white] people. 'Cause my best friend was white. I never told her what happened. But her sister goes to Midtown [the school that was with us on the field trip] and was on the team. And I know she told her.

VJ: Had you planned on going to a historically black college before the shooting?

Stephanie: No. I had planned on going to either Mercer or Converse. And as a matter of fact, [Converse] gave me 10,000 dollars to come and offered to help take care of my out-of-state fees. And I applied to Cameron [the HBCU Stephanie now attends] . . . and [Cameron] gave me a full scholarship.

VJ: Did the event influence your decision?

Stephanie: Yes. And when I told the white guidance counselor [at the high school], she was like, "No. No. No. You need to go somewhere like Mercer or Wesleyan." She was like, "You need to go to a mixed school."

VJ: Did you get the message that you shouldn't go to a black school?

Stephanie: Definitely.

Amari and Eurocentric Resistance

Amari on the other hand, has decided that he has no use for white people in his life. Amari's resistance embodies elements of Eurocentric episte-mology. Within Eurocentric epistemology, "Autonomy has become cham-pioned and individualism revered. Authority is lifted up to a romantic heroism waged against a raw, half-savage natural and mental landscape" (Miles 2003, 12; Morrison 1992). In the comments below, Amari shows how he made the conscious choice to essentialize white people:

VJ: And what about your attitude towards white people?

Amari: I don't know. I read a quote by Sigmund Freud. It was something along the lines of the way people feel by a certain age, they'll never change. So I feel like, I might see a white person . . . they fifty years old. So, I think they were alive back in the 60's. He racist even though he might not show it. [Freud] says it's in your subconscious. So even though you can repress it the majority of the time it'll manifest itself. And like the [guard] coming 'round the corner, he might repress it most of the time, but when he see a group of young black people, that's when it manifest itself. [The guard assumes] "Oh. They some drug dealers." So, then he chased and shot at us.

VJ: So how does that affect how you feel about white people?

Amari: I'm on guard. But I mean white people . . . I would say they're violent because they scared of black people now. But yet and still the things they do, kinda sneaky. You know racism not just as overt as it used to be.

VJ: So how do you resist that?

Amari: Make them mad.

VJ: [Why?]

Amari: They racist.

VJ: What does that mean?

Amari: They give the white people the good stuff and the black people the bad stuff. Like back in the 50's and 60's, the black people had a little raggedy school with the hand me down books and the white people had all the first rate things.

VJ: Do you feel that's still true today?

Amari: Still the same thing. Just in a lesser degree.

VJ: So would you ever attend a white college?

Amari: No. I wouldn't want to be around people like that.

Africanist perspectives are not focused on whiteness. This might seem like an obvious fact, but I must stress it here in order to explain why I believe Amari uses Eurocentric discourse to resist the results of the shooting. Africanist perspectives focus on ways of being Africanist, not on ways of dealing with, or perspectives regarding, whiteness specifically. Toni Morrison (1992), James Baldwin ([1963]1993), Lewis Gordon (1997), and other Africanist writers have explicated the problem of focusing on whiteness when documenting the black experience. The problem with focusing on whiteness when discussing blackness is that it casts blackness in relief to whiteness. In other words, black people only have an identity as long as white people continue to recognize them as Other.

When a black person operates within the idea he or she is black because white people have created blackness through colonialism and slavery, it is difficult for this black person to speak outside the discourse of Eurocentrism, even when speaking in opposition to white privilege. This black person must use the master's tools because they are the only ones he or she knows. This black person's discourse mirrors that of the master—when he speaks about white people, one could substitute "blacks" for every critique of "whites" and be convinced that a white person was speaking. This is why I believe Amari uses Eurocentric discourse to resist the effects of the shooting.

BLACK TEACHERS IN WHITEFACE

When I began teaching at the majority African American school where I met Stephanie, Amari, Michelle, Josh, and Roseanne, I knew how discourses operated and was aware that I should not marginalize Africanist discourses or ways of being. Even though I knew this on a cognitive level, something about having lived in dominant discourse communities permeated much of what I said and did when engaging with these students. Oppression and subjugation do not necessarily imply intent. In my case, I intended to help students appreciate their own uniqueness. What I did was another matter entirely.

I discovered through this study that I reflected what Toni Morrison (1996) calls the "white gaze." As Morrison explains it, some people of color operate with a constant and censoring white consciousness. Therefore, these people unwittingly operate out of a white supremacist discourse. I feel that I have been guilty of this in many of my dealings with students. Morrison suggests, "Maybe I'm wrong in my feelings about the impact of the white gaze on African-American[s] . . . but I know that eliminating it from my imagination was an important thing'" (McHenry 2003, 28–32). This study was my method of resistance to the white supremacist operating within my own discourse and consciousness.

As I seek to identify how the white gaze affects the way I deal with black students, some things I have done come immediately to mind. I have a deep understanding of what causes one to be raced black since I attended majority-white schools from fifth grade through my doctoral program. First, I knew that many white people thought blacks were loud, so I constantly told my team members not to be loud in public. Blacks, especially those of the hip-hop generation, are also raced because they wear baggy pants and oversized shirts. Consequently, I did not allow my team members to dress in this fashion when we went to tournaments. Ironically, we often saw that white students from other schools at these tournaments spoke loudly and wore baggy clothing, but *as they were white, they were not raced* because of their clothing or manner of speaking. I felt that when my students did these things, they were judged differently by the white gaze. I would look askance at any of my students who wore what I thought was excessive or gaudy jewelry. If I felt their appearance was *different* enough to draw attention to them, I required them to remove the violating adornments.

I felt that I had to watch my students constantly, especially when we were in public places of business. I would not tell them that they could not go into the gas stations or upscale mall stores when we traveled. I simply kept an eye on them when they went to these places, and as we traveled through small Southern towns, I was careful to linger inconspicuously about as they did their shopping. I felt I had to do this because, as a product of the segregated Sixties, I knew that many white people assumed that black people entered these businesses in order to steal merchandise. Even though I knew none of my students would steal, I placed my gaze on them in the hopes of preventing some white person from accusing them of violating the law.

What I did to, and with, my students was shameful. In my attempt to theorize my actions, I believe that my discourse was unknowingly colonized. I used Eurocentric discourse, specifically the discourse of academic rationalism and assimilation, when I disciplined my students. Race as we know it in the Americas is a Eurocentric construct. I was not conscious of racing my own students—of standing as proxy for the white supremacists. Nevertheless, my continual monitoring of their dress, speech, and behavior affected the way these young people negotiated the Event. My subjective impact became clear once I realized that these students had agreed among themselves not to tell me about the shooting because they were afraid that I would be angry with them. In addition, they agreed that they would not tell anyone at their home school about the shooting Event even after it became public. The students were ashamed. Consequently, I had effectively transferred that part of my Eurocentric consciousness to them. When I asked Michelle why they were ashamed, even though they had done nothing wrong, she responded that they "just looked guilty." I have to take responsibility for my role in making young people feel embarrassed by a situation in which they held no culpability.

CONCLUSION

Although the guard who shot at these young people was guilty of racing them, within Africanist epistemology it is the duty of the elders—elders like me and other educators—to teach students the kinds of discourses they should use to resist racing and subjugation. It is our duty to help young people learn *Sankofa*. Those of us who work and live within microborders in this country must reach back to the ancestors for tools to equip young people for resistance. Not only must we look to the ancestors, but we must also look to the future, to the vision for people of color in an age of magic realism, where they have learned not only discourses for resistance but also discourses that do not other Others.

NOTES

1. For the purposes of this article, I will refer to the 1997 shooting as the "Event" using capital letters to distinguish it from other events.
2. *Sankofa* is the Andinkra word interpreted as "return and get it." It is often translated as "never forget the lessons of the past."
3. For a critique of the Eurocentric discourse used by Africans and African Americans such as W. E. B. DuBois, Anthony Appiah, and Alexander Crummel, see Jones 2004.

REFERENCES

Abrams, J. J. 2002. Aesthetics of self-fashioning and cosmopolitanism: Foucault and Rorty on the art of living. *Philosophy Today* 46 (2): 185–92.

Aguirre, A., Jr. 2004. Profiling Mexican American identity: Issues and concerns. *American Behavioral Scientist* 47 (7): 928–42.

Akintunde, O. 1999. White racism, white supremacy, white privilege, and the social construction of race: Moving from modernist to postmodernist multiculturalism. *Multicultural Education* 7 (2): 2–8.

Allen, T. 1994. *The invention of the white race.* London: Verso.

Anderson, V. 1995. *Beyond ontological blackness: An essay on African American religious and cultural criticism.* New York: Continuum.

Anzaldúa, G. 1999. *Borderlands/la frontera.* 2nd ed. San Francisco: Aunt Lute Books.

Asante, M. K. 1998. *The Afrocentric idea.* Rev. and exp. ed. Philadelphia: Temple University Press.

Baldwin, J. [1963]1993. *The fire next time.* 1st Vintage int. ed. New York: Vintage International.

Bentham, J. 1812. Panopticon versus New South Wales, or the Panopticon penitentiary system and the penal colonization system compared containing, 1. Two letters to Lord Pelham. 2. Plea for the constitution [microform]. London: Sold by R. Baldwin.

Bhabha, H. K. 1997. Life at the border: Hybrid identities of the present. *NPQ: New Perspectives Quarterly* 14 (1): 130–31.

Braidotti, R. 2001. Once upon a time in Europe. *Signs: Journal of Women in Culture and Society* 25 (4): 1061–64.

Crittenden, C. 2002. Self de-selection: Technological annihilation via cyborg. *Ethics and the Environment* 7 (2): 127–53.

Cruz, C. 2001. Toward an epistemology of a brown body. *International Journal of Qualitative Studies in Education (QSE)* 14 (5): 657–69.

Daniel, J. L., and G. Smitherman. 1976. How I got over: Communication dynamics in the black community. *Quarterly Journal of Speech* 62 (1): 26–39.

Delpit, L., and P. White-Bradley. 2003. Educating or imprisoning the spirit: Lessons from ancient Egypt. *Theory into Practice* 42 (4): 283–89.

Derrida, J., and A. Dufourmantelle. 2000. *Of hospitality.* Palo Alto, CA: Stanford University Press.

Dillard, C. 2000. The substance of things hoped for, the evidence of things not seen: Examining an endarkened feminist epistemology in educational research and leadership. *International Journal of Qualitative Studies in Education (QSE)* 13 (6).

Diop, C. A. [1960]1987. *Precolonial black Africa: A comparative study of the political and social systems of Europe and black Africa, from antiquity to the formation of modern states,* trans. H. J. Salemson. Brooklyn, NY: Lawrence Hill Books.

Foucault, M. [1972]1980. *Power/knowledge: Selected interviews and other writings, 1972–1977,* trans. L. M. Colin Gordon, John Mepham, and Kate Soper. New York: Pantheon Books.

———. [1976]1990. *The history of sexuality.* New York: Vintage Books.

———. 1977. *Language, counter-memory, practice: Selected essays and interviews,* trans. D. F. B. S. Simon. Ithaca, NY: Cornell University Press.

———. [1977]1995. *Discipline and punish: The birth of the prison*, trans. A. Sheridan. 2nd ed. New York: Vintage Books.

———. [1997]2003. *"Society must be defended": Lectures at the college de France, 1975–76*, trans. D. Macey. 1st ed. New York: Picador.

Foucault, M., and J. Miskowiec. [1984]1986. Of other spaces. *Diacritics* 16 (1): 22–27.

Freire, P. 2000. *Pedagogy of the oppressed*. 30th anniv. ed. New York: Continuum.

Futrell, R., and P. Simi. 2004. Free spaces, collective identity, and the persistence of U.S. white power activism. *Social Problems* 51 (1): 16–42.

Goldstein, J. E. 1994. Foucault and the postrevolutionary self: The uses of cousinian pedagogy in nineteenth-century France. In *Foucault and the writing of history*, ed. J. E. Goldstein, 99–115. Cambridge, MA.: Blackwell.

Gordon, L. R. 1997. *Her majesty's other children: Sketches of racism from a neocolonial age*. Lanham, MD: Rowman & Littlefield.

Gordon, L. R. 2000. *Existentia Africana: Understanding Africana existential thought*. New York: Routledge.

hooks, b. 1992. *Black looks: Race and representation*. Boston: South End Press.

———. 1994. *Teaching to transgress: Education as the practice of freedom*. New York: Routledge.

Howard-Hamilton, M. F. 2000. Creating a culturally responsive learning environment for African American students. *New Directions for Teaching and Learning* 82:45, 49.

Jones, V. J. 2004. *Race is a verb: An effective history of young adults subjected to racial violence*. Unpublished qualitative dissertation, University of Georgia, Athens, GA.

Lyotard, J. F. [1979]1984. *The postmodern condition: A report on knowledge*. Minneapolis: University of Minnesota Press.

Mbiti, J. S. 1990. *African religions and philosophy*. 2nd rev. enl. ed. Portsmouth, NH: Heinemann.

McHenry, S. 2003. Lady laureate: Meet the great Toni Morrison in an exclusive BIBR kitchen-table chat. *Black Issues in Higher Education Book Review*, 28–32.

Meehan, A. J., and M. C. Ponder. 2002. Race and place: The ecology of racial profiling African American motorists. *JQ: Justice Quarterly* 19 (3): 399–430.

Miles, S. 2003. Playing in the dark: Whiteness and the bioethics imagination. *American Journal of Bioethics* 3 (2): 12.

Morrison, T. 1992. *Playing in the dark: Whiteness and the literary imagination*. Cambridge, MA: Harvard University Press.

———. 1996. *The dancing mind: Speech upon acceptance of the National Book Foundation Medal for distinguished contribution to American letters on the sixth of November, nineteen hundred and ninety-six*. 1st ed. New York: Alfred A. Knopf.

Rella, F. 1994. *The myth of the Other: Lacan, Deleuze, Foucault, Bataille*. Washington, DC: Maisonneuve Press.

Spivak, G. C. 1993. *Outside in the teaching machine*. New York: Routledge.

Villenas, S. 1996. The colonizer/colonized Chicana ethnographer: Identity, marginalization, and co-optation in the field. *Harvard Educational Review* 66 (Winter): 711–31.

4

Latino Youths at the Crossroads of Sameness and Difference: Engaging Border Theory to Create Critical Epistemologies on Border Identity

Cynthia L. Bejarano

This chapter examines the largely unspoken and unexamined divisions among youths of Mexican descent whose identities are located along a wide continuum of Mexicanness. This analysis is based on a four-year ethnography conducted at a metropolitan high school that is the catalyst for an upcoming book exploring Latino[1] youth cultures through a border theoretical lens. Border theory provided the template for exploring these identity constructions and the new epistemologies and pedagogies that celebrate difference and begin looking toward the extreme margins of what is hegemonic or conventional thinking. By establishing strong foundational structures to discuss the intellectual spaces and lived experiences of those considered to be different or "Other," we can better understand the mosaic of youth cultures that intersect, merge, and create anew the lives and perspectives of youths of Mexican descent in the borderlands.

Youths of Mexican descent grapple with identity issues, a sense of belonging, and acceptance at the U.S.-Mexico border. Negotiating identity for Chicana/o and Mexicana/o[2] teenagers creates divisive relationships that often escalate into verbal and physical forms of violence at Altamira High School.[3] Embroiled fourteen- through eighteen-year-old Mexicana/o and Chicana/o youths struggle with questions of Mexican authenticity, nationalism, discrimination, and cultural bias, with little respite for sharing common ground with one another. Cultural strife between Latina/o boys and girls is misunderstood and oftentimes overlooked by educational practitioners who fail to understand the subtle differences between who is perceived as Mexicana/o and Chicana/o.

These identity clashes are salient since the differences among Latinas/os are commonly overlooked or denied by people, especially in the borderlands where they represent a significant demographic presence. Subgroups of Latinas/os are often homogenized by those unfamiliar with their vast differences. Consequently, all youths of Mexican descent are frequently thought of as having identical experiences. M. Houston (1992) suggests that "scholars tend to reduce complex social phenomena to their simplest terms in order to study them. This includes treating social groups that are internally diverse as if they are homogenous" (54). Not only scholars but also school teachers and staff, other ethnic/racial students, and U.S. society in general assume that these Mexicana/o and Mexican American/Chicana/o youths have the same experiences.

Four years of ethnographic fieldwork revealed the deep creases of cultural tensions between young Latinas/os at Altamira High and the pronounced differences between what it means to call oneself Mexicana/o or Chicana/o.[4] Field notes were filled with overwrought examples of resentment between Mexicano and Chicano boys and girls. For instance, Javier[5] and Arturo stated they had problems with the Chicanos because they were racist (i.e., prejudiced against Mexicanas/os). Javier explained, "The Chicanos will make fun of us because of our language and customs." Both boys said that last year the Chicano and Mexicano boys got into a fight, and Arturo was involved in it because he was tired of the Chicano boys calling the Mexicanos "wetbacks." He said they were at school and were about to get into a physical fight on school grounds but left because the security guards were approaching. Arturo still ended up getting jumped by ten Chicanos. Administrators and teachers were often puzzled by how Latino boys could fight so incessantly when they were seemingly so much alike. Interestingly enough, the security guards seemed to understand fully how identity issues often triggered these explosive responses by young people, but they were rarely ever asked for their opinion. They spent more one-on-one time with students while navigating the hallways, lunch areas, and hang-out spots. Driving around campus in golf carts with T-shirts, shorts, and walkie-talkies made them much more approachable than those in the principal's office.

Both Chicanos and Mexicanos instigated the verbal and physical fighting. I even saw "Fuck Chicanos" or "Mexicans rule" on the notebooks of some Mexican boys, and I heard about Chicano boys attempting to monitor whom the Chicanas spoke to, warning them to stay away from the "wetbacks." When I asked the Mexicanas and Chicanas why the boys would physically fight, both would say, "Because they are immature" or "Because they are just dumb." Despite their condemnation of the boys' violence, occasionally the girls also fought. Isabel, a Mexican immigrant who had recently arrived in the United States, relayed the story of fighting off four Chicanas who called her a "wetback" on her first day of school. Most girls' propensity, however, was to "mad dog" each other, that is, glare at one another from a distance, and gossip about each other's actions and dress. The phrases and metaphors they used about one another, the whispers shared across the schoolyard, and the cutting stares were provocative clues about the clashes between these students. Overall, the confrontations remained relatively constant throughout the years and led to my interest in understanding why the divisions between these youths cut so deeply.

Ironically, strong identity ties among these youths of Mexican descent served as a source of both strength and conflict. Racial/ethnic friction arose between Mexicana/o immigrants who exuded a strong sense of pride in their Mexican heritage and identity and their Chicana/o counterparts who strongly identified with American popular culture, while holding on to their Latina/o roots. Problems spiraled into confrontations and intragroup tensions at Altamira High and in other public spaces when these young people reinforced and affirmed their identities.

FINDING A MIDDLE GROUND OF IDENTITY

Other groups of youths of Mexican descent seemed caught in the middle of the tensions between Chicana/o and Mexicana/o groups since they claimed some aspects of both identities. In one sense, it was ostensibly impossible to pinpoint exactly who this middle group was, even though both Chicana/o and Mexicana/o groups occasionally referred to an "in-between" group. For example, in-between youths were different from Leslie and Evelyn, Mexican Americans who claimed both Mexicana/o and Chicana/o identities, depending on their situation but who nevertheless chose to "hang out" with Mexicanas/os. This in-between group also did not fall into the Chicana/o group, like Blanca, who identified as Mexicana since she was born in Mexico but spent all her time with Chicanas/os.

The in-between group, rather, spent time apart from the other predominantly Mexicana/o and Chicana/o groups. I gathered from these youths that they were not necessarily one coherent group or several groups but represented smaller, tributary Latina/o groups. These were students of Mexican descent who might have come to this country when they were very young and grew up claiming to be "American." Some did not acknowledge that they understood Spanish when ESL students spoke to them, asked for assistance, or simply wanted to strike up a conversation. They did, however, manage to identify themselves at any given time as Mexicana/o and Chicana/o.

Some were first-generation Mexican Americans who spoke both languages perfectly and vacillated between a Mexicana/o and Chicana/o, or even an interracial, group of friends. Cisco provides a perfect example. He could move from his mixed-race group of friends, sitting at one cafeteria table, to the other side of the cafeteria to sit at the Mexican table with his second cousins from

Mexico, saying, *Yo soy puro Mexicano por vida* (I am pure Mexicano for life), then finish the school day at a Movimiento Estudantíl Chicano de Aztlan (MEChA) meeting with Chicana/o friends. His English accent was absent when he spoke Spanish, and his Spanish accent was untraceable when he spoke English. Unlike Cisco, very few students could "pull this off." Others who attempted to transcend borders came across as "fake" or as "dissing their own *raza*," like the Mexican girls who claimed "Chicanismo" while not speaking Spanish, even though others claimed they spoke Spanish in their homes. The Chicanas engaged in a discussion about this.

> *Blanca:* I believe that some people, they don't say they're Mexicans. . . . Most of them are ashamed to admit that they are actually Mexican. To me it is like, Chicana, okay, you're a Chicana [says this to Angel, who's part Mexican American and Anglo]. But that's like more of a white . . . like an English word for it, you know what I'm saying? It's like most people are Mexicans, they are straight up Mexicans. They are born in Mexico, but they don't consider themselves Mexican because they are ashamed. I don't know why, but they are ashamed of saying they are Mexican.
>
> *Leticia:* Well, they don't want to get criticized.
>
> *Blanca:* By the society.
>
> *Leticia:* Yeah.

The contradictions in identities were messy and confusing for some, while others comfortably subscribed to an assortment of labels: Mexicana/o, Hispanic, Latina/o, Chicana/o, or Mexican American. There were students who struggled with their biculturalism, as recent immigrants or as second-, third-, or fourth-generation youths born in the United States. Several saw themselves as a little bit of both, but not quite enough of one or the other, which further complicated their identity-seeking process and their establishment of borders around who they felt they were. Clearly, youths of Mexican descent grappled with cultural differences and found themselves locked in a tug-of-war over their identity. This phenomenon left some Latinos adrift in a middle zone along the continuum of Mexicanness that could be ambiguous and challenging to identify.

Viewed differently, this middle zone may hold some answers as to how youths can negotiate their identities successfully and avoid some difficulties in claiming only one identity as Mexicana/o or Chicana/o. Perhaps success is fluidity and living "sandwiched" between contradictions (Anzaldúa 1987). For instance, Leslie uses the labels interchangeably when she feels it is appropriate:

> Many identify as Chicanas because they don't know how to speak in Spanish. I think that is the reason. I want to consider myself as Mexicana, but I am not sure if I am in that category. I use Chicana because that way people wouldn't

say she is Mexicana but she can't speak or write in Spanish. I use it to my preference, for example, on an application I write down that I'm Chicana because this way they know I'm here legally. I have my Social Security number so they can't discriminate for any reason. That's when I use Chicana more, or when they ask me, I say I'm Chicana so that they will know that I have my legal papers. But when we go out to have a good time and go out to dance, then I am a Mexicana.

Using both labels at any given time is expected: one is applied in certain situations, and possibly both are even used to describe oneself with a slash in between the two labels (Mexicana/Chicana). The students who found a common middle ground in using both ethnic labels circumvented the lure to engage anyone in physical or verbal confrontations. Most students, however, were locked in an oppressive cycle of criticizing, ridiculing, and Othering (perceiving others to be less desirable than those in one's own social category), which created divisive circumstances through reinforcing categories of being American or not American. In this process, hierarchies were created where Chicanos were viewed as legitimizing their social and cultural place at Altamira High as U.S. citizens, while perpetuating feelings of not belonging in their Mexican immigrant counterparts.

OTHERIZATION

The Othering process by Chicanas/os toward Mexicanas/os reflects and parallels the discrimination faced by Latinas/os from many American citizens and the xenophobia of the larger U.S. society. At the same time, Chicanas/os engaged in Othering Mexicanas/os, while these same Chicanas/os were often Otherized by fellow U.S. citizens. Once again, the social hierarchy present at Altamira High managed not only to stratify the groups but also to make the two less powerful groups (Mexicanas/os and Chicanas/os) feel insignificant and foreign. Francisca González claims,

> Historically and to the present day, Mexicanas[/os], as well as all women[/men] of color, are textually represented as the "other.". . .Consequently, because of these differences, Mexicanas[/os] and women[/men] of color are named inferior to both European American men and women and are subordinated through rejection because of race/ethnicity and class differences. (1998, 83)

This passage applies to youths of Mexican descent who feel inferior to dominant "American" youths. Consequently, these feelings of "inferiorization" are manifested through their Othering of one another:

> Samantha: Creo que hay algunos grupos de Chicanos que cuando nos ven nos miran para abajo. Aunque yo se que en el mismo grupo hay mexicanos y

Chicanos que fueron nacidos en México pero han vivido aquí y son esos gru-
pos que nos dan esas miradas. Yo no se, los jóvenes de hoy están algo perdi-
dos. No saben lo que quieren. Ellos no te ayudarían, todo lo que ellos
quieren es pasarla bien, usar drogas, pelear y tener sexo.

[I feel there are some small groups of Chicanos that when they see us, they
look down on us, even though I know that in that same group, there are Mexicanos and Chicanos who were born in Mexico, but they have lived here, and
it is that group that gives us dirty looks. I don't know. The youths these days are
somewhat lost. They don't know what they want. They won't help you, all they
want is to have a good time, do drugs, fight, and have sex.]

Distinct messages of Otherization were relayed back and forth from
dominant groups to Chicanas/os and down to Mexicanas/os. Ultimately,
the messages trickle downward, impacting all youths of Mexican descent.
Margaret Montoya (1999) aptly describes their situation when she speaks
of her own experiences: "I felt isolated and different because I could be exposed in so many ways—through class, ethnicity, race, gender, and the sub-
tleties of language, dress, makeup, voice, and accent" (210). The overarching questions of identity and legitimacy are related to Franz Fanon's
poignant query asking, "Where am I to be classified? Or, if you prefer,
tucked away?" (1967, 113).

Interestingly enough, even though Chicanas/os maintained their status as
Americans and had more privileges than Mexicanas/os in the United States,
they often felt like "second-class citizens" in the country of their birth.
Some Chicanas/os, dismayed by their status as second-class citizens, began
to view their Mexican heritage as less significant and allowed dominant
American culture to consume their Mexicanness. And although there were
some pockets of resistance by Chicana/o youth through the MEChA organization, oftentimes Chicana/os single-handedly planned Latino-based fes-
tivities on campus, like a Cinco de Mayo luncheon and dance, and excluded
Mexicana/o students from organizing the events. Many students, however,
were firmly rooted in their primary culture and thrived on this exposure
and proximity to the border.

Despite their rich cultural perspective on living near the border, Mexicana/o
students also understood the pain experienced by Chicana/o border dwellers
who did not want to identify as Mexicanas/os so close to the border. Chicanas/
os confronted the same situation with other Americans who considered
them foreign and more closely a part of Mexico than the United States. Both
Mexicana/o and Chicana/o youths seemed to battle constantly for some acceptance, whether this meant remaining loyal *a lo Mexicano* (to anything
Mexican) or demonstrating American-like qualities to save face with others
in the United States.

Regardless of the tactics they chose, the Othering process for all youths of
Mexican descent was a common one that placed them on the margins, the

very physical boundaries of living in the borderlands, and wrapped them in the oppositional dialectics they were entangled in. A. Arteaga (1994) asserts that "the Other is more fully relegated to the realm of absence. . . . The Other is exteriorized, frozen, inscribed. Effectively, the Other is silenced, existing only as defined by a rigid and prescribed alterity or not existing at all" (21). Those who do not succumb to the pressures of assimilating, who are not lured by the calls of success according to U.S. standards, sustain their lives on the borderlands but with great marginalization from dominant groups. Gloria Anzaldúa explains,

> I have so internalized the borderland conflict that sometimes I feel like one cancels out the other and we are zero, nothing, no one. . . . Yet the struggle of identities continues, the struggle of borders is our reality still. One day the inner struggle will cease and a true integration will take place. (1987, 63)

In the borderlands, some of the most reoccurring questions asked are, "Where are you from?" "Are you a U.S. citizen?" or, more offensively, "What are you?" Irrespective of the question asked, the same vestiges of discrimination and prejudice and the construction of social hierarchies found in the larger American culture were also present at Altamira High.

FREIRE AND OPPRESSION

Hegemonic forces pulled at the cultural strings of these Latino youths at Altamira High, even though they managed to maintain a stronghold on their cultural backgrounds and languages. School hallways and lunchrooms were still spaces infiltrated by hegemonic rhetoric on assimilation and identity and therefore influenced how youth were willing to identify. Inevitably, a Mexican American identity (emphasis on American) was perceived as carrying more social and cultural clout than a Mexican identity alone. For some youth and school personnel, the label "Mexican" was more dubious and hinted at something foreign and "different." Oftentimes, adults easily perpetuated these understandings, knowingly or not, thus deepening tensions that existed between Latina/o youths.

Latino youths became what Paulo Freire (1970) describes as "receptacles" of learning, simply regurgitating everything fed to them from teachers and larger educational systems. Freire states, "The more completely she [he] fills the receptacles, the better a teacher she [he] is. The more meekly the receptacles permit themselves to be filled, the better students they are" (53). In some instances, Mexicana/o and Chicana/o youths did succumb to the messages that teachers and school officials filled them with. The demands to conform are greater than those to preserve culture and language within school grounds. Nonetheless, once students are outside the school grounds, they make concerted efforts to return to what is natural and secure for them: they reimmerse themselves in the familiar contours of what they understand as Mexicanness.

Despite overt difficulties, border youths lived within the spectrum of Mexicanness that was central to their identity making. However, their border narratives reveal pressures complicating any possibility of a clear-cut path toward identity. Oftentimes, the messages they received claimed they were not members of U.S. society but simply shadows of a dominant culture or a mere immigrant nuisance. Language differentials (i.e., Spanish or English), for instance, positioned them in strategic places along a fence, either looking out at a First World "frontier" or looking into the faces representing the Third World. Similarly, stepping outside of their American barrios for Chicana/os, or outside of their mother country and over the U.S. threshold, called the border for Mexicana/os, consequently left both Mexicanas/os and Chicanas/os and other youths in between these two labels vulnerable to multiple negative forces, including social stratification, internal colonization, and distancing by "Othering." These forces and the discourses about citizenship together produced in-between groups of Latina/o youths struggling to maintain ties to both Mexicanas/os and Chicanas/os or, alternatively, preferring one to the other. The complexity under which these youths functioned was astounding.

A struggle was apparent in the Chicanas' relationships with Anglos during these conversations. They quickly pointed to these examples and said they had to compete with Anglo whites and, as Angel stated, "step on" Mexicanas/os in order to succeed. They refused to return to the "hole" that they had climbed out of. There was a pervasive attempt to penetrate the highest level of this hierarchy by some Chicanas/os, even though they remained socially wedged between Mexicanas/os and Anglos. Freire states,

> The oppressed, instead of striving for liberation, tend themselves to become oppressors, or "sub-oppressors." . . . This is their model of humanity. This phenomenon derives from the fact that the oppressed, at a certain moment of their existential experience, adopt an attitude of "adhesion" to the oppressor. (1970, 27)

The preoccupation with acceptance and upward mobility at Altamira High School, therefore, blinds Chicana/o students from recognizing the role and nature of their relationships with Mexican and Anglo students. Oftentimes, Chicana/o and Anglo white students, for instance, are classified as mainstream students by school officials and have no opportunity to dialogue with or engage Mexican students who are highly isolated in ESL classrooms. At Altamira, while mainstream and ESL students were segregated from one another in the classroom, the students also segregated themselves by establishing Chicana/o and Mexicana/o enclaves in the cafeteria and throughout the school grounds.

BORDER PEDAGOGY AND EDUCATORS

Educational inequities were rampant in school settings and classroom structures. According to Anna Nieto Gomez (1997), "All institutions in a Capitalistic society perpetuate myths of racism and sexism. The educational institution reinforce[s] the division between people of different races, cultures, sex, and class, and define[s] these divisions as natural" (98). Many of these divisions are lived out in educational systems, which have varied influences on youths and their cultures, as reflected in their multiple experiences.

Even though educational institutions are meant to provide equal opportunities for all students, this is rarely the case. At Altamira High School, several dedicated faculty members and staff worked with ESL students and mainstream students. There were, however, quite a few adults who were not as actively involved with these ESL students' educational endeavors. Many were oblivious to the intraethnic tension in their school:

> When I went to the administration office and I spoke to one of the school secretaries, she called the fight [the fight mentioned at the beginning of this chapter] "a fight over name calling between an American-born Hispanic and a Hispanic from Mexico." She assured me that they had taken care of the problem. A white male math teacher who was in the office said, "There aren't too many problems with students at [names the school]. You should study youth at other schools that have more problems."

Some adults at this school did not perceive intraethnic conflicts as highly problematic. When fighting between Latino youths ensued, many Anglo teachers and administrators placed the bulk of the responsibility to diffuse the situation on the few Latina/o faculty and staff on campus. As harmless as it may have seemed, by this practice some Anglo faculty and staff Otherized and socially stratified the Latina/o faculty and staff. The Latina/o adults were compartmentalized and reduced to solving the troubles that were perceived to reflect issues unique to their ethnic group. These problems were framed as "Latino problems," therefore shedding the responsibility of other faculty, staff, and administrators to help resolve these issues. Non-Latino faculty frequently had an aversion to recognizing these issues as deeply embedded societal and educational problems that pierced the school infrastructure and impacted everyone.

Another dilemma for Latina/o youths was created by the tracking systems at Altamira High that often erratically placed them in educational pathways that were less fruitful for some students than others. Nellie, for instance, was a Mexican American student who spoke, read, and wrote perfect English but was placed in an ESL class because as she said she got "lost between the cracks of the system." She believed it was because teachers heard her speak Spanish, and she hung out with the Mexicana/o students. Her classes were much easier than mainstream classes, and she "had no complaints"; however, her learning process was placed in tremendous jeopardy.

This lack of educational opportunities largely limited many students' futures and divided groups of youths according to their school and socioeconomic experiences. Factors like English-language deficiencies, official school labels like ESL or mainstream (regular class status), social class, and citizenship status also contributed to the ill effects of educational systems on many youths. In addition, pressuring Mexican American teachers and staff, especially ESL teachers, to cope with the youths' identity issues and conflicts greatly burdened these individuals. The pressure should have been shifted onto the entire school community (i.e., administration, teachers, and students) to work together in concert to stop the conflict that was prevalent between Chicanas/os and Mexicanas/os.

A reeducation of school administrators and teachers addressing identity conflict must begin so that they understand the roots of violence in schools, which can be avoided if they know the impetus for violent behavior. Violence often stems from identity searching (i.e., name calling, adopting clothing and styles, challenging others' belief systems and experiences) and the tensions spawned between youths as a result of this process. By collectively taking an active role in learning about the nuances between groups of Latino youth, much of the physical violence between these young people could be dissipated. Training faculty and staff about Latino identity and language issues would enhance student-teacher relationships, alleviate tensions between faculty and staff of color versus other faculty and staff, and work toward more fully integrating marginalized students, who would otherwise continue to be isolated. Latino youth are an untapped resource that, if cultivated, could serve as a tool to diversify the school setting through their full involvement in the classroom, after-school activities, and rich cultural exchanges.

These suggestions echo what Henry A. Giroux (1992) and Alejandra Elenes (1997) suggest about integrating critical and border pedagogies into the schooling process. Giroux speaks of the need to "create pedagogical conditions where students become border crossers to understand otherness in its own terms" (28). This approach will broaden the knowledge base of not only Latino students but also all students, faculty, and staff that embrace difference and its educational contributions. The subtle differences between these youths are difficult for others to interpret and understand. "Border pedagogy offers the opportunity for students to engage the multiple references that constitute different cultural codes, experiences, and languages" (Giroux 1992, 29). This type of "border thinking" is perhaps the most challenging of epistemologies and pedagogies because it forces people to look at the margins of knowledge and understanding, which have otherwise been taught as culturally, socially, and educationally insignificant. As Elenes (1997) explains, "[Border identity] is a discourse and identity of difference and displacement" (359). It takes courage for educators and students to engage these discourses that have always been portrayed as foreign, irrelevant, and nonacademic.

These suggestions are rooted in presenting Latina/o youths with a more holistic education by fully including them in the educational process and articulating a sense of dignity and appreciation for their culture and identity. This process would have to begin by discarding the first-grade *Jack and Jill* books for ESL students found in the school library and replacing them with literature by authors who write about themes these students can relate to, like immigration issues for newcomers, the experiences of multigenerational families, and the stresses found among people of Mexican descent, including tense race relations with other multicultural groups. Mentorship programs for youth from multiple generations, for instance, could serve as a promising possibility between first- and second-generation youth. Establishing youth-centered workshops on culture and violence for faculty and staff and organized by youth is another idea. The suggestions are boundless, but school administration must first identify youth conflict as part of an educational problem and a form of institutional violence, rather than framing Latina/o youth conflict as simply a Latino issue or problem.

Establishing change in the school setting is the first step, but it is only one "space and place" that needs reexamination. Although the school setting is a critical and especially salient place where youths affirm and perform their identities, the larger institutions and ideologies of family, neighborhood, racism, discrimination, and poverty circumscribing their lives also shape these identities. It is necessary to examine the underlying notions of power within ideologies and institutions that function, both intentionally and unintentionally, to further fragment and compartmentalize youths through identity politics. As Craig Calhoun (1995) suggests, "because our various identities may be contested, and because a range of agents seek to reinforce some and undermine others, there is always a politics to the construction and experience of identity" (233). The categories of sameness in which these youths often find themselves obscure the vast differences that, consequently, have the potential to erupt into devastating intragroup tensions.

CONCLUSION

This analysis endeavored to deconstruct the perceived sameness of Mexicana/o and Chicana/o youths. It was not meant to compartmentalize them into strictly Mexicana/o or Chicana/o identities but to explain the different paths youths of Mexican descent take toward Mexicana/o, Chicana/o, or mixed identities. Pablo Vila (2000) criticizes Anzaldúa's (1987) and Renato Rosaldo's (1989) border theorizing, claiming that both border scholars homogenize border identities. However, I view their interpretations, as well as Vila's, as a starting point to explain the difficulties and nuances of these identity-seeking processes for youths of Mexican descent in the U.S. borderlands. These struggles remain embedded within the fabric of the desert landscapes and the skin of all Mexicanas/os and Chicanas/os *que luchan* (that struggle) to define themselves along the line of Mexicanness so pervasive within the greater borderlands.

What continues to happen on the physical borderlands provides a map, a blueprint, to understanding what happens to other youths of Mexican descent found in metaphorical and physical borders within the interior crevices of the United States. I do not claim that the phenomena taking place in the borderland is exclusive to this area, but I do believe that the patterns of identity making in the Southwest are replicated in other U.S. cities. Mexicana/o and Chicana/o identities are defined according to the physical boundaries of the international border where people's racial and/or ethnic status is politically, socially, culturally, and legally magnified.

The identities of the young Mexicanas/os and Chicanas/os from this high school were ingrained in the borderlands. The use of border theory provided the framework in examining the construction of Mexicanness that these youths cultivated. Border theory is understood by these youths since they intimately know and understand the conceptualizations of borders. It serves as a tool for future policy making since it addresses the needs of youths through educational policies and the border transformative pedagogies that Elenes (2001) advocates.

These youths may best be served by applying border theory not only to their identity making but also in comprehending their marginalized position in American society and their need for inclusion within the United States through educational endeavors that can integrate border pedagogies into the classroom, which educates all youth, not simply youth of Mexican descent. Border theory can serve as the tapestry that will weave together educational practitioners, linguists, cultural and social brokers, youth advocates, and youths themselves to begin a dialogue about borders, education, and identity to jointly construct innovative ways of thinking and teaching through border pedagogy and border epistemology.

Borders are commonsensical. People are generally defined, identified, and categorized through social, cultural, economic, political, educational, and national borders. Paradoxically, this matrix of border discourse serves both to separate and to bind people together. The strength of this theoretical framework is its durability and plasticity; it can be stretched and molded to fit and analyze numerous circumstances. Perhaps by exploring all of our nuances, we can come to the conclusion that borders are part of our identities, and some borders can be transcended and used for good. Perhaps we can even see that we all reside at the border crossroads of sameness and difference.

NOTES

1. I use Latina/o to refer to Mexicana/o and Chicana/o students together.
2. Chicana/o refers to Mexican Americans who are second generation or beyond. The Chicana/o youth who participated in this study are second-, third-, and fourth-generation Mexican Americans. Mexicana/o refers to Mexican immigrant youth who have either recently arrived in the United States or are first-generation immigrants regardless of the amount of time they have spent here.
3. Altamira High is a pseudonym to protect the identity of the actual high school where the research was conducted.
4. This research was heavily influenced by other high school studies and ethnographies examining identity issues and education. Other scholars have explored identity and the reception of immigrants in the United States, immigrant youths' experiences and segmented assimilation, ethnic self-identities, language use, length of stay in the United States, neighborhoods, educational experiences, and exposure to U.S. popular culture. Many of these factors figured prominently in Californian studies by Maria Eugenia Matute-Bianchi (1986) regarding youths of Mexican and Japanese descent and Norma Mendoza-Denton's (1999) research on girl gang members of Mexican descent. Other important contributors include high school ethnographies like Angela Valenzuela's (1999) work, which explores academic achievement and schooling orientations between Mexican and Mexican American high school students in Texas. Laurie Olsen's (1997) ethnography gages immigrant students' racial categories and identity negotiations, and their social and academic success and exclusion from mainstream language development and curriculum. Penelope Eckert's (1989) high school ethnography is a broader yet extremely significant study of social categories and identity in a Midwestern high school, which examines social group inequalities among various student groups. These last five studies more closely resemble the inquiries, objectives, and findings of this research.
5. All names in this chapter have been changed to protect the identities of the students who participated in this ethnography.

REFERENCES

Anzaldúa, G. 1987. *Borderlands/La frontera: The new mestiza*. San Francisco: Aunt Lute Books.

Arteaga, A. 1994. An other tongue. In *An other tongue*, ed. A. Arteaga, 9–34. Durham, NC: Duke University Press.

Calhoun, C. 1995. *Critical social theory: Culture, history, and the challenge of difference*. Oxford: Blackwell.

Eckert, P. 1989. *Jocks and burnouts: Social categories and identity in the high school*. New York: Teachers College Press.

Elenes, A. 1997. Reclaiming the borderlands: Chicana/o identity, difference, and critical pedagogy. *Educational Theory* 47 (3): 359–75.

———. 2001. Border/transformative pedagogies at the end of the millennium: Chicana/o cultural studies and education. In *Decolonial voices: Chicana and Chicano cultural studies in the 21st century*, ed. A. J. Aldama and N. Quiñonez, 1–26. Bloomington: Indiana University Press.

Fanon, F. 1967. *Black skin, white masks*. New York: Grove Press.

Freire, P. 1970. *Pedagogy of the oppressed*. New York: Continuum.

Giroux, H. A. 1992. *Border crossings: Cultural workers and the politics of education*. New York: Routledge.

Gomez, A. N. 1997. Chicana feminism. In *Chicana feminist thought: The basic historical writings*, ed. A. M. Garcia, 52–57. New York: Routledge.

Gonzalez, F. 1998. Formations of Mexicananess: Trenzas de identidades multiples (Growing up *Mexicana*: Braids of multiple identities). *International Journal of Qualitative Studies in Education* 11 (1): 81–102.

Houston, M. 1992. The politics of difference: Race, class, and women's communication. In *Women making meaning: New feminist directions in communication*, ed. L. F. Rakow, 45–59. New York: Routledge.

Matute-Bianchi, M. E. 1986. Ethnic identities and patterns of school success and failure among Mexican-descent and Japanese-American students in a California high school: An ethnographic analysis. *American Journal of Education* 95 (1): 233–55.

Mendoza-Denton, N. 1999. Fighting words: Latina girls, gangs, and language attitudes. In *Speaking Chicana: Voice, power and identity*, ed. D. L. Galindo and M. D. Gonzales, 39–56. Tucson: University of Arizona Press.

Montoya, M. 1999. Máscaras, trenzas, y greñas: Un/masking the self while un/braiding Latina stories and legal discourse. In *Speaking Chicana: Voice, power, and identity*, ed. D. L. Galindo and M. D. Gonzales, 194–211. Tucson: University of Arizona Press.

Olsen, L. 1997. *Made in America: Immigrant students in our public schools*. New York: New York Press.

Rosaldo, R. 1989. *Culture and truth: The remaking of social analysis*. Boston: Beacon Press.

Valenzuela, A. 1999. *Subtractive schooling: U.S.-Mexican youth and the politics of caring*. Albany: State University of New York Press.

Vila, P. 2000. *Crossing borders, reinforcing borders: Social categories, metaphors, and narrative identities on the U.S.-Mexico frontier*. Austin: University of Texas Press.

5

Unraveling the Heart of the School-to-Prison Pipeline

Tyson Lewis and Elizabeth Vázquez Solórzano

INTRODUCTION

Recently, educational theorists have begun to analyze the relationship between the growing prison-industrial complex and U.S. education, referring to this phenomenon as the "school-to-prison pipeline" (see Advancement Project 2005; Wald and Losen 2003). Through a variety of zero-tolerance measures (e.g., mandatory suspension, referral to law enforcement), many urban, low-income schools create social conditions that criminalize students (predominately African American boys), leading from the classroom to the cellblock. While making strides in our understanding of how the pipeline works, current research in this area is lacking in two important respects. First, as we discuss below, the literature on the pipeline highlights the surface similarities between the penitentiary and the playground (Noguera 1995, 2003; Giroux 2001), yet fails to address the specific modality of power underlying this connection. Here, we suggest that, at their most extreme, the use of surveillance equipment, physical violence, zero-tolerance policies, and lockdown procedures transform schools from disciplinary institutions into exceptional spaces of sovereign force. Drawing on G. Agamben's theory of the concentration camp (1995, 2005) as the spatiotemporal inscription of sovereign violence in the modern era, we argue that the preconditions establishing the school-to-prison pipeline are informed by the exceptional logic of the camp. Redefining urban schooling in relation to the camp is more than simply a provocation. Rather, this analogy will give new urgency to educational activism and, more importantly, help to theorize further the relationship between discipline, sovereignty, and pedagogy at the heart of schooling.

Second, the current pipeline literature does not adequately frame the discussion within a historical materialist understanding of late capitalism. Thus, it is imperative that educational studies be positioned in relation to the economic and political functions that prisons play within our postindustrial society. Furthermore, the extended, or seemingly "invisible," damage caused by this pipeline has broad implications—implications that educational theorists must be aware of if they are to see the extent to which the school-to-prison pipeline is a concentrated representation of the internal contradictions of capitalism. Here, we employ Fredric Jameson's theory of "cognitive mapping" (1995) to understand how modalities of power and their relational/spatial configurations intersect with the global system of capitalism. In agreement with Jameson's project, we argue that cognitive mapping is central to educational reform, enabling those battling the pipeline to understand the overdetermined relationship that exists between schools, prisons, and the economy. By analyzing the pipeline, we demonstrate that the school has become a pedagogical space of exceptionality, creating one of the central preconditions for sustaining an ever-expanding prison industry: a criminalized population.

CONSTRUCTING THE PIPELINE: FROM THE LOGIC OF THE CAMP TO THE LOGIC OF THE PRISON

P. Noguera has asked, "What stands in the way of better relations between teachers and students, and why do fear and distrust characterize those relations, rather than compassion and respect?" (1995, 205). In answering this question, Noguera argues that urban schools breed a culture of fear and paranoia, which translates into militarized solutions to school violence. As such, school disruption is contained through penitentiary procedures and "lockdown" facilities that merely increase the very social conditions that lead to escalating violence. The security measures employed by schools are similar to those used in jails and prisons, prompting scholars to suggest that schools operate more like prisons than schools (Noguera 2003). Thus, what stands in the way of better relations is an overarching ideology of "maximum security" (Devine 1996) or "education as enforcement" (Saltman 2003). The question becomes, How are we to understand maximum security in terms of educational power between students, teachers/institutions, and social relations? In this section of this chapter, we examine the interlocking discourses and practices that reconfigure the school as a sphere wherein sovereign violence is enacted against educational life.

First, we must make a crucial analytical distinction that will help to clarify the difference between discipline and punishment in contemporary urban schooling. As opposed to Michel Foucault's description of the panoptic, or disciplinary, society (1979), the camp, for Agamben (2005), does not function to create docile, self-regulating, and productive bodies. Rather, it is an exceptional zone provoked through the language of war and siege, where laws and social norms operate only through their suspension. In the camp, power does not circulate through an invisible, subtle, and almost imperceptible economy but rather through the force of the sovereign's decision to grant life or to take life away. Whereas disciplinary power relations produce subjects through the discrete tabulation and compartmentalization of their internal potentialities, the camp punishes through judgment, reducing the subject to nothing but bare life, or life lacking rights and civic duties. The excessive force of the sovereign that Agamben describes in the camp does not produce normalized, internally regulating, disciplined subjects of the state but rather life whose only function is survival. For Agamben, spaces of sovereign force have become increasingly prevalent, ranging from refugee camps (where victims of genocide or famine reside) to concentration camps (as in the terrorist camps in Cuba) to airports (where customers can be detained for extended periods of time without due process). Bearing this distinction in mind, the overt display of military might in terms of police force and unforgiving zero-tolerance sanctions in urban schools index the return of repressed sovereign force into pedagogical space, transforming the urban school into a camplike structure.

This trend toward sovereign force against disciplinary power began in the mid-1990s when the national zero-tolerance war on drugs "trickled down" to the U.S. school system. Originally implemented to eliminate weapons and drugs in schools, these policies rapidly expanded to cover a wide variety of seemingly minor disciplinary infringements. As R. Casella reports, federal policies such as the Gun-Free Schools Act of 1994 resulted in absurd and unjustifiable abuses of power in schools (2001). Case in point: in a Mississippi school, five African-American boys were arrested on felony assault charges for accidentally hitting their white bus driver in the head with a peanut. As this one example illustrates, most of these extreme cases of zero-tolerance target youth of color. A. C. McFadden and colleagues' longitudinal study on discipline referrals and punishment reinforces these startling statistics. Black pupils have higher rates of referrals (36.6 percent) than would be expected based on their school population (22 percent) and are more likely than their white counterparts to receive out-of-school suspension and corporal punishment (McFadden et al. 1992). In South Carolina, Black students make up 42 percent of the public school enrollment but represent 61 percent of all children charged with disciplinary-code infractions (Advancement Project and the Civil Rights Project 2000). The evidence is clear: there are huge disparities in the frequency and severity of disciplinary referrals and punishments meted out to Black students in contrast to their white classmates. Since the federally imposed zero-tolerance law requires the involvement of law enforcement for specific matters, schools that lack campus police channel many school-related incidents to the juridical system. Black and Latino youth are more likely to enter the criminal justice system as it becomes increasingly common for school offenses to be referred to the police (Nolan and Anyon 2004). Here, the racial economy of in-school detentions amounts to the reduction of educational life to bare life (where the mere physical presence of the body is substituted for education), and expulsion and arrest amounts to absolute educational abandonment rather than disciplinary normalization.

George W. Bush's No Child Left Behind Act (2001) provided a new incentive to expand zero-tolerance policies even further. The overwhelming focus of states to avoid test-driven accountability sanctions has led to increased reports of schools that "push out" low achieving students (Orfield et al. 2004). As A. Fuentes has argued, No Child Left Behind exacerbated the problematics of school discipline:

> Zero tolerance critics believe the current emphasis on standardized testing is one reason harsh policies continue even as school crime plummets. . . . The fixation on testing and a growing population of lower-income, mostly Latino, children in Texas public schools are incentives for suspension and exclusion. (2003, 20)

In the interest of quality measures, excluding children from test-taking exercises has become a necessity for school districts. Rather than lower achievement scores on standardized tests, teachers and principals are choosing simply to remove "problem" children. Thus, institutional survival takes precedence over the mandate to teach those students most in need of help. Here, children must be left behind, or abandoned, in order to (paradoxically) sustain the law that no child be left behind. In other words, the school must defer to the mandate of the state in order to ensure its funding and thus its ability to continue to educate the nation's poor precisely by no longer educating them. As in Agamben's description of the camp, the norm of the state only operates in such exceptional spaces through its suspension.

A discourse of war, terror, and siege justifies or legitimates the transformation of the school into a camplike space where a culture of violence and neglect is not curbed but sustained, where students are not taught but rather policed or simply expunged from the educational system, and where behaviors that disrupt the "normal" functioning of learning become the dysfunctional norm. A recent example of this state of siege occurred in 2003 at Charlestown High School in Boston. After a student was shot in the leg close to the school's campus, police inaugurated "Operation Clean Slate." As a result of this action (no doubt justified in part by the door opened by zero-tolerance measures), seventeen students were arrested, lockers were raided, the school was placed in lockdown, and suspects were detained and interrogated in the principal's office. Mariellen Burns, a spokesperson for the police, said that this *"war* was done for the safety of the students and the faculty and to send a message at the beginning of the school year that anyone who has issues like this [related to school violence] needs to deal with them immediately [our emphasis]" (Tench 2003). Here, Foucauldian technologies of disciplinarity such as interrogation are not implemented to train, normalize, or rehabilitate so much as to punish students through the shock-and-awe tactics of war. Thus, a terrain opens up in schools between the panoptic, disciplinary model and the logic of the camp, where discipline is exchanged for sovereign force. Zero tolerance enacts what Agamben would refer to as a sovereign's ban legitimated by the discourse of moral, or just, war (1995)—a power over life and death, or in the case of education, a power over whose life is worthy of being educated. Education is no longer a panoptic apparatus in a Foucauldian sense, and the sovereign's ban is precisely the "savage" power that J. Kozol (1991) has described—a savage power that exposes the bare life of poor students of color to social abandonment rather than educational enrichment.

And there is a disturbing correlation between school zero-tolerance practices and those of the adult and juvenile detention facilities. Casella demonstrates that zero-tolerance policy as a form of criminal prevention is closely linked with the criminalization of students and the crippling of student access to educational resources, effectively relegating such students to a prison track (2003, 55). This system of early detection and prosecution "accelerates youths' movement to outplacements, sometimes boot camps and lockdown facilities, and finally to prison" (Casella 2003, 56). The Sentencing Project reported that, in 1997, 68 percent of state prisoners in Massachusetts never completed high school, thus establishing a strong correlation between student drop-out rates, suspension rates, and future prison time (Iafolla 2004). L. Lochner and E. Moretti (2004) concur that dropping out of high school greatly increases the likelihood of later imprisonment. Because of the correlations between testing, zero-tolerance suspension, and incarceration, the links between standardization and prisons cannot be overshadowed by a national rhetoric of "educational equity" and safety. Rather, the structure of the camp underlying the implementation of prisonlike technologies in education forms the central mechanism that facilitates a pipeline from the classroom to juvenile detention to adult incarceration.

As Agamben (2005) argues, the camp is a site of indistinction or indifferentiation between violence and law; as such, it is a paradoxical location. In the second half of this chapter, we argue that the particular paradoxes of the school as camp (e.g., the promise of safety and the reproduction of violence, the moral claim to justice and the perversity of abandonment, the social responsibility to reform and the degradation of punishment) reveal their true significance only in relation to the overall contradictions of late capitalism.

THE REPERCUSSIONS OF THE PIPELINE: TRACING ITS SEISMIC EFFECTS

Wages of Incarceration

According to A. Davis, American prisons are rooted in bourgeois ideology, racism, sexism, and the logic of capitalist production (2003, 43). There is in Davis's genealogy a direct lineage linking slavery, the post–Civil War convict lease system (which controlled back labor via "moral" instructions of correction and reform), and the current-day privatization of prisons. Further complicating Foucault's argument that prisons function to "save the soul" or rehabilitate the criminal, Davis (1998) asserts that in the United States, the prison system has functioned largely to concentrate and control Black labor power. Rather than an enlightened tool of correction, systems of incarceration have worked to maintain the social relations of slavery under the guise of "social welfare." At the base of contemporary prison "serfdom" is the educational system, which functions as a "prep school for prison" for many poor students of color (Davis 2003, 39; see also Smith 2002). In other words, abandonment of students potentially leads to a particular type of bound labor: prison labor. Thus, the camp as the spatial logic of late capitalism in Agamben's model is connected with the production of a surplus labor force that is absorbed into the prison system. If discipline directly conditions educational life as labor power, then abandonment only contingently leads to economic viability through its structural relation to the prison system.

In his book *The Perpetual Prisoner Machine*, Dyer (2000) uncovers the nefarious connections between incarceration and capitalist profiteering. Summarizing his position, Dyer states, "the motive behind the unprecedented growth in the U.S. prison population is the $150 billion being expended annually on criminal justice, much of which eventually winds up in the bank accounts of the shareholders of some of America's best known and most respected companies" (2). Business has commodified prisoners, transforming the suffering of the incarcerated into a marketplace for both product consumption and product production. So, who exactly is benefiting? Dyer's list of corporations with major investments in the propagation of prison construction and prison maintenance is staggering. Construction firms—such as Turner Construction, Brown and Root, and CRS—with substantial ties to prison industry are only the tip of the iceberg. With the end of the Cold War, defense industries are redirecting their markets toward prisons, retooling military equipment such as night-vision goggles for use in prison surveillance. Furthermore, a list of corporations—including Dial, AT&T, and health-care providers—lease prison labor to manufacture cheap goods, and thereby profit from prisons. In fact, according to Dyer, by 1998, there were twenty-five hundred prison industries in America. Companies such as Microsoft, Victoria's Secret, IBM, Compaq, and others take advantage of the low-wage bonanza that prisons offer to corporate America. With salaries ranging from $0.20 to $1.20 per hour and with no health care and no way to organize against human rights abuses, this labor pool is ideal for companies seeking to downsize factories in the United States.

Those who support prison labor argue that it is a form of job training. Yet, P. Wright argues that the intimation of social justice by corporations employing prisoners is nothing more than an ideological smoke screen (2003, 116). Corporations favor lifers and long-timers, as well as those who already have job training. Furthermore, Wright sarcastically observes that prisoners would be prepared upon release only for further exploitation in First World sweatshops. As such, the goals of prison labor have less to do with the future of the prisoners themselves and more to do with corporate imperatives.

But the aftermath of the pipeline does not end there. L. Baker (1999) argues that the existence of "Fourth World" labor practices inside of U.S. prisons benefits the larger system of postindustrial capitalism through a complex dialectic. Baker writes that capitalism uses prison labor "for union busting and for supplanting well-paid skilled labor, both processes that can reduce the general level of wages and benefits" (1999, 152). Employers, freed from paying a living wage, turn to prison labor as a proxy for Third World labor, thus effectively sustaining a labor force that causes a decrease in wages generally and further escalates labor control, both inside and outside of prisons (Baker 1999; Lafer 2003). Overall, the moral discourses of "education," "correction," and "social justice" cloak this situation within an ideological web of mystification, which deflects attention from the overall economic benefits being extracted from a seemingly disorganized, chaotic, and corrupt system of educational abandonment, incarceration, and labor exploitation.

Even if prisoners are not exploited as an incarcerated labor force, the need for bodies to fill up beds in our expanding prison-industrial complex serves an important economic function, ensuring a sustainable source of income for citizens who are in some way employed by prisons. In *Freedom for Some, Discipline for Others*, E. Brown states, "As the criminalization of the poor escalates, the prison industry is housing the cast-offs, employing the unemployed in cities devastated by de-industrialization, and creating profits for private corporations" (2003, 114). Reliance on prisons to sustain local economies produces an incentive to continually build prisons and keep them filled with "criminals," thus blurring the lines between profit and justice. More importantly, the bare life of the prisoners is what is commodified, not their labor power. Survival itself enters into the sphere of exchange. Thus, Davis's argument concerning Black labor power is inadequate to explain the full reach of capitalism in our postindustrial society.

Nullified Social Contract

Political disenfranchisement is another "invisible" effect resulting from the school-prison pipeline. In most U.S. states, felons or ex-felons have severe voter restrictions. Thus, as M. Mauer aptly points out, "Given vast racial disparities in the criminal justice system it is hardly surprising, but shocking nonetheless, to find that an estimated 13 percent of African-American males are now disenfranchised" (2002, 51). Mauer further argues that this phenomenon has its historical roots in post–Reconstruction attempts to curb Black political participation. During the late 1800s, many Southern states explicitly targeted crimes (e.g., burglary, arson) frequently attributed to African-American men for disenfranchisement. Likewise, the war on drugs similarly targets crimes linked with poor communities of color (Mauer 2002, 52). Then, as now, the result is an overrepresentation of minorities in prisons, many of whom are serving ridiculously long sentences for minor crimes of possession, and an underrepresentation of minority votes during elections. Mauer summarizes, "The irony of the combined impact of American disenfranchisement policies along with the massive expansion of the prison system is that a half century after the beginnings of the civil rights movement, increasing numbers of African Americans and others are losing their voting rights each day" (2002, 58). Thus, voting restrictions for convicts and "those who have served their time" create a subaltern group whose potentially damming critique of the prison-industrial complex remains politically silenced. In other words, those subjected to prison life are silenced, rendered as bare life rather than full citizens.

Considering the complex relationship between education, capital, and prisons, it is not at all surprising that the overwhelming pedagogical logic of urban schooling is predicated on a sustained state of sovereign force where education transforms into social abandonment. The school as an exceptional space (whose function is not to normalize, discipline, or rehabilitate but to punish, thus render educational life inoperable) plays an integral role in constructing and maintaining the overall preconditions of a pipeline that funnels the victims of deindustrialization, globalization, and political disenfranchisement into a prison-industrial complex. The interrelation between urban schools, prisons, and capital forms a dehumanizing economy that is predicated on producing bare life. In conclusion, we suggest that the proper strategy to combat this pipeline is to pool the resources now being mobilized separately to reform or abolish the prison system and to revolutionize the U.S. school system.

CONCLUSION

As Davis argues, "This focus on incarceration coincided with a shift toward incapacitation and retribution and away from rehabilitation and deterrence as the preferred goals of the criminal justice system. Instead of utilizing modes of punishment that would rehabilitate, such as treatment, community service, and fines, policy makers have changed the criminal laws and policies in ways that have often mandated prison terms for many types of criminal offenses" (2002, 61). Is not the very same ideology of retribution (or, to use Agamben's terminology, the revenge of sovereign force) at work in contemporary low-income, urban schools? As a result, education turns into its opposite, resulting in a crisis that cannot be solved according to the practices of abandonment. And yet, as our analysis demonstrates, this negation of education reveals the fundamental truth of schooling within late capitalism: schooling is for many of the nation's poor a site of abandonment and institutional violence existing in excess of disciplinary regulation. This shift is, as argued above, the result of an economic move from industrialization (where disciplined, normalized bodies were necessary) to postindustrialization (where bare life itself becomes a commodity). Thus, what might appear to be exceptions to the general rule are not simply glitches in the social fabric but rather the return of the internal antagonism of the social—an antagonism that cannot be accounted for by the dominant logic of "equal opportunity," "safety," or "no child left behind."

While the overwhelming negativity of sovereign violence is one of the central stumbling blocks preventing the full realization of the potentials of education, it is also the moving principle motivating social transformation and resistance. In response to these conditions, scholars such as T. Ambrosio and V. Schiraldi (1997) have proposed a five-point plan that cuts back on prison construction while simultaneously instituting localized community correction plans and educational rehabilitation programs as viable alternatives to the current school-to-prison pipeline. D. Osher, Poirier, and Rutherford offer an economic argument against the pipeline: "Cost-benefit analysis suggests that the monetary benefits of effective prevention exceed the costs of such programs. Research has pointed to the comparative benefits of effective preventative and community interventions, as well as the cost of unnecessary incarceration, boot camps, and shock incarceration in terms of reducing recidivism and promoting productive citizenship" (2003, 92). Escalating prison costs are a burden to the community and a drain on taxpayers, limiting funds that could be channeled into educational programs. This contradiction is nowhere more apparent than in California. Riding a twenty-year prison explosion, California spends $5.1 billion on prisons annually to lock up more than 160,000 people. In fact, through the 1980s, California's spending on prisons increased 95 percent, while spending on higher education decreased 6 percent, and from 1973 to 1993, state corrections spending increased 1,200 percent, while higher education increased by only 419 percent (Ambrosio and Schiraldi 1997, 6–7). Because of a strong prison-guard union, California has recently been shutting down health clinics, firing teachers, and cutting other social services, while the prison budget has decreased by a measly 1 percent (Jones 2004). While public schools are crumbling, the state has been hard at work building twenty-three prisons since 1980 (Jones 2004). All in all, "compared to prisons, prevention costs less and pays far greater dividends" (Osher, Poirier, and Rutherford 2003, 112). As V. Jones argues, "We [in California] are spending $80,000 per kid in the youth authority. . . . You can send two kids to Yale for the cost of sending one kid to jail, and yet there's a 91 percent recidivism rate" (2004, 211). Rehabilitation and preventative therapy are less expensive and have a higher success rate than traditional incarceration, thus alternatives to incarceration support community renewal as opposed to corporate profit.

We would add to this growing body of suggestions that in order to be successful, rehabilitation programs and educational reform policies have to take into account the spatial nomos of contemporary society: the camp. While individual counseling and institutional restructuring are important and necessary, the broader power relations reproducing the conditions of violence and abuse have to be addressed. In other words, as opposed to sovereign violence and its articulation in the form of the camp, educators cannot simply retreat into disciplinary normalization and its accompanying panoptic model. Rather, the triadic relation between disciplinarity-sovereignty-education (linked as it is to modifications in the mode of production) has to be effectively broken by a new notion of educational power.

Engaging youth in critical ethnographies and action research is appropriate since they feel the immediate effects of school practices that lead into the pipeline. Collaboration between the researcher, community activists, and affected youth can help to identify different aspects of the pipeline and can also help to develop more constructive solutions to exclusionary practices. Youth are a vital resource for the movement against criminalizing and exclusionary school-discipline practices. Already students are taking action against the pipeline. Books Not Bars is a youth-based organization in southern California that uses rap music, protest poetry, and rallies to protest the California Youth Authority (CYA) prison complex. As opposed to the brutality, sexism, and racism endemic to the CYA, Books Not Bars calls for investment in small-scale rehabilitation centers run by educators and counselors rather than prison guards and private companies. Such organizations breach the gap between prison and educational activism, mobilizing students against forms of oppression within school, within the CYA, and within their communities. An emphasis on youth movements in relation to the pipeline recognizes students not simply as victims of their environments—not simply as passive bare life abandoned by the educational system—but as active agents responding to the contradictions and paradoxes of the state of exception with creativity and a "militant optimism" (Bloch 1995) in the possibility for overcoming the inherent crises within the present.

Yet, such efforts need to be informed by an overall critique of capitalism and the sovereign logic of the police. The function of the pipeline within the totality of social relations would enable student activists to conceptualize the economic, political, and social links that connect violence against youth in CYA and the execution of educational life in urban centers. In other words, the global state of exception, through which law is suspended, resulting in the pure force or violence of the sovereign, has to be mapped in relation to the underlying presence of the sovereign decision concerning whose life is worthy of being educated. Exposing these connections reveals a powerful potential to organize school reformers, student activists, and prison abolitionists into a counterhegemonic bloc capable of fighting not only for youth but also for prisoners. Through cognitive mapping, prison abolitionists would realize how youth are a resource in their struggles; likewise, students battling the pipeline could merge with a larger community of prison activists. In the words of L. Althusser, the tensions within the school-to-prison pipeline could become an "explosive" locus where the "moment of unstable global condensation induc[es] the dissolution and resolution of the whole" (1969, 216). While still lacking such a revolutionary perspective, Books Not Bars does offer inspiration to educators concerned with the school-to-prison pipeline, as well as a vision of change and transformation that empowers students to join the fight for freedom against structures of oppression, exploitation, and subjugation.

REFERENCES

Advancement Project. 2005. *Education on lockdown: The schoolhouse to jailhouse track,* available at www.advancementproject.org/publications.html (accessed June 21, 2005).

Advancement Project and the Civil Rights Project, 2000. *Opportunities suspended: The devastating consequences of zero tolerance and school discipline policies.* Cambridge, MA: Harvard University.

Agamben, G. 1995. *Homo sacer: Sovereign power and bare life.* Palo Alto, CA: Stanford University Press.

——. 2005. *State of exception*. Chicago: University of Chicago Press.

Althusser, L. 1969. *For Marx*. Middlesex, UK: Penguin Books.

Ambrosio, T., and V. Schiraldi. 1997. *From classrooms to cell blocks: A national perspective*. Washington, DC: Justice Policy Institute.

Balfanz, R., K. Spiridakis, R. C. Neild, and N. Legters. 2003. High-poverty secondary schools and the juvenile justice system: How neither helps the other and how that could change. In *Deconstructing the school-to-prison pipeline*, ed. J. Wald and D. Losen, 71–81. New Directions for Youth Development 99. San Francisco: Jossey-Bass.

Bloch, E. 1995. *The principle of hope*, Vol. 1. Cambridge: Massachusetts Institute of Technology Press.

Brown, E. 2003. Freedom for some, discipline for others. In *Education as enforcement*, ed. K. Saltman and D. Gabbard, 127–52. New York: Routledge Falmer.

Baker, L. 1999. Prison labor: Racism and rhetoric. In *Race and ideology: Language, symbolism, and popular culture*, ed. A. Spears, 133–63. Detroit, MI: Wayne State University Press.

Casella, R. 2003. Punishing dangerousness through preventive detention: Illustrating the institutional link between school and prison. In *Deconstructing the school-to-prison pipeline*, ed. J. Wald and D. Losen, 55–69. New Directions for Youth Development 99. San Francisco: Jossey-Bass.

——. 2001. *At zero tolerance: Punishment, prevention, and school violence*. New York: Peter Lang.

Davis, A. 1998. Racialized punishment and prison abolition. In *The Angela Davis reader*, ed. J. James, 96–110. New York: Blackwell.

——. 2002. Incarceration and the imbalance of power. In *Invisible punishment: The collateral consequences of mass imprisonment*, ed. M. Mauer and M. Chesney-Lind, 61–78. New York: New York Press.

——. 2003. *Are prisons obsolete?* New York: Seven Stories Press.

Devine, J. 1996. *Maximum security: The culture of violence in inner-city schools*. Chicago: University of Chicago Press.

Dimitriadis, G., and C. McCarthy. 2003. Creating a new panopticon: Columbine, cultural studies, and the uses of Foucault. In *Foucault, cultural studies, and governmentality*, ed. J. Bratich, J. Packer, and C. McCarthy, 273–92. New York: State University of New York Press.

Dyer, J. 2000. *The perpetual prisoner machine*. Boulder, CO: Westview Press.

Foucault, M. 1979. *Discipline and punish*. New York: Vintage Books.

Fuentes, A. 2003. Discipline and punish. *The Nation* (December 26), 17–20.

Goldberg, E., and L. Evans. The prison industrial complex and the global economy. *JusticeNet Prison Issues Desk*, December 26, available at www.prisonactivist.org/crisis/evans-goldberg.html (accessed July 11, 2005).

Giroux, H. 2001. *Public spaces, private lives: Beyond the culture of cynicism*. Lanham, MD: Rowman & Littlefield.

Iafolla, B. 2004. School to prison pipeline, part I: Do not pass go . . . Go directly to jail. *Weekly Dig* (September 10), available at www.weeklydig.com/dig/content/3765.aspx (available at October 23, 2004).

Jameson, F. 1995. *Postmodernism, or the cultural logic of late capitalism*. Durham, NC: Duke University Press.

Jones, V. 2004. Interview. *Democracy Now* (April 16), available at www.democracynow
.org/article.pl?sid=04/04/16/1536232 (accessed January 2, 2005).
Kozol, J. 1991. *Savage inequalities: Children in America's schools.* New York: Crown
Publishing.
Lafer, G. 2003. The politics of prison labor: A union perspective. In *Prison nation: The
warehousing of America's poor,* ed. T. Herivel and P. Wright. London: Routledge.
Lewis, T. 2003. The surveillance economy of contemporary schooling. *The Review of
Education, Pedagogy and Cultural Studies* 25 (4): 335–55.
Lochner, L., and E. Moretti. 2004. The effects of education on crime: Evidence from
prison inmates, arrests, and self-reports. *American Economic Review* 94 (1): 155–89.
Mauer, M. 2002. Mass imprisonment and the disappearing voter. In *Invisible punishment: The collateral consequences of mass imprisonment,* ed. M. Mauer and M. Chesney-Lind. New York: New York Press.
McFadden, A. C., G. E. Marsh, B. J. Price, and Y. Hwang. 1992. A study of race and
gender bias in the punishment of school children. *Education and treatment of children* 15 (2): 140–46.
Noguera, P. 1995. Preventing and producing violence: A critical analysis of responses to school violence. *Harvard Educational Review* 65 (2): 189–212.
———. 2003. Schools, prisons, and social implications of punishment: Rethinking
disciplinary practices. *Theory into Practice* 42 (4): 341–50.
Nolan, K., and J. Anyon. 2004. Learning to do time: Willis's model of cultural re-
production in an era of postindustrialism, globalization, and mass incarceration.
In *Learning to labor in new times,* ed. M. Dolby and D. Gabbard with P. Willis. New
York: Routledge Falmer.
Orfield, G., D. Losen, J. Wald, and C. B. Swanson. 2004. *Losing our future: How mi-
nority youth are being left behind by the graduation rate crisis.* Cambridge, MA: Civil
Rights Project at Harvard University.
Osher, D., M. Quinn, J. Poirier, and R. Rutherford. 2003. Deconstructing the pipeline:
Using efficacy, effectiveness, and cost-benefit data to reduce minority youth incar-
ceration. In *Deconstructing the school-to-prison pipeline,* ed. J. Wald and D. Losen,
91–113. New Directions for Youth Development 99. San Francisco: Jossey-Bass.
Reed, C. 2004. An ugly prison record. *Toronto Star,* May 10, available at www
.commondreams.org/views04/0510–03.htm (accessed June 2005).
Saltman, K. 2003. Introduction. In *Education as enforcement,* ed. K. Saltman and D.
Gabbard. London: Routledge Falmer.
Sandronsky, S. 2001. California's crisis of black incarceration, census shows. *Common
Dreams New Center,* August 11, available at www.commondreams.org/views01/
0811–03.htm (accessed August 21, 2001).
Skiba, J. R., R. S. Michael, A. C. Nardo, and R. L. Peterson. 2002. The color of disci-
pline: Sources of racial and gender disproportionality in school punishment. *The
Urban Review* 34 (4): 317–42.
Schlosser, E. 1998. The prison-industrial complex. *The Atlantic Online* 282 (6):
51–77, available at www.theatlantic.com/issues/98dec/prisons.htm (accessed Au-
gust 20, 2001).
Smith, G. 2002. "Remorseless young predators": The bottom line of "caging children." In *Growing up postmodern,* ed. R. Stricklan, 65–85. Lanham, MD: Rowman
& Littlefield.

Tench, M. 2003. Police conduct sweep of several schools. *Boston Globe,* September 11, B3.

To cope with violence, schools divide and conquer. 2000. *USA Today,* April 19, 26A.

Wald, J., and D. Losen. 2003. Defining and redirecting a school-to-prison pipeline. In *Deconstructing the school-to-prison pipeline,* ed. J. Wald and D. Losen, 9–15. New Directions for Youth Development 99. San Francisco: Jossey-Bass.

Wright, P. 2003. Making slave labor fly: Boeing goes to prison. In *Prison nation: The warehousing of America's poor,* ed. T. Herivel and P. Wright, 112–19. New York and London: Routledge.

II

THEORETICAL CONCERNS

6

Some Reflections on Critical Pedagogy in the Age of Global Empire

Peter McLaren

This chapter comprises a series of reflections (which I originally presented as a keynote address but which has since served as the basis of numerous recent publications) on what it means to attempt to fashion a critical pedagogy here in the United States at a time when the Bush administration is reshaping what it means to live in a democracy. Here, I attempt to elucidate some of the most compelling contradictions around which the struggle for democracy is taking place, not the least of which speaks to the dynamic tension between democratic rights and responsibilities and the reproduction of capitalist social relations. In doing so, I attempt to underscore the importance of critique and the need to recover the contributions of Marxist theory—both of which, I argue, are important for the development of a philosophy of praxis that is the engine of revolutionary critical pedagogy.

At this particular historical moment, democracy seems acutely perishable. Its contradictions have become as difficult to ignore as sand rubbed in the eyes. Although dressed up as a promise, democracy has functioned more as a threat. Spurred on by feelings of "righteous victimhood" and by a "wounded and vengeful nationalism" (Lieven 2003) that has arisen in the wake of the attacks of 9/11, and pushing its wars on terrorism to the far reaches of the globe (with what Terry Eagleton calls a "world-hating hubris" [2003, 227]), the United States is shamelessly defining its global empire as an extension of its democratic project. The U.S. National Security Strategy of 2002 states that the United States will not hesitate to act alone and will "preemptively" attack "terrorists" who threaten its national interests at home or abroad.

One of its national interests is to bring free market democracy to the rest of the world. What used to be called gunboat diplomacy is being rewritten as a diplomatic gunning down of any and all opposition to the unfettered movement of finance capital in and out of new markets. Sidestepping the inconvenient possibility that Iraq had no connection to Al Qaeda, the Pentagon hawks swept through the streets of Baghdad and arrived at the near culmination of their civilizing mission by enacting a negation as one-sided as the positivity they opposed. It was the aftermath of "Shock and Awe." Paul Brennan skillfully uses Shock and Awe to probe America's heart of darkness:

> Shock and Awe—and, indeed, the whole Bush idea that flexing our high-tech military might in the Middle East will remake the wicked everywhere into models of democratic values—sounds like nothing so much as Mr. Kurtz's report to the International Society for the Suppression of Savage Customs (the Victorian equivalent of the Project of the New American Century), which Marlowe recounts for his listeners in Chapter 2 [of Joseph Conrad's *Heart of Darkness*]: *He began with the argument that we whites, from the point of view of development we had arrived at, "must necessarily appear to them [savages] in the nature of supernatural beings—we approach them with the might as of a deity," and so on and so on. "By the simple example of our will, we can exert a power for good practically unbounded," etc, etc.* (2003, 1–2)

But Marlowe says the report was missing something:

> *There was no practical hint to interrupt the magic current of phrases, unless a kind of note at the foot of the last page, scrawled evidently much later, in an unsteady hand, may be regarded as the exposition of a method. It was very simple, and at the end of that moving appeal to every altruistic sentiment it blazed at you, luminous and terrifying, like a flash of lightning in a serene sky: "Exterminate all the brutes!"* (2003, 1–2)

Meanwhile, at home, we are exterminating the brutes in a different, but no less effective, way. Witness the general intensification of labor by the overextension of the working day, cutbacks in resources and social programs, combined with tax breaks for the very rich, relentless violations of laws by corporate executives, and the lack of waged work, all under the banner of the preferred euphemism for imperialism: fighting terrorism and bringing about free market democracy. It is hard to put pen to paper without feeling like Sisyphus with his block of stone toiling in the realm of the dead.

Recently Americans celebrated the 212th anniversary of the ratification of the Bill of Rights; yet, we are all presumed guilty until proven innocent. And since now we can be denied the opportunity to prove our innocence, then guilt and innocence lose their meaning. In fact, by becoming their opposite, they cancel each other out. They cease to exist. Only Sauron's eye of the security state remains. Inside, we all wear the hoods that the U.S. military places over the heads of its prisoners. We all wait to be sent to Guantánamo

Bay. We are all forced to stand for hours with our hands raised over our heads. We are all forced to listen to tapes of rabbits being slaughtered.

In the security state, lies are now "creative omissions" or "misstatements," while truth is whatever it needs to be to secure the strategic interests of the United States. Global prosperity means tearing up the Kyoto treaty; preventing nuclear threats by rogue nations means threatening to use nuclear weapons in "preemptive" strikes; creating global support against terrorism means blocking a UN investigation of the Israeli assault on the Jenin refugee camp; bringing war criminals to justice means preventing the establishment of an international criminal court. Today, the preferred choice of Bush policy makers is deceit and deception. It is important to recognize that increasingly, within the security state, nothing carries the aura of truth as much as deception; nothing is as real today as that which is fake. Naomi Klein captures this phenomenon—hardly restricted to the United States—in the following description:

> The blacklisting of the almanac was a fitting end for 2003, a year that waged open war on truth and facts and celebrated fakes and forgeries of all kinds. This was the year when fakeness ruled: fake rationales for war, a fake President dressed as a fake soldier declaring a fake end to combat and then holding up a fake turkey. An action movie star became governor and the government started making its own action movies, casting real soldiers like Jessica Lynch as fake combat heroes and dressing up embedded journalists as fake soldiers. Saddam Hussein even got a part in the big show: he played himself being captured by American troops. This is the fake of the year, if you believe the *Sunday Herald* in Scotland, as well as several other news agencies, which reported that he was actually captured by a Kurdish Special Forces unit. (2004)

Most frightening is the chillingly preordained character of the Bush plutocracy given supernatural ballast by Bush's claim to be a special envoy of God. His assertion, with clairvoyant confidence, that God appointed him president and has called on him to lay waste to the evildoers of the world (at least those evildoers who sit on both untapped and fully operational oil reserves) has, for many God-fearing Christian Americans, given Bush the moral authority to turn the carnage inflicted by the world's most fearsome military machine into sacred wrath. With his ideological twin, Tony Blair, playing Lord Curzon, the Bush/Blair alliance does not bode well for peoples the world over who worship "false" prophets (i.e., who are non-Christian).

With the mighty chains of this Christian faith, Bush has hoisted his conscience onto the biblical back of God, to whose wrath he has faithfully committed himself and his armies of invasion. Bush wraps his depleted uranium shells in the "divine right of kings" and the U.S. doctrine of Manifest Destiny before hurling them into the theater of war with the deftness of a Super Bowl quarterback. As U.S. weapons of mass destruction effortlessly saw through tendon and bone, blast apart organs, and incinerate flesh with a vengeful fury, Bush sleeps as soundly as the ten thousand innocent Iraqi civilians that he has recently killed, but remains oblivious to the wails and shrieks of the countless numbers that he has left orphaned and crippled. After his routine three-mile jog and bedtime prayers, the former governor of Texas, who set the record for most executions by any governor in American history, has learned to unburden his heart by invoking the Lord for help in directing the nation's foreign policy. His mind unmercifully devoid of functioning synapses and unencumbered by the power of analysis, Bush unhesitatingly made his decision to invade and occupy Iraq "because he believes, he truly believes, that God squats in his brainpan and tells him what to do" (Floyd 2003, 4). The Israeli newspaper *Haaretz* was given transcripts of a negotiating session between Palestinian prime minister Mahmoud Abbas and faction leaders from Hamas and other militant groups. In these transcripts, Abbas described his recent summit with Ariel Sharon and Bush. During the summit, Bush allegedly told Abbas,

> God told me to strike at Al-Qaeda and I struck them, and then He instructed me to strike at Saddam, which I did, and now I am determined to solve the problem in the Middle East. If you help me I will act, and if not, the elections will come and I will have to focus on them. (Regular 2003, 1)

When, on the freshly mopped deck of the carrier, USS *Abraham Lincoln*, the U.S. warrior president emerged in a snug-fitting flight suit from an S-3B Viking aircraft. His trademark swagger and petulant grin were greeted by patriotic cheers from throngs of wild-eyed officers and sailors. Appearing topside before a bold banner that announced "Mission Accomplished," our boy emperor declared the "battle of Iraq" a "victory" in the ongoing "war on terror." This event was carefully choreographed by Bush's team of seasoned image makers that included a former ABC producer, a former FOX News producer, and a former NBC cameraman, paid for out of an annual budget of $3.7 million that Bush allots for his media coordinators. Bush's speech on the carrier paraphrased chapter 61 of Isaiah, the very book that Jesus used when proclaiming that Isaiah's prophecies of the Messiah had come true, suggesting perhaps that Bush believes the Second Coming has begun (Pitt 2003) and that his war on terror is playing an important role in this biblical prophecy. Leftist commentators have noted that the Pentagon's Shock and Awe bombing strategy was copied from the Nazi strategy of *Blitzkrieg* (lightning war) and the Luftwaffe's doctrine of *Schrecklichkeit* aimed at terrorizing a population into surrender, and that the Bush Doctrine of preventive war mirrors the rationale behind Hitler's march into Poland (Hitler had claimed Poland was an immediate threat to the safety of the Reich). And while Bush padre's vow to establish a new world order and

Hitler's vow to create a *Neue Ordung* have to be seen in their historical and contextual specificity, the comparison of the Bush dynasty to the Third Reich does extend beyond fascist aesthetics, media spectacle, and the police-state tactics of the Office of Homeland Security. It can be seen in the machinations of capital and the role of the military-industrial complex in imperialist acts of aggression disguised as "freedom."

Bush will continue to represent those loyal minions who were outraged by Janet Jackson's exposed breast at the Super Bowl, but who sat down with their families to watch with patriotic pride the spectacle of the Shock and Awe bombing of Baghdad on CNN. The hawks around Bush genuflect at the intellectual altar of the late philosopher-king and University of Chicago classicist Leo Strauss, who maintained that only an elite few in the government warrant the sacred custodianship of the truth and are thereby charged with using "noble lies" to keep the truth from the unwashed masses by preoccupying everyday citizens not only with real or perceived external threats to the nation but also with the task of developing nationalist or militantly religious sentiments fanatical enough to ensure their willingness to die for the nation.

Straussians are first and foremost pragmatists who will resort to whatever works best to secure control. Karl Rove, the president's political adviser, not only puts Straussian strategy to work, but he is also reported to "reread Machiavelli the way the devout study their Bibles" (Maertens 2004). As Tom Maertens asserts,

> It was the Bush-Rove team that deployed the scurrilous push-pull techniques against Senator John McCain in the 2000 South Carolina primary. (Sample question: "Would you be more likely or less likely to vote for John McCain for president if you knew he had fathered an illegitimate black child?" In reality, the brown-skinned child with McCain was his adopted Bangladeshi daughter, but the race-baiting worked and McCain was defeated.) (2004)

The new Orwellian ambience in the United States can be sniffed in the words of prominent right-wing journalist Charles Krauthammer: "America is no mere international citizen. It is the dominant power in the world, more dominant than any since Rome. Accordingly, America is in a position to reshape norms—How? By unapologetic and implacable demonstrations of will" (cited in McMurtry 2001). Sound Nietzschean? Readers who are fans of *Zarathustra* might be emboldened by the words uttered by David Rockefeller at the June 1991 Bilderberg meeting in Baden, Germany: a "supranational sovereignty of an intellectual elite and world bankers . . . is surely preferable to the national auto-determination practiced in past centuries" (cited in McMurtry 2001). When you put Krauthammer and Rockefeller together, you complete the circuit of totalitarian logic involving "full-spectrum dominance" set in train by the juggernaut of globalized capital.

The following characterization of the United States by John Bellamy Foster may be unsettling to some, but it is certainly not far-fetched to anyone acquainted with U.S. cold war history over the past half-century: "By any objective standard, the United States is the most destructive nation on earth. It has killed and terrorized more populations around the globe than any other nation since the Second World War" (2001, 8). It is precisely this question that critical educators need to engage, as morally repellent as it may be to some. As U.S. tanks roll over the dead and dying in Baghdad and other Iraqi cities, I assert that one of the principle contradictions today is between the criminal ruling class of U.S. imperialism, on the one hand, and the exploited and oppressed peoples and nations around the world on the other. Regardless of the recent so-called Shock and Awe victory of Bush and his quislings in Iraq, I argue that the working out of this contradiction constitutes one of the major forms of motion that will eventually determine human history and geography.

LIBERAL CAPITALIST DEMOCRACY IN RUINS

It is my profound conviction that capitalism is not something that can be fixed, or humanized, because, as Dave Hill, Mike Cole, Paula Allman, and Glenn Rikowski have argued, its very value form is premised on the exploitation of human labor. Yet, even in progressive circles, scholars on the Anglo-American left have dismissed Marxist educators calling for a socialist democracy as extremists or juvenile leftists. Consequently, critical revolutionary educators need to pose to their progressive liberal counterparts some searching questions. Can liberal reformers—even World Bank dissenters such as Jeff Sachs, George Soros, and former senior vice president and chief economist of the World Bank and Nobel Prize recipient Joseph Stiglitz (2002)—rebuild and redirect the capitalist financial system in the interests of the poor and powerless? Can they prevent the rationality of financial capital, which is more interested in short-term profits than investing in fixed capital and long-term technological progress, from prevailing over what is rational from the standpoint of society as a whole? Can they prevent the suffering of workers due to the dismantling of protectionist trade barriers? Can they stop privatization from resulting in oligopolies and monopolies? Can they stop the International Monetary Fund from bailing out international investors and granting elites the opportunity to protect their financial assets by massive capital flight, while placing the burden of repaying loans, in the words of Tony Smith, "on the very group that benefited least from them, working men and women" (2002)? Do they have the power to prevent the gangster capitalists of Russia, for instance, from buying up most of the privatized assets and natural resources of the country?

Can they stop the multilateral agencies from advancing the particular interests of the United States? Can they prevent new nation-state-driven racisms that follow in the wake of the new U.S. phallomilitary warrior nationalism currently providing ideological ballast for its practices of primitive accumulation via cluster-bombing Iraq? Can they transcend the creation of plutocratic political subjectivities from above in order to combat the uneven development of epidemics such as AIDS and SARS in the equal-opportunity inevitability of death? Can they reverse the systematic tendencies to crises of overaccumulation and financial collapse or the structural mechanisms generating uneven development? Can they prevent speculative bubbles from expanding and bursting? Can the balance of power in capital/wage labor relations shift in favor of labor? Can the fundamental dynamic of capitalist property relations be challenged? Questions such as these cut to the roots of the capitalist system. From the perspective of our analysis, honest answers to these questions will lead to a resounding no. Liberal capitalist reformers in the main fail to comprehend "that money is the alien form of appearance of abstract labor," and they refuse to challenge the money fetish as the master trope of capitalist social relations (Smith 2002). Of course, liberal reform efforts to make global capitalism more "humane" are welcome, but it still remains the case that, in the last instance, they cannot prevent financial disaster from being visited upon developing countries or the poor in general because these problems are inherent in the system of property and productive relations that constitute the very blood and gristle of the capitalist system (Smith 2002).

Let me offer a Lacan-inspired description of the liberal democracy that I have been describing. The key point is that liberal capitalist democracy sustains the alibi that the corrupt behavior of corporate bosses is an aberration and not the "spectral double" of law-abiding business leaders; it sustains the myth that the real American corporate leader is a church-going philanthropist who wants to contribute to making the United States a better place for working men and women. Liberal democracy occludes the fact that violence (of corporate leaders, police, and criminals) is a symptom of liberal democracy's failure to respond to the suffering of others (Zizek 2002). If we see liberal democracy as a totality, then we can recognize it as a dialectical unity of itself and its other. The notion that we live in a meritocracy is the form of appearance of its very opposite: the absence of equality in a society divided by race and class. Liberal democracy, as a master signifier of "America," constitutes an imaginary supplement or, in Lacanian terms, a "big Other" that acts on behalf of all citizens, an excess that serves ideologically to justify all acts in its name on the basis that it is ultimately for the common good of humanity. This supplement enables U.S. citizens to endure America's unbearable contradictions, such as its lack of medical insurance for the poor; its growing homeless population; its corporate scandals; its institutionalized forms of racism; its torture training center at the School of the Americas in Fort Benning, Georgia; its support in the past of a long list of fascist dictatorships in Guatemala, El Salvador, Iran, Indonesia and Chile; its past funding and training of the Contra terrorists; its invasions of Panama and Grenada; and its recent role in the coup attempt in Venezuela, not to mention financial and military aid to the ruthless Colombian regime.

The seemingly inexorable advance of capitalism, against which workers and their school-age children have little, if any, redress, has led many educators to despair. Few educational critics would deny that the last several decades of school reform have not had their professed effect, and that working-class and ethnic minority students for the most part are faring badly on standardized tests and in securing any jobs at all, let alone what could be described as decent work. Much contemporary educational criticism on the Left is postmodernist in orientation and disposition, and while it would be wise not to characterize this work as mere flummery, even the best of it has, nevertheless, signaled a discernible shift "from politics to culture" (Eagleton 2003, 12), and in the main, such criticism has had a nugatory effect overall on educational change. The failure of the political order is embodied in the desperate lives of the world's suffering and homeless populations. As Eagleton notes,

> The dispossessed are a living sign of the truth that the only enduring power is one anchored in an acknowledgement of failure. Any power which fails to recognize this fact will be enfeebled in a different sense, fearfully defending itself against the victims of its own arrogance. (2003, 176)

My own position within the anticapitalist and Marxist humanist alliance falls within the purview of *socialist anticapitalism*. To this end, I have tried to develop a rematerialized approach to critical pedagogy that Paula Allman (1999, 2001) has named "revolutionary critical pedagogy." Such an approach to pedagogy insists on understanding social life from the standpoint of the strategic centrality of class and class struggle. This contrasts with the postmodernized cultural studies approach that is fixated on discourse and power.

The Strategic Centrality of Class

I agree with E. San Juan Jr. (2003a, 2004) that the United States continues to function not as a democratic polity but as a class-divided racial polity, as racial exclusion and differential entitlements to whites based on property relations are firmly at the center of the neoliberal capitalist system. Racism, as such, can be considered the ideological correlate of the modern social order premised on the global division of labor.

Within the sociology of education there exists the much-vaunted race-class-gender triptych found in the "intersectionality thesis" that maintains that race, class, and gender mutually inform each other, producing the hybrid, or mestizaje, subject (subjects that are oppressed in different ways, according to where they are located within the triptych, given certain contexts or relational conditions with the social order). It is important to underscore that oppression by class is not more important than other forms of oppression, such as acts of racism or homophobia. But class exploitation can be considered the material armature or material basis or material conditions of possibility for other forms of oppression within capitalist society. You can talk about racism and sexism but not "classism." There is no "classism" since class exploitation is not simply one form of oppression among others but constitutes the ground upon which other "isms" of oppression are sustained within capitalist societies (Scatamburlo-D'Annibale and McLaren 2003).

Race, class, and gender, while they invariably intersect and interact, are not coprimary. This triplet approximates what the philosophers might call a "category mistake." On the surface, the triplet may be convincing—some people are oppressed because of their race, others as a result of their gender, and yet others because of their class—but this is grossly misleading, for as Eagleton points out, "It is not that some individuals manifest certain characteristics known as 'class' which then results in their oppression; on the contrary, to be a member of a social class just *is* to be oppressed" (1998, 289), and in this regard, class is a wholly social category. Furthermore, even though class is usually invoked as part of the aforementioned and much vaunted triptych, it is usually gutted of its practical, social dimension or treated solely as a cultural phenomenon—as just another form of difference. In these instances, class is transformed from an economic and, indeed, social category to an exclusively cultural or discursive one, or one in which class merely signifies a subject position. Class is therefore cut off from the political economy of capitalism, and class power is severed from exploitation and a power structure "in which those who control collectively produced resources only do so because of the value generated by those who do not" (Hennessy and Ingraham 1997, 2).

When we claim that class antagonism or struggle is one in a series of social antagonisms—"race," class, gender—we often forget the fact that *class sustains the conditions that produce and reproduce the other antagonisms*, which is not to say that we can simply reduce racism or sexism to class. In other words, class struggle is the specific antagonism, the generative matrix, that helps to structure and shape the particularities of the other antagonisms. It creates their conditions of possibility. Thus, racism, sexism, and homophobia are not simply the effects of asymmetrical relations of power. Of course, racism, sexism, and homophobia do often take on a life of their own. This is quite true. But their material basis can be traced to the means and relations of production within capitalist society—to the social division of labor that occurs when workers sell their labor power for a wage to the capitalist (i.e., to the owner of the means of production). To ignore class exploitation when you are talking about racism and sexism—something educationalists are wont to do—is a serious mistake (the same is true when discussing class exploitation—you can't ignore other modalities of oppression, such as racism and sexism). However, class exploitation is a topic that is very often ignored within schools of education. If it is discussed, it is often reduced to a discussion of unequal "resource distribution," and this ignores the fact that exploitation is a fundamental character of capitalism, that it is constituent of the labor/capital relation. The unwillingness of many educators to understand or accept this relationship (class as a social relation) has caused even the educational Left to evacuate reference to historical structures of totality and universality. Class struggle is a determining force that structures "in advance" the very agonistic terrain in which other political, racial, and gender antagonisms take place.

A politics that reduces class exploitation to one form of oppression among others renarrates class struggle against economic exploitation and between exploiters and the exploited as cultural struggles against the dominant discourses of the "haves" against those of the "have nots," thus camouflaging continuing efforts by the capitalist state to subsidize the wealthy few at the expense of the many and disguising in cultural garb the reality of class as the unmet needs of the majority.

This is not to say that cultural discourses are secondary to economic relations; nor is it to maintain that symbolic production has no political significance or potential or that resistance at the level of culture is merely a "natural" occurrence. I am saying that it is politically, pedagogically, and conceptually mistaken to reduce the reality of class struggle, the social division of labor, and relations of production to a terrain of unstable constellations of meaning and indeterminate and incommensurable discourses that seemingly bear little relationship to the messy terrain of capitalist social relations.

As San Juan (2003a, 2004) makes clear, by separating race and racism from the social relations of production and treating them mainly as issues of ethnicity and the politics of "difference" and "diversity," the multiculturalist problematic operates effectively as a hegemonic scheme of peacefully managing the crisis of race, ethnicity, gender, and labor in countries such as the United States, a way of neutralizing the perennial conflicts in the system, of containing diversity in a common grid, of selling diversity in order to preserve the ethnocentric paradigm of commodity relations that structure the experience of life-worlds within globalizing capitalism. According to San Juan (2004a, 2004b), an understanding of the hegemony of the

United States as a racial polity must begin with a historical materialist approach grounded in the labor/capital dialectic, where class is seen as an antagonistic relation between labor and capital and where "race" is understood historically as a manifestation of the class-conflicted structure of capitalism and its political/ideological/judicial process of class rule (San Juan 2003a, 2004a, 2004b).

Consequently, is important to bring educational reform movements into conversation with movements that speak to the larger totality of capitalist social relations and that challenge capital's social universe. We need to keep our strategic focus on capitalist exploitation if we want to have effective antiracist, antisexist, antihomophobic struggles. We need to challenge global capitalism universally, which does not mean we ignore other social antagonisms and forms of oppression, the horizon of which capitalism functions to sustain.

Regrettably, much of critical race theory and multicultural education has been marked by the absence of an explanatory primacy of class analysis. Analyses of class exploitation from a Marxist perspective have been substituted by a neo-Weberian focus on status and lifestyle. What effectively gets lost as a result is the notion of class as a structural determinant. Because the antagonistic relationship of class—so central to Marxist analysis—has been displaced by neo-Weberian notions of status, lifestyle, and other cultural contingencies, scholars such as San Juan have argued that a methodological individualism and normative functionalism prevail to this day in humanities and cultural studies approaches to antiracist initiatives. Viewed from the prism of "static nominalism," class is reduced to an economistic factor of identity. Jettisoning the Marxist view that class, as a social relation, serves as the only structural determinant of ideologies and practices sanctioning racial and gender oppression in capitalist society, critical race theory and multiculturalism do not foreground the fundamental importance of the social division of labor in the capitalist production process as a key factor in understanding racism. This dilemma has especially important consequences today as capital's vampirelike drive for self-expansion is accumulating more surplus value in the unproductive sections of the labor market and, in doing so, is further devastating the crumbling infrastructures left behind by previous modes of capitalist value augmentation that were declared unholy by the Thatcher and Reagan administrations. The reason we need to focus on a critique of political economy in our antiracist efforts is that racism in capitalist society results from the racialization of the social relations of capitalist exploitation. In San Juan's view (2003a, 2004), multiculturalism has deliquesced into a disavowed, inverted, self-referential form of racism, a "racism with a distance"—it "respects" the identity of the Other, conceiving of the Other as a self-enclosed, "authentic" community toward which he or she, the multiculturalist, maintains a strict distance, rendered possible by his or her privileged universal position as white. Thus, dominant forms of liberal multiculturalism constitute, in some cases, a form of indirect racism insofar as the dominant imperial white subject retains the position as the privileged empty point of universality from which one is able to appreciate (and depreciate) properly other particular cultures.

The conclusion to be drawn, according to San Juan (2003a, 2004), is that the problematic of multiculturalism is the form of appearance of the totalizing presence of capitalism as universal world system. Here, in this world of ersatz revolutionary resistance, multiculturalists can fight for cultural differences while at the same time leaving the basic homogeneity of the capitalist world system intact.

While we surely must recognize the integrity and value of peoples' cultures and life forms, and for their collective right to exist and flourish, the key issue is how universalize this multiplicity and autonomous singularities. This process of universalization cannot exist as long as the global logic of corporate accumulation determines the everyday life of people on this planet. The key is to abolish class divisions and to struggle for a socialist alternative to capitalism. However, I want to stress that in no way does this position ignore forms of nonclass domination. John Bellamy Foster makes an important observation when he writes,

> The various forms of non-class domination are so endemic to capitalist society, so much a part of its strategy of divide and conquer, that no progress can be made in overcoming class oppression without also fighting—sometimes even in advance of the class struggle—these other social divisions. (2005, 17)

THE POLITICS OF DIFFERENCE

A historical materialist approach that drives the critique offered by revolutionary critical pedagogy understands that categories of difference are social/political constructs that are often encoded in dominant ideological formations and that they often play a role in moral and legal state-mediated forms of ruling. It also acknowledges the material force of ideologies, particularly racist ideologies, that assign separate cultural and/or biological essences to different segments of the population, which, in turn, reinforce and rationalize existing relations of power. But more than this, a historical materialist understanding foregrounds the manner in which difference is central to the exploitative production/reproduction dialectic of capital, its labor organization and processes, and in the way labor is valued and remunerated.

The real problem is the internal or dialectical relation that exists between capital and labor within the capitalist production process itself, a social relation in which capitalism is intransigently rooted. This social relation, essential to the production of abstract labor, deals with how already existing value is preserved and new value (surplus value) is created (Allman 2001). The process of actual exploitation and the accumulation of surplus value is best understood as a state of constant manipulation and as a realization process of concrete labor in actual labor time, within a given cost-production system and a labor market. Difference (racial as well as gender difference) is encapsulated in the production/reproduction dialectic of capital. It is this relationship that is mainly responsible for the inequitable and unjust distribution of resources. A deepened understanding of this phenomenon is essential for understanding the emergence of a polarized labor market and the fact that disproportionately high percentages of people of color are trapped in the lower rungs of the domestic and global labor market (McLaren and Farahmandpur 1999a, b). Difference in the era of global capitalism is crucial to the workings, movements, and profit levels of multinational corporations, but these types of complex relations cannot be mapped out by using truncated ways in which people of color (and, more specifically, women of color) provide capital with its superexploited labor pools, a phenomenon that is on the rise all over the world. Most social relations constitutive of radicalized differences are considerably shaped by the relations of production, and there is undoubtedly a radicalized and gendered division of labor whose severity and function vary depending on where one is situated in the capitalist global economy (Meyerson 2000).

SOCIALISM RELOADED

Socialism is not a discredited dream. It is a current that runs through periods like the menacing present and that is animated by, and in struggle against, all forms of oppression and exploitation. While the antiwar movement will undoubtedly have to overcome certain internal problems to grow much larger and to curb future wars in Syria, Iran, or Venezuela, what we are seeing today is the emergence of a completely new quality of social consciousness that could provide the concrete basis for an internationalist political movement. What matters here is that, against the backdrop of U.S. imperialism, the only way students are ever going to win lasting "peace" or the right to a decent education or job is through the linking of their struggles with all the victims of the vicious ruling class, including workers whose blood, sweat, and toil are the living fuel that makes the economy run.

In creating the conditions for social change, then, the best pedagogy recognizes the limits of traditional reformist pedagogical practice by prioritizing the need to question the deeper problems, particularly the violent contradictions (e.g., the gap between racism and the American dream) under which students are forced to live. Critical revolutionary pedagogy raises the question, Do we know whose hands ground the capitalist lenses through which we comprehend the world, and do we know whence came the bloodstains on the lens grinder's workbench?

Against tremendous odds, the challenge over the last several decades has been to humanize the classroom environment and to create pedagogical spaces for linking education to social justice initiatives, and to that end, we are indebted to critical pedagogy. Yet, faced with the urgency for change, approaching social transformation through the optic of revolutionary critical pedagogy ratchets up the struggle ahead. Revolutionary critical pedagogy dilates the aperture that critical pedagogy has struggled to provide for teachers and students over the last several decades by further opening up the pedagogical encounter to its embeddedness in globalized social relations of exploitation, as well as to the revolutionary potential of a transnational, gender-balanced, multiracial, anti-imperialist struggle. A revolutionary critical pedagogy raises the following questions for consideration by teachers, students, and other cultural workers: How can we liberate the use-value of human beings from their subordination to exchange-value? How can we convert what is least functional about ourselves as far as the abstract utilitarian logic of capitalist society is concerned—our self-realizing, sensuous, species-being—into our major instrument of self-definition? How can we make what we represent to capital—replaceable commodities—subordinate to who we have also become as critical social agents of history? How can we make critical self-reflexivity a demarcating principle of who we are and critical global citizenship the substance of what we want to become? How can we make the cultivation of a politics of hope a radical end in itself? How can we decommodify our subjectivities? How can we materialize our self-activity as a revolutionary force and struggle for the self-determination of free and equal citizens in a just system of appropriation and distribution of social wealth? How can we make and remake our own nature within the historically specific conventions of capitalist society so that we can make this self-activity a revolutionary force to dismantle capitalism itself and create the conditions for the development of our full human potential? How can we confront our producers (i.e., the social relations of production, corporate media, cultural formations, and institutional structures) as an independent power?

Completely revolutionizing education does not depend upon the great white men that capitalist education teaches us are our presidents, heroes, and role models. It relies upon the broad masses of people recognizing that the whole system must be transformed to reflect their interests. This is the strength of a revolutionary critical pedagogy, that it is fighting for the interests of the multiracial, gendered working class and indigenous peoples all the way through. It seeks to transform schools into political and cultural centers, where crucial questions, from international affairs to education policy, are debated and struggled over openly. It is a pedagogy that not only conjures up the audacious urges of the oppressed but also enables them to fight back against the system's repeated attacks by raising people's understanding of their political opponents and developing their organization and fighting position. It is a call to battle, a challenge to change this monstrous system that wages permanent warfare against the world and the planet, from state terror in the homeland to the dumping of toxic chemicals on Native American lands and in communities of color, to devastating bombing campaigns against sovereign nations. It is a pedagogy of hope that is grounded in the unfashionable reality, history, and in the optimism of oppressed peoples and nations everywhere.

Critical pedagogy is secured by the most effective of revolutionary tools: critique. It is focused not only on the practice of critique but also on the critique of pedagogical practice. Unfortunately, many resisting subjects and agents mistake discursive empowerment for social and economic enablement. Their coming to voice and the politics of self-affirmation and self-identity fails to challenge the gross materiality of exploitation. Certainly, the question of developing voice and the politics of self-assertion are fundamentally important, but often the autonomous individual of bourgeois ideology is misrecognized as the voice of the organic intellectual.

The practice of discursive democracy that equates democracy with the affirmation of voice substitutes verbal empowerment and individual expression for material democracy—for the equal access of all to social and economic resources through collective social struggle to transform existing social relations.

According to Teresa Ebert (n.d.),

> Critique is that knowledge-practice that historically situates the condition of possibility of what empirically exists under patriarchal-imperialist-capitalist labour relations and, more importantly, points to what is suppressed by the empirically existing: what could be (instead of what actually is). Critique indicates that what is, is not necessarily the real/true but rather only the existing actuality, which is transformable. . . .
>
> Quite simply then, critique is a mode of knowing that inquires into what is not said, into the silences and the suppressed or missing, in order to uncover the concealed operations of power and underlying socioeconomic relations connecting the myriad details and seemingly disparate events and representations of our lives. In sum, materialist critique disrupts that which represents itself as what is, as natural, as inevitable, as the way things are, and exposes the way "what is" is historically and socially produced out of social contradictions and how it supports inequality. Critique enables us to not only explain how class, race, gender and imperialist oppression operate so we can change it, but also to collectively build the emancipatory subjectivities we need to carry out the revolutionary struggle.

Critique is often difficult to execute and requires the development of historical material analysis of one's own self-constitution as a social agent within the totality of capitalist social relations. We often fail to recognize our responsibility to others because we are preoccupied with the others' relations to us. We forget our network of obligations. Insofar as we, in the words of San Juan, "claim to live in a community of singular persons who alternatively occupy the positions of speakers and listeners, I's and you's, and who have obligations to one another, and reciprocal accountabilities" (2003b, 5), we mistake the struggle for liberation with the pursuit of subjective, autonomous self-identity, failing to realize that subjective self-identity is impossible outside of our relation to the Other and that we can never be free of our obligations to others.

As long as capitalism is not dead, neither is the heart of Marxism and class struggle. At the same time, we must remember that socialists work not for Marxism as a theory but for socialism—Marxism is a tool, not an end in itself. It is, however, an essential tool in attempting to conceive of capitalism and its attendant forms of oppression as a whole. That is not to say that everything Karl Marx said or anticipated has come true. That is certainly not the case. But Marx did provide us with fundamental insights into class society that have held true to this day. Rather than jettisoning Marx and decentering the role of capitalism in creating misery around the globe and discrediting socialist struggle, there is a need to challenge vigorously the assumptions that have come to constitute the core of contemporary radical theory, pedagogy, and politics.

To defeat capitalist globalization and the accumulation of corporate profits by private owners means developing a philosophy that can help us to organize praxis to this end. Our position as revolutionary critical educators is to support continentwide mobilizations against the neoliberal offensive and the Washington consensus, whose objective is to turn back all of the social rights achieved over the past half-century. We advocate a gender-balanced, multiracial opposition to imperialism, to war, to capitalist globalization, and to the law-and-order policies that have made a mockery of our democratic freedoms and that institutionalize violence against the most vulnerable groups in our society. We challenge the productivist model of development that puts the future of humanity at risk, and we demand democratic control over choices of development and of production. In doing so, we steadfastly refuse to submit to social liberalism, which controls the institutions of the state in the interests of the minority, who own all the wealth, and we work toward a socialist alternative to capitalism so that social needs are satisfied. Here, we advocate the politics of internationalism, especially in light of the rise in power of social movements and continental social forums. We refer to diverse groups that include the *piqueteros* in Argentina, the *cocaleros* in Bolivia, the landless workers in Brazil, the Packakutik indigenous movement in Ecuador, the Zapatistas in Mexico, and the Bolivarian Circles in Venezuela. The convergences necessary to give true credibility to the conviction that another world is possible will not just happen on their own; they must be struggled for, and guided by, all of our efforts. This is the challenge of researchers, scholars, and activists working together for global justice and peace.

Marx's new society based on being rather than having, creating rather than controlling, relating rather than dominating, will emerge neither from endless negation nor from the spontaneous activities of the multitude, but, as Peter Hudis notes, it will require an articulation of a positive vision of the new, a competing vision of a future alternative to capitalism. This means taking seriously the notion of praxis and recognizing that theory is more than the trajectory of ideas moving from theoreticians to the masses. It also means recognizing that movements from practice by the masses are also forms of theory. As Marx wrote in *The German Ideology*, historical materialism "does not explain practice from the idea but explains the formation of ideas from material practice" (1978). For Marx, "not criticism but revolution is the driving force of history" (1978, 164). While it is surely true that activists who have warmed their political hands in the urban bonfires of Spanish Harlem winters have never read Georg Wilhelm Friedrich Hegel's *Philosophy of Right*, they nevertheless are theoreticians implicitly.

History needs a more powerful ally than the left-liberalism of today's postmodernized academic Left. Left unreconciled, capital propels progress to a higher level of disunity. We do not seek an imageless metaphysical truth where thought thinks itself, but we seek transformation of the conditions of social reproduction where the struggle preserves, yet overcomes, past struggles to emerge at a point where a new social universe can be imagined and a new vision of the future can be won, where the corporate walls of oppression and the ramshackle edifice of capital crumble into dust.

What has become clear is that the real threat to the security state is not terrorism but the struggle for socialism and democracy. For it is the self-movement and self-management of working people struggling for socialism and democracy that poses the greatest challenge to the transnational robber barons who administer the security state and who have acquired an unquenchable, vampirelike thirst for finance capital.

Critical revolutionary pedagogy can serve the important purpose of generating new ways of thinking about the state and its relationship to the production of and possibilities for human agency, both now and in the crucial years ahead of us. Humans are conditioned by structures and social relations, just as humans create and transform those structures and relations. Everything in human history passes through the realm of subjectivity, and it is through this dance of the dialectic that we create our future. The democracy in which we live is indeed at a tragic crossroads, and we must fiercely question its present historical course in order to outlast despair and hold on to the vision that first brought this worthy concept into existence.

NOTE

This article has served as the basis of numerous publications, sections of which have appeared throughout many of my recent writings, including those that appear in Peter McLaren, *Capitalists and Conquerors*, Lanham, Maryland: Rowman and Littlefield Publishers, 2006.

REFERENCES

Allman, Paula. 1999. *Revolutionary social transformation: Democratic hopes, political possibilities and critical education.* Westport, CT: Bergin and Garvey.
———. 2001. *Critical education against global capitalism: Karl Marx and revolutionary critical education.* Westport, CT: Bergin and Garvey.
Barber, Benjamin. 2002. Beyond jihad vs. McWorld: On terrorism and the new democratic realism. *The Nation* 274 (2) (January 21): 11–18.
Bennett, William. 2002. *Why we fight: Moral clarity and the war on terrorism.* New York: Doubleday.
Brennan, Paul. 2003. Mistah Kurtz's new job: America's heart of darkness. *OC Weekly* 8 (31) (April), available at www.ocweekly.com/ink/03/31/books-brennan.php.
Cole, M., D. Hill, G. Rikowski, P. McLaren. 2000. *Red chalk: On schooling, capitalism and politics.* London: Tufnell Press.
Eagleton, Terry. 1996. *The illusions of postmodernism.* Cambridge, MA: Blackwell.
———. 1998. Defending the free world. In *The Eagleton Reader*, ed. Stephen Regan, 285–93. Malden, MA: Blackwell.
———. 2003. *After theory.* New York: Basic Books.
Ebert, Roger. 2004. Less is Moore in subdued, effective "9/11." *Chicago Sun-Times.* May 18, available at www.suntimes.com/output/eb-feature/cst-ftr-cannes18.html.
Ebert, Teresa. n.d. Subalternity and feminism in the moment of the (post)modern: The materialist return, available at www.geocities.com/CapitolHill/Lobby/2072/AOVol3-3Subalterity.html.
Floyd, Chris. 2003. The revelation of St. George. *Counterpunch*, June 30, available at www.counterpunch.org/floyd06302003.html.
Foster, John Bellamy. 2001. Imperialism and "empire." *Monthly Review* (December), available at www.monthlyreview.org/1201jbf.htm.
———. 2005. The renewing of socialism. *Monthly Review* 57 (3) (July–August): 1–18.
Hennessy, Rosemary, and Chrys Ingraham, eds. 1997. Introduction: Reclaiming anticapitalist feminism. In *Material feminism: A reader in class, difference, and women's lives*, 1–14. New York: Routledge.
Hudis, Peter. 2003. *Organizational Responsibility for Marxist-Humanism in Light of War, Resistance, and the Need for a New Alternative.* Report to National Plenum of News and Letters Committees, August 30, 2003.
Klein, Naomi. 2004. The year of the fake. *The Nation* 278 (3) (January 26), available at www.thenation.com/doc/20040126/klein.

Landau, Saul. 2004. Is Venezuela next? *Progreso Weekly*, March 25, available at www.progresoweekly.com/index.php?progreso=Landau&otherweek=1080194400.

Lieven, Anatol. 2003. The empire strikes back. *The Nation* (June 19) www.thenation.com/doc.mhtml?i=20030707&s=lieven.

Lind, Michael. 2004. Churchill for dummies. *The Spectator*. (April 24), available at www.antiwar.com/spectator/spec280.html.

Maertens, Tom. 2004. Clarke's public service. *Star Tribune*, March 28, available at www.truthout.org/docs_04/033004B.shtml.

Marx, Karl. 1978. The German ideology, part one. In *The Marx-Engels reader*, ed. Robert C. Tucker, 146–200. 2nd ed. New York: W. W. Norton.

McLaren, P., and R. Farahmandpur. 1999a. Critical pedagogy, postmodernism, and the retreat from class: Towards a contraband pedagogy. *Theoria* 93:83–115.

———. 1999b. Critical multiculturalism and globalization. Some implications for a politics of resistance. *Journal of Curriculum Theorizing* 15 (3): 27–46.

McMurtry, John. 2001. Why is there a war in Afghanistan? Opening address, Science for Peace Forum and Teach-in, University of Toronto, Ontario, Canada, December 9, 1–13.

Meyerson, Gregory. 2000. Rethinking black Marxism: Reflections on Cedric Robinson and others. *Cultural Critique* 3 (2), available at http://eserver.org/clogic/3-1%262/meyerson.html.

Pitt, William. 2003. George W. Christ? *Truthout* (May 5), available at www.truthout.org/docs_03/050503A.shtml.

Regular, Amon. 2003. "Road map is a life saver for us," PM Abbas tells Hamas, *Haaron*, August 11, available at www.haaretz.com/hasen/pages/ShArt.jhtml?itemNo=310788&contrassID=2&subContrassID=1&sbSubContrassID=0&listSrc=Y.

San Juan, E., Jr. 2003a. Marxism and the race/class problematic: A re-articulation. *Cultural Logic* 6, available at http://eserver.org/clogic/2003/sanjuan.html.

———. 2003b. U.S. war on terrorism and the Filipino struggle for national liberation. *Dialogue and Initiative* (Fall): 2–6.

———. 2004a. Post-9/11 reflections on multiculturalism and racism. *Axis of Logic*, November 13, available at www.axisoflogic.com/cgi-bin/exec/view.pl?archive=79&num=13554.

———. 2004b. *Working Through the Contradictions: From Cultural Theory to Critical Practice*. Lewisburg, PA: Bucknell University Press.

Scatamburlo-D'Annibale, Valerie, and Peter McLaren. 2003. The strategic centrality of class in the politics of race and "difference." *Cultural Studies/Critical Methodologies* 3 (2): 148–75.

Smith, T. 2002. An assessment of Joseph Stiglitz's *Globalization and Its Discontents*, department seminar, Philosophy Department, Iowa State University, October 29, 2002; teach-in sponsored by Alliance for Global Justice, Ames, Iowa, October 16, 2002, available at www.public.iastate.edu/~tonys/Stiglitz.html.

Stiglitz, J. 2002. The roaring Nineties. *The Atlantic Monthly* (October), available at www.theatlantic.com/issues/2002/10/stiglitz.htm.

Tabb, W. 2001. Globalization and education as a commodity, available at www.psc-cuny.org/jcglobalization.htm.

Turner, Denys. 1983. *Marxism and Christianity.* Oxford: Basil Blackwell.

Wilden, Anthony. 1980. *The imaginary Canadian: An examination for discovery.* Vancouver, Canada: Pulp Press.

Zavarzadeh, M., and D. Morton. 1994. *Theory as resistance: Politics and culture after (post)structuralism.* New York: Guilford Press.

Zizek, S. 2002. *Revolution at the gates: Selected writings of Lenin from 1917.* New York: Verso.

7

Youth Alienation in Everyday Life: The Promise of Critical Pedagogy

Benjamin Frymer

The alienation and anomic disengagement of youth has been a major source of concern in the United States since World War II, generating continual public anxiety and sustained scholarly attention. In fact, during the 1950s and 1960s, "alienation" became a frequent buzzword employed by television and print media and the source of renewed interest in the social science research of the day. Both media and scholarly accounts continually associated the term with youth and, indeed, the life phase of "adolescence" in and of itself. This link between alienation and youth was firmly established when influential public writers such as Paul Goodman (1960) and Kenneth Keniston (1965) published dramatic accounts of the perceived legions of "disaffected youth" sprouting up in all geographical corners of the United States.

Since the 1960s, "youth alienation," both real and imagined, has continued to be a source of fear and institutional reaction as reflected in the many channels of U.S. cultural discourse and those institutions responsible for socializing the young for participation in adult life—namely, the family, schools, and the criminal justice system. Drug use, teen pregnancy, gangs, school dropouts, suicide, violence, political apathy, casual sex, rock and rap music, and, more recently, depression, video games, raves, and the Internet have all been taken as signs of an underlying existential estrangement, or even nihilism, in the lives of youth and the expressions of youth cultures. While these empirical indicators are taken to reflect an essential interior emptiness, distress, or turmoil in the inner lives of adolescents, rarely are they or their everyday experiences connected to the larger social, economic, and cultural formations that give rise to the substance of everyday life and that are the basis of specific historical relations of domination and resistance. Imagined as essentially Other in relation to those who conform, and compared to hegemonic models of psychological maturity, social progress, and individual development (Lesko 2001), alienated youth are positioned outside arenas of history, relations of power and domination, and social change. Their alienation, as in the 1960s, is considered a more or less transitory form of individual or group deviance, if not an inherent vulnerability to the risks of adolescence itself.

In contrast to this dominant discourse on youth alienation, the group of critical theorists in education grouped under the rubric "critical pedagogy" has made a significant contribution to a contemporary critical understanding of youth alienation in schools as part of their overall project to illuminate the politics of education. Beginning with and inspired by the pioneering work of Paulo Freire in the philosophy and sociology of education, critical pedagogy has used an interdisciplinary empirical and theoretical project to critique the dominant perspectives in the field of education and in public discourse. Since much of Freire's philosophy of education is itself based on an analysis and critique of student alienation or "objectification," critical pedagogy seamlessly moved toward an investigation of this phenomenon in contemporary schooling. Incorporating the Frankfurt School, Pierre Bourdieu, Antonio Gramsci, structural Marxism, and the Birmingham School, critical pedagogy, as reflected in the early work of Henry Giroux (1981, 1983), Paul Willis (1977), and Peter McLaren (1986), revitalized and extended Freire's critical theory into a critical social theory of education. More recent work in cultural studies and critical ethnography (Bettie 2002; Dimitriadis 2003; Fine 1991; Gaines 1991; Valenzuela 1999; Weis 1990; Wexler 1992) has broadened the field and brought attention to numerous forms of alienation in U.S. schools. Thus, the result, until a recent split in the field between cultural studies and political-economic approaches, was a plethora of empirical and theoretical interrogations of contemporary ideology and practice in capitalist schooling. However, despite critical pedagogy's initial interest in the problems of culture, subjectivity, and ideology in education, the current division between interrogation of representations in popular culture and the reconstruction of materialist frameworks necessitates work that links student alienation in everyday life, understood as both a material and cultural phenomenon, to the larger social structure and culture of American schooling and late capitalist society. This chapter asserts that Freire's critical pedagogy, with its central theme of alienation in all relations of social life and being, may provide one of the bases for a renewed critical social theory of youth alienation.

Freire's analysis of alienation in education is rooted in the same theoretical and empirical trajectory as the philosophical and social category *entfremdung* (estrangement), one of the key concepts in the development of the Western

Marxist project. From its origins in Georg Wilhelm Friedrich Hegel's analysis of the historical subject's attempt to attain the object in different forms of consciousness, the Hegelian-Marxist tradition has sought to understand alienation in terms of the numerous forms of separation that prevent the subject from realizing its historically conditioned humanity. Since Ludwig Andreas Feuerbach and Karl Marx, Hegelian-Marxism has proceeded to locate these separations dialectically in the cultural, phenomenological, and material existence of life in capitalist society. From Marx (1964) and Georg Lukács (1971), to Theodor Adorno (1973), Eric Fromm (1955), Herbert Marcuse (1964), Guy Debord (1994), Henri Lefebvre (1971, 1991), and Raoul Vaneigem (1994), the analysis of alienation has targeted the capitalist mode of production for inverting the relationship between subject and object in the totality of social life. Whether in Marx's uncovering of commodification or Lukács's reification thesis, the deformation of the subject into an object in all spheres of everyday life has been the crucial phenomenon of critical theory and the crux of the imperative for revolutionary transformation.

Yet, contemporary theories of alienation, including those pertaining to youth, must be reconstructed and positioned within a renewed critical theory and critical pedagogy project. Alienation has to be thought anew for the age of late or postmodern capitalism. The modern industrial capitalist society that circumscribed youth identity and everyday life for over a century has given way to a new, dizzying, postindustrial landscape of bewildering communications and information technologies, massive transformations in the nature of work, the proliferation and circulation of commodity images on an unprecedented scale, and the steady decay of uprooted foundational norms and dislocated ethical narratives. Just as youth in the late nineteenth century were forced to undergo dramatic reorientation in adjusting to the new era of modern industrial capitalism, contemporary youth will either form new identities and bases of meaning and participation in the early stages of today's postmodern capitalist social order or dissolve into a fragmented simulacrum. At stake is not simply the speed and character of the transitional process but the very possibility for creating youth identity, meaning, and participation in everyday life under advanced capitalist modes of domination—a possibility that has been systematically denied in previous modern periods. Before outlining some of the essential features of a critical theory of youth alienation, it is important to elaborate on Freire's seminal critique of the modes of oppression and alienation of everyday life.

FREIRE'S ANALYSIS OF ALIENATION

Critical pedagogy's promise for confronting youth alienation is rooted in Freire's critical theory. A return to the centrality of the phenomena of alienation and dehumanization found in Freire's "pedagogy of the oppressed" can provide critical pedagogy with a renewed basis for the political transformation and illumination of the everyday alienation stunting the humanity and social participation of large groups of contemporary youth. Freire's focus on both the social and existential subordination of the oppressed, as reflected in phenomenological experience and the objective socioeconomic conditions of individual lifeworlds, is central to a critical social theory of youth alienation in everyday American life. In fact, Freire's project, his pedagogy of the oppressed, is specifically concerned with the transcendence of alienation and oppression through the development of a critical literacy with revolutionary intent. However, unlike previous traditions of critical theorizing, Freire's pedagogy, with its roots in Marx, is based on praxis, dialectically combining theory and practice in its program.

As best evidenced in his major work, the *Pedagogy of the Oppressed* (1972), Freire's problematic was constructed out of a complex combination of historically distinct theoretical, philosophical, and political traditions. Among the more influential strands of Freire's writings, it is possible to identify strong influences from Hegelian Marxism, existentialism, liberation theology, phenomenology, and some form of critical hermeneutics. Shaull, in his introduction to the English translation of *Pedagogy of the Oppressed*, quotes Freire's own statement on his intellectual roots as including "Sartre and Mounier, Eric Fromm and Louis Althusser, Ortega y Gasset and Mao, Martin Luther King and Che Guevara, Unamuno and Marcuse" (1972, 11). Other Freire scholars have indicated his indebtedness to Hegel (Torres 1994) and the humanist existentialism of Buber, Jaspers, and Marcel (Peters and Lankshear 1994). Certainly, the figure of Marx, especially the early Marx, remains a significant, if not the most significant, and powerful influence throughout Freire's work. But what these intellectual and political figures share is a concern with the problem of alienation and existential and social oppression.

At the foundation of Freire's pedagogy is a philosophical anthropology about the nature of human being. For Freire, as for Marx, human nature is radically historical. It is only capable of being defined and understood as potentiality, as possibility within conditions of freedom. Human nature cannot be abstracted from the specific and powerful social relations and structures within which we live at any given historical moment. Freire asserts, with Marx, that our nature is defined by the potential for imagination, creativity, meaning, and the free exercise of our productive powers through unalienated work. We *are* who we can potentially *become* through our capacity to think, feel, and work under conditions of our own choosing. "Human" being only becomes realized when the individual and community are actualized together in a reciprocal process.

Freire asserts that the "ontological vocation" to be human depends upon the potential for reflective, intentional activity, or "praxis." For Freire, to be human in any meaningful sense is to be a subject, a conscious social actor who has the desire and the opportunity to participate in social and political life. However, a subject is not just a citizen who performs perfunctory tasks in a formal democracy. Rather, a full subject is an intellectual who continuously "reads the world" as she or he simultaneously reads the word. The preconditions for individual engagement, democracy, and social freedom are therefore "educational." Alienation is the separation of the subject from her ontological vocation of active human participation in the world.

The subject-object distinction takes on additional meaning for the oppressed. In fact, it is very difficult to understand Freire's conception of subjectivity independently of his analysis of objectification and dehumanization in the condition of oppression. The oppressed, submerged in conditions of existential violence, do not exercise their human capacities. They do not reflect on their lives, their experiences, their misery, or the reasons they find themselves among the dominated.

What then is the social and phenomenological condition of oppression for Freire? To answer this is to "penetrate" the political and philosophical core of his pedagogy of the oppressed. Freire argues that the oppressed are living under conditions of pervasive existential violence, which have essentially blocked the emergence of their humanity. Therefore, the ultimate significance of social and economic domination is the establishment of a class of dehumanized and alienated "objects." Objectification of potential subjects is a form of violence for Freire since it is a process that violates the human essence at all levels of its being and expression: psychological, existential, political, and ontological. The oppressed are turned from potentially active subjects into dominated objects, from critically reflective actors, who participate in society democratically, into passive instruments of elite authoritarian control.

Freire's pedagogy of the oppressed is based on Marx's critique of alienation as commodification. However, instead of limiting his focus to production and labor, Freire, like prior theorists such as Lukács and Marcuse, sees objectification as a pervasive social phenomenon saturating the totality of capitalist societies. The individual is turned into an object, not only as a laborer but also through a whole constellation of objectifying forces, such as the state, schools, the media, the family, and other cultural spheres. The oppressed are particularly vulnerable to objectification given their marginal and subordinate status, and their general submersion in a "culture of silence." They are not expected to participate in the political affairs of their societies and are valued only as menial laborers. Freire argues,

> The oppressed, who have been shaped by the death-affirming climate of oppression, must find through their struggle the way to life-affirming humanization,

which does not lie *simply* in having more to eat. . . . The oppressed have been destroyed precisely because their situation has reduced them to things. In order to
regain their humanity they must cease to be things and fight as men. This is a
radical requirement. They cannot enter the struggle as objects in order *later* to become men. (1970, 55)

As objects, the oppressed have been prevented from becoming human
subjects. They are not actors but are acted upon. They do not desire freedom
but live in constant fear of it. They do not reflect on their lives and their social conditions but are told what to think and who to be. In short, their
being-in-the-world is a nonbeing, like that of any other dead object.

The goal of the pedagogy of the oppressed is to transform objects into full
subjects through dialogical learning. The oppressed must develop critical
consciousness of their objective situation, but they must also simultaneously struggle to become subjects capable of creating a free society. According to Freire, "The struggle begins with men's recognition that they have
been destroyed" (1970, 55). In other words, critical consciousness of the
world, thus subjectivity, must emerge from an awareness of one's own oppression and alienation. Without such awareness, objectification remains a
seemingly natural state.

Moreover, education for liberation cannot be imposed on, or imparted
to, the oppressed; it can only be created with them in the process of humanization. Dialogical education is based on the assumption that human
beings are potentially active, conscious agents capable of knowing and
transforming the worlds they live in. Drawing on Husserl, Heidegger, and
Jaspers, Freire argues that libratory pedagogy must recognize that students
can learn to think actively and with intentionality and purpose, in other
words, with a critical consciousness. Authentic praxis consists of a movement of the oppressed to simultaneously understand and change the conditions of oppression. In this regard, Freire argues,

Problem-posing education is revolutionary futurity. Hence, it is prophetic (and
as such, hopeful). Hence, it corresponds to the historical nature of man. Hence,
it affirms men as beings who transcend themselves, who move forward and
look ahead, for whom immobility represents a fatal threat, for whom looking
at the past must only be a means of understanding more clearly what and who
they are so that they can more wisely build the future. Hence, it identifies with
the movement which engages men as beings aware of their incompletion—an
historical movement which has its point of departure, its subjects and its objective. (1970, 72)

Thus, in contrast to "banking education," which seemingly craves a kind of
existential death and affirms the inevitability of a violent present, the pedagogy of the oppressed loves life, development, and the flourishing of the

individual through collective understanding and historical struggle to transcend the condition of estrangement.

FREIRE AND CONTEMPORARY YOUTH ALIENATION

A critical pedagogy capable of confronting present-day youth alienation needs to expand the scope of Freire's thought while still drawing upon his most seminal contributions to educational praxis. While maintaining Freire's understanding of alienation as objectification and dehumanization and the denial of active participation in political life and intellectual activity, it must chart new historical forms of youth alienation in everyday life and create a new relationship between a contemporary analysis of estrangement and critical pedagogy. In particular, I argue that a critical theory of late capitalist youth alienation must (1) interrogate the cultural logic of everyday life, (2) confront the production of existential nihilism and loss of meaning amid commodification and spectacle in capitalist society, and (3) investigate the subordination of education as a political and social project, as well as an ethical end, amid an intensification of the spectacle society. A renewed critical pedagogy's project of emancipation must envision a response to pervasive youth and student alienation and a vision of transcendence in and through education. This return to the core problem of alienation brings critical pedagogy back to the social, philosophical, and political project of Paulo Freire in the context of a late capitalist, postindustrial, spectacle society. This new social formation has been explored by a number of critical theorists over the past two decades.

Social theorists of postmodernity, such as Guy Debord (1994), Fredric Jameson (1991), Douglas Kellner (1995, 2003), David Ashley (1997), and Jean Baudrillard (1983), have concentrated their attention on the cultural and social impact of new mass-communications technology and the mass media to define the novel conditions that have emerged in capitalist societies since the modern industrial era. Together, the body of work known as postmodern theory has been preoccupied with the power of mass-mediated images and messages to transform, if not dissolve, social life, individual consciousness, and identity. The power of a new media age to construct and simulate social reality is said to have dislodged the modern foundations of identity, the self, morality, and the real. In fact, according to Baudrillard, the transition from modern to postmodern is said to occur when the real referents of signs are lost in the endless proliferation and circulation of media images and representations. For Baudrillard, postmodernity consists of the production of endless series of simulacra—copies of copies with no authentic original.

How have young people adapted to these new conditions? Too often, everyday life in postmodernity generates new forms of estrangement and anomie that make growing up, to borrow Paul Goodman's telling phrase, even more "absurd" (Strickland 2002). Contemporary youth alienation must be understood within the context of dramatic new material and cultural conditions that generate social fractures and undermine stable bases of meaning and identity for the self, even as these same conditions create different forms of estrangement by race, class, gender, and sexuality. While the alienation of groups marginalized by these modes of oppression must be connected to earlier modern forms of Freirean oppression, economic exploitation, racial domination, and patriarchy, the near universal cultural and economic transformations of the postindustrial digital age, with its corresponding malaise and fragmentation of identity, transcend class, race, gender, and sexuality. Youth alienation goes beyond the boundaries of subculture, as well as "objectification" in Freire's sense. It is part of the very logic of postmodernity and late capitalism.

Thus, for many U.S. youth, the problem of adolescence continues to revolve around the creation of some form of transcendent, yet stable, identity, but in the contemporary society of the spectacle, this task has become even more difficult. While the possibility for struggle and resistance still lies in the spirits of youth, just as it does for Freire's "oppressed" classes, the advanced development of consumer capitalism has changed the landscape of alienation and the possibility of its transcendence. The process of struggle with society and the meaning of identity are now more obscure and confusing. Authenticity and rebellion are more difficult even to locate and strive for in "spectacular" society. The conditions in which the young must define themselves and their purposes have become more abstract and absurd, beyond the everyday objectification Freire attempted to address.

Absurdity lies in the fact that youth identity in the society of the spectacle has become a commodity that is bought by media conglomerates and sold back to young people themselves. The production and circulation of mass-mediated images has become the defining ground upon which adolescents must locate a sense of self. Their selves are always already presented to them in the spectacle, and these images conform to a restricted range of choices that young people are allowed to integrate and express. The struggle to define one's self that Edgar Friedenberg (1959) asserts to be the central task of adolescence is itself incorporated into this preselected set of images for public consumption. Youth style, rebellion, and marginality are hunted down and integrated into the media before any authentic cultural roots can spread and stable identities can form.

Thus, just as in Freire's diagnosis of oppression and estrangement in everyday life, contemporary youth alienation speaks to a multidimensional cultural and existential crisis for all groups of youth, including those privileged by class, gender, and race. It is a crisis of identity, of the self, of human recognition, and of the possibility of growing up on terms that oppose the commodification of contemporary life. New suburban and rural estrangement witnesses the struggle of young men and women to maintain the integrity of self in the face of the larger alienated society of spectacular life. This is particularly the case for boys and young men. The anomic detachment, anger, resentment, and isolation of groups of vulnerably masculine youth outsiders forms in response to the perceived mediocrity, meaninglessness, and absurdity of life in the society of the spectacle.

Paradoxically, the horizons of everyday life appear limited to these boys in the exact historical moment when new worlds of communication, knowledge, and images in the age of new media have opened up. Many young men see no future and no alternative past the momentary gratifications of violence and mediated diversions from boredom in the hollowed-out world of suburbia or rural towns. Cruelty, hypocrisy, and absurdity appear to them to be impossible to change; they are just part of the "way things are." Thus, the problem of postmodern alienation exemplifies, above all, the power of historically specific capitalist relations to commodify everyday life and subjectivity itself. Both the quotidian practices and experiences of young people are profoundly shaped by the overlapping, internally related estrangements of self and society in the spectacle society's abstract world of commodities.

For many middle-class youth, particularly white suburban and rural kids who drift toward or are pushed to the margins, the problem of postindustrial life is the pervasive anomie and absurdity of consumerism, suburbia, and abstract social life. It is the set of conditions creating widespread fragmentation of identity within hyperreal media worlds. The society of the spectacle can make growing up more absurd, especially when disciplinary projects attempt to reinforce the abstract identities they promote. Thus, when identity crises are fueled or reinforced by cultural waves of hostility and punishment, the alienation of marginal youth only intensifies. The frequent result is depression, rage, detachment, and, for some, homicide or suicide. Thus, nearly half a million American teenagers attempt to kill themselves every year, and the "rate of teenage suicide . . . has tripled in the past thirty years" (Gaines in Spina 2000, 107).

Finally, Freire's pedagogy can contribute to analyzing the subordination of education, as a process and ideal, to bureaucratic and capitalist schooling in the spectacle society. For Freire, any educational experience worthy of the name necessarily entails active engagement on the part of the learner as part of a dialogical, problem-posing movement of critical awareness into the world. Education ceases to exist when the learner is transformed into a passive object, such as in traditional "banking" methods of instruction. Just as for Freire this form of existential and social negation is the essence of oppression, according to Debord, passivity is the very mode of "life" sanctioned by the society of the spectacle. In fact, for Debord, the ubiquitous channels of mass communication promote the desire for passivity in all spheres of (former) activity. The modern individual is encouraged to be a mere spectator, a passive viewer of life as it is mediated for the public by corporations and political elites. She is to renounce the attempt to control her own learning or to construct the ground of meaning by which her life becomes a transcendent project. As students in large bureaucratic school systems, and with their leisure time governed by the production and circulation of commodity images, contemporary youth are typically confronted by wide gaps between schooling and authentic education in Freire's sense. Education has become systematically alienated from the institution of schooling and overwhelmed by pervasive cultures of consumption and entertainment with their corresponding production of continually circulating desires and fantasies for status, power, and "happiness."

Thus, the everyday life of schools becomes a kind of spectacle in itself, based on modes of abstraction that create the separation of schooling from the process of education. In other words, as Freire argued about traditional teaching, postindustrial schooling has been alienated from the purposive end of education itself. Despite the best intentions of many dedicated teachers, education takes place in the vast majority of U.S. schools only through a profound struggle by a much smaller group of teachers and administrators against the forces of the market, rationalized accountability schemes, and media culture. Therefore, in the face of historical transformations in late capitalist educational discourse and practice, the United States has witnessed the gradual discursive erosion of learning as even one of the main goals, let alone the central purpose, of schooling. The now entrenched ideological linkages between schooling and competition, whether for national superiority in a globalized economy or individual market attainment in a consumer society, have submerged the substantive ends of schooling beneath layers of instrumental rationality.

In conclusion, with a renewed sense of purpose and a return to its origins in Freire's critical theory, a contemporary critical pedagogy could address this youth crisis and become an important analytic and political force tackling the problem of alienation and its transcendence once again. Just as Freire's pedagogy of the oppressed understood the dehumanization of the learner to reside in objectification, forced passivity, and the undermining of active intellectual and political engagement in the everyday lives of the poor and downtrodden, a contemporary critical pedagogy could help interrogate current forms of youth objectification, passivity, and disengagement. By placing the alienations of late capitalism at the center of its core concerns, critical pedagogy would be able to speak to the lives of youth in more powerful and transformative ways. Equipped with a sociology of everyday life, critical pedagogy might once again speak to the economic, cultural, existential, and political constellations of estrangement that undermine the active participation of youth in their lifeworlds and the larger political and economic life of contemporary societies.

REFERENCES

Adorno, T. 1973. *Negative dialectics*. New York: Seabury.

Ashley, D. 1997. *History without a subject: The postmodern condition*. Boulder, CO: Westview.

Baudrillard, J. 1983. *Simulations*. New York: Semiotext (e).

Bettie, J. 2002. *Women without class: Girls, race, and identity*. Berkeley: University of California Press.

Davis, N. 1999. *Youth crisis: Growing up in the high-risk society*. Westport, CT: Praeger.

Debord, G. 1994. *The society of the spectacle*. New York: Zone Books.

Dimitriadis, G. 2003. *Friendship, cliques, and gangs: Young black men coming of age in urban America*. New York: Teachers College Press.

Fine, M. 1991. *Framing dropouts: Notes on the politics of an urban high school*. Albany: State University of New York Press.

Freire, P. 1970. *Pedagogy of the oppressed*. New York: Continuum.

Friedenberg, E. 1959. *The vanishing adolescent*. Boston: Beacon Press.

Fromm, E. 1954. *The sane society*. New York: Rinehart.

Gaines, D. 1991. *Teenage wasteland: Suburbia's dead end kids*. New York: Pantheon.

Giroux, H. A. 1981. *Ideology, culture, and the process of schooling*. Philadelphia: Temple University Press.

———. 1983. *Theory and resistance in education: A pedagogy for the opposition*. South Hadley, MA: Bergin and Garvey.

Goodman, P. 1960. *Growing up absurd: Problems of youth in the organized society*. New York: Vintage.

Jameson, F. 1991. *Postmodernism, or the cultural logic of late capitalism*. Durham, NC: Duke University Press.

Kellner, D. 1995. *Media culture: Cultural studies, identity, and politics between the modern and the postmodern*. New York: Routledge.

———. 2003. *Media spectacle*. New York: Routledge.

Keniston, K. 1965. *The uncommitted: Alienated youth in American society*. New York: Harcourt, Brace, and World.

Kozol, J. 1991. *Savage inequalities: Children in America's schools*. New York: Crown.

Lefebvre, H. 1971. *Everyday life in the modern world*. New York: Harper and Row.

———. 1991. *Critique of everyday life*. New York: Verso.

Lesko, N. 2001. *Act Your age! A cultural construction of adolescence*. New York: Routledge Falmer.

Lukács, G. 1971. *History and class consciousness: Studies in Marxist dialectics*. Cambridge: Massachusetts Institute of Technology Press.

Marcuse, H. 1964. *One dimensional man: Studies in the ideology of advanced industrial society*. Boston: Beacon.

Marx, K. 1964. *Economic and philosophic manuscripts of 1844.* New York: International Publishers.

McLaren, P. 1986. *Schooling as a ritual performance: Towards a political economy of educational symbols and gestures.* Boston: Routledge and Kegan Paul.

Peters, M., and C. Lankshear. 1994. Education and hermeneutics: A Freirean interpretation. In *Politics of Liberation: Paths from Freire,* ed. P. McLaren and C. Lankshear. London: Routledge.

Spina, S. U., ed. 2000. *Smoke and mirrors: The hidden context of violence in schools.* Lanham, MD: Rowman & Littlefield.

Strickland, R., ed. 2002. *Growing up postmodern: Neoliberalism and the war on the young.* Lanham, MD: Rowman & Littlefield.

Torres, C. A. 1994. Education and the archaeology of consciousness: Freire and Hegel. *Educational Theory* 44 (4): 429–45.

Valenzuela, A. 1999. *Subtractive schooling: U.S. Mexican youth and the politics of caring.* Albany: State University of New York Press.

Vaneigem, R. 1994. *The revolution of everyday life.* Seattle, WA: Left Bank Books.

Weis, L. 1990. *Working class without work: High-school students in a de-industrializing economy.* New York: Routledge.

Wexler, P. 1992. *Becoming somebody: Toward a social psychology of school.* London: Falmer Press.

Willis, P. 1977. *Learning to labour: How working class kids get working class jobs.* Farnborough, UK: Saxon House.

8

Is Religion Still the Opiate of the People? Critical Pedagogy, Liberation Theology, and the Commitment to Social Transformation

César Augusto Rossatto

During the 2004 U.S. presidential elections, just like in the Middle East, Ireland, and in many other parts of the world, religion and politics were mixed together within an extremely dangerous fanatical spectrum. Historical experience accounts for this kind of symbiotic regime change into theocratic fundamentalism, which generates a dosage of intolerance for those that oppose it. Like it is popularly said, "Going to war over religion is like arguing over who has the best imaginary friend." Faith loses, and the society has nothing to gain, when religion is used as a political weapon. Faith in this context is not a world conception but a way of appropriating and acting in it (Rabaça 2004).

Therefore, this chapter intends to critically uncover the current relationship of religion and politics, with its consequences to education. Despite the school and church separation, how does critical pedagogy examine teachers' religious affiliations and challenge their positionalities in schooling? What is the influence of religion in education? Even with liberation theology, is religion still the opiate of the people? How is liberation theology understood in the United States in contrast to Brazil and Latin America? This chapter examines some of these questions and others affecting our world today by bringing about cross-cultural studies (Brazil and the United States, mainly), a literature review on the topic, and combining it with an analysis of El Paso and Juárez current border issues (along the U.S.-Mexico border). Finally, besides being white and Christian, and therefore able to talk as an inside member, I also use my autobiographical experience of seven years in the seminary, studying for the priesthood, in addition to two years of university liberation theology studies, and my continual membership in the critical liberation theology congregation for more than twenty-five years.

RELIGION SHAPING POLITICS

Religion was definitely used as an ideological instrument for political action that shaped the results for George W's. reelection, in addition to the culture of war impregnated in the U.S. society, which is also another pathological patriot doctrine (Wise 2005a) that gives only the United States the permission to invade and dominate other countries and seek their interests. If all countries were to assert these "rights," we would have endless wars; as it is, we do anyway, at the hands of the United States. This culture says "God bless America," "forgetting" to ask God to bless each and every country in the world without exception (Chomsky in Rossatto 2004; Wise 2005b). This oblivious, religiously constructed practice was the catalyst hegemonic apparatus that drove millions to believe they were doing the "right thing" during the 2004 elections. Even though the rest of the world demonstrated its disappointment with and disapproval of George W.'s administration, masses of people were blinded enough to choose who they perceived as the "lesser of two evils," dismissing overwhelming evidence to the contrary. This kind of mentality pushed people to believe in specious "facts" as alibi. People would only hear what they wanted to hear, comprising an indoctrinating way of thinking, which, for many affiliated with various conservative religious groups, seemed to be a normal undertaking.

Religions today, just like in the past, enable wealthy, powerful, capitalist, corporate power to expand its neoliberal empire; for instance, in the U.S. Congress, most elected officials are members of Religious Right institutions. Yet, why do people allow themselves to be manipulated? Where is located the belief that drives people to act out of a naive faith rather than cognizant and rationalized dispositions? Without trying to blame victims for their victimization, it is obvious that the responsibility lies with the dominant group's interests that inculcate the masses to think and act according to their interest and not with people who are subjugated to such outcomes. For instance, T. Whitehurst (2004), in her article "Careful Not to Get Too Much Education . . . Or You Could Turn Liberal," points out that religious fundamentalist students were instructed to be cautious not to lose their moral and religious values if they wanted to pursue higher levels of education, leading one to think that the question must be about how and why people in positions of power control those in underprivileged conditions.

Noam Chomsky, in *Hegemony or Survival: America's Quest for Global Dominance* (2003), asserts that dominant groups are concerned with not allowing the "great beast" (referring to masses of people) to go astray and how they might maintain these people properly confined in "their place." The implications of such a task developed a huge enterprise industry to tame the beast and coerce these people through control mechanisms that manufactured their consent, opinions, and attitudes. In other words, this complex hegemonic system and its doctrine try to safeguard the privilege and power exercised by a white, patriarchal, capitalist society. Religion in such contexts has played a key function to divide the masses and facilitate the establishment of the upper classes' dominance. Religion, not spirituality, is a human-organized institution; yet, despite controversial and painful historical outbreaks, humans for centuries have continued to embrace it.

RELIGION AND SPIRITUALITY WITHIN DIFFERENT CULTURES

Humans look inward and outward for spiritual relationships with deities to be able to better understand themselves and justify their experience in the universe. Few people know, though, that the inside search can be just as dangerous as the outside search, since passion and fanaticism can blind them to what is perceived as common sense. For example, in the inside search, many people can lose themselves with deceitful religious ideologies or fanaticism. In the outside search, many can also blind themselves with the "kingdom of God in heaven," fervor for materialistic consumption, or the struggle for money, power, and prestige as a filling for spiritual voids.

Regardless, any spiritual experience precludes an inside or outside search that connects the person with the universe and what it has to offer, and through religion this experience can materialize. For example, for some it can be nirvana/transcendence, the kingdom of God, or a combination of both (Boff 2000). Nevertheless, Leonardo Boff says that according to the Dalai Lama, it is spirituality, not religion, that provokes an inside transformation. Religions started with this idea of translating messianic people's encounter with themselves and their god. Thus, religions can translate these experiences people have with the divine, guide them into mystical encounters, or show them paths to ethical or coherent beliefs and approaches to religious life, but religion cannot be the translation of spirituality since spirituality is a personal experience, which provokes an inner transformation, not a doctrine that can be transmitted, even though religions' main purpose should be the guidance to spirituality (Boff 2001). But religion, from the Latin *religare* (reconnect), became an institutionalized or organized doctrine in an attempt to connect humans and their higher spiritual sources.

Liberation theology, with its Marxist roots, announces a deep commitment to social justice and rejects the notion that organized religion can become the opium (an alienating mechanism) of the people if it doesn't guide them to spirituality or critical consciousness. For instance, it becomes the opium when the word "god" translates into a political power or money-making mobilization. In many instances, religious power can be a source of violence and hegemonic control, as history had shown. However, spirituality is not a monopoly of religions or codified spiritual paths. Spirituality has an individual human dimension. According to Boff (2001), this spiritual dimension, which every individual can have, reveals itself through one's capacity to dialogue with one's own self and one's ability to love, which translates into sensitivity, compassion, listening to the "other," responsibility, and care as a fundamental attitude. In other words, it is not about "thinking" god but "feeling" god.

Different groups or cultures believe and experience spirituality in diverse ways. For instance, First Nation people (i.e., Native Americans) differ from the white European, Westernized Jews and Christians and the ancient Asian religious cultures. Many indigenous populations believe that we are spiritual beings born in human bodies; therefore, our function on this planet is not to be more spiritual but to be more human, or better human beings, which also means being spiritual. Better yet, by being spiritually conscious, one can act more humanely. The Aboriginals in Australia also had a hard time understanding why the white man thought that the sacred was only inside church walls. They would say, "For us, all around us is sacred, the air we breathe, the scents we smell, what we see and hear in nature." Some Afro-Brazilian religions believe in the concept of *Axé*, defined as a cosmic energy that permeates the whole universe and concentrates on human beings to brighten their reality. They also believe in the concept of *Exú*, defined as the messenger for excellence of the Axé, the universal energy that lives inside people as the strength of radiation, which leaves a breathing space to capture more energy and, for that reason, to be of service to others. In other words, one can be the strength and the other the movement; one cannot be without the other since one gives movement to the energy of the other (definitions taken from personal interviews in *terreiros de candomble*, a popular spiritual gathering in Bahia, Brazil; also see Cone 1997; Boff 1998).

THE CONSEQUENCES OF RELIGION
AND THE REINVENTION OF CRITICAL PEDAGOGY

Besides different cultures' positive religious perspectives and contributions, a critical examination of religions' manipulative doctrines, along with their consequences, must always be revisited by critical pedagogy. When social practices go unchallenged, they can often lead to a dogmatic predicament with devastating collective repercussions—such as the Heaven's Gate in Los Angeles and Jim Jones's mass suicide in Guyana—justifying the need for critical leftist interventions. Religion has evidently contributed positively to society, but even with this rapport, according to Muller (2004), in some *favelas* (slums) in Brazil, while religion had pushed out the drug dealers, yet it seemed that one addiction was substituted for another, with the hope that the latter was less harmful. For example, some religions promote a blind fanaticism, where oppressed people are exploited; some go to extremes, to even laundering money, and crimes are committed in name of religion; some become like a good-old-boys' system. It is even worth mentioning that under globalization, developed countries like the United States are exporting some of these religions to Brazil, such as the Mormon, Protestant, Evangelical, and Baptist denominations, among others. Some of these religions go to Brazil and other developing countries with millions of dollars to expand their hegemonic dominance.

Because of religiously motivated catastrophic consequences to humanity, such as those that induce fanaticism, alienation, passivity, and crime, critical educators need to denounce and deconstruct religious practices, which in the past, just as today, maintain the status quo. Why hasn't religion led to true liberation? For instance, historians point out that during World War II, the pope had an agreement with Hitler not to speak out against the war and his crimes and atrocities in exchange for keeping the Vatican and other Catholic buildings intact. In this way, religious leaders, just like intellectuals, become complicitous in their silence. Where were the intellectuals and highly educated religious leaders during slavery? Didn't they know that was atrocious treatment of humans? As were the killings of indigenous people? Religious leaders, just like intellectuals, need to speak up and oppose injustices, such as the war in Iraq. Isn't the fact that hundreds of thousands have died and hundreds of billions of dollars have been wasted enough reason to push any intellectual or religious leaders into collective opposition? For instance, Don Helder Camera, an internationally known community activist and bishop from Brazil, gave up the amenities offered by the church to live in the favelas. He used to say, "When I feed the poor, they call me a saint, but when I ask why the poor are without food, they call me a communist." Nevertheless, when people question or try to change the status quo, most of the time, they pay a high price, but this is the duty of critical pedagogues, liberation theologians, and any critical leftist educator committed to social justice. Nevertheless, a language of critique must be followed by a language of possibility since, for a few in extreme levels of oppression and poverty, religion can represent a last ray of hope.

Nonetheless, a call to question everything that happened in the past and in the present is an intrinsic necessity with today's schooling challenges due to religion and historical consequences. Even though the past is a reference memorandum and not a breathing space to live in, its influence on the present and the future must be everyone's concern, especially when we talk about actions and guiding doctrines dictated by global hegemony (Chomsky 2003). For instance, it is imperative to question why Christians suffered oppression and brutal treatment in the past, but when raised to a position of power and privilege, they also inflict the same or worse atrocities on others. This can lead one to think that the oppressed, when raised to a position of power, can also become oppressors if they don't regain their humanity and develop critical consciousness (Freire 1993). Moreover, white patriarchal Christians also learned rather quickly that in order to have political power and maintain themselves in such a structure, they needed economic power as well. For this reason, the concept of purgatory was established, to legitimize a money-making mechanism, even without any biblical basis. This unsubstantiated and deceiving concept supposedly gave those who were financially secure the assurance to move the souls of their loved ones from purgatory into heaven if they would pay for a mass with such intentions. In other words, this version converted God into a capitalist figure who made the wealthier feel good about themselves and gave them the "right" to buy heaven (Ferder 1993). Similarly, I observed many times in Los Angeles, after fifteen years of living there, that in some poor communities the parish services (with exceptions) would focus on the idea of God's punishment or guilt, while in Malibu, Bel Air, Beverly Hills, or other more affluent communities, the parish services often made the people feel good about themselves. In these territories, the idea of God was love, forgiveness, and caring, which ultimately legitimized a guilt-free environment.

Religion has always been an intrinsic part of human life and human destiny's makeup. It has accompanied important events and key decisions that at times were perceived as inappropriate: case in point, George W.'s reelection. This confirms the fact that religion today, just like in the past, is still the catalyst for hegemonic historical decisions. George W. claimed to be a born-again Christian, opposed to gay marriage and abortion; that alone was very appealing for religious people, for whom these were major priorities for the presidency. Consider also the Republican initiative to pass a bill in Congress to designate the membership to their political party as unquestionable membership—to critique it would be unconstitutional, just as if it were a religious affiliation, which many interpret also as an association that must be accepted and respected as an absolute—the initiative didn't go anywhere.

According to S. Waldman and J. Green (2004), the overwhelming majority of Evangelicals and Protestants, like the majority of Catholics and moderately religious voters, were very important in this election, as were the very religious "born agains" or the Religious Right. It goes without saying that the so-called red states, which voted for George W., were considered the poorest ones and those with the highest rates of religious fanaticism and of divorce. Ironically, little did people know that they voted for the candidate with the least intention of helping them. Case in point: the U.S. $300 billion invested to kill people in Iraq and the small amount of $300 million to save the tsunami victims in Asia. The implications of such historical cases give enough reasons for critical leftist educators today to reinvent critical pedagogy, because educators, thus our society as a whole, need to better understand religious and political analysis or discourses and their mischievous cover-ups. The call for the reinvention of critical education is necessary to denounce any sort of deceitful manipulation since critical pedagogy must serve as an instrument of approximation to the "truth," not the absolute truth, but educators and the society as a whole ought to understand political and religious past and current contexts and their implications for schooling. For instance, the so-called saint inquisition (an evil rather than sainted initiative) preached the reproduction of a given manipulated knowledge, not its discovery. Besides being driven by dogma, the inquisition period gave birth to the so-called dark ages, where the Catholic religious regime established a system of dictatorial supremacy to eliminate any conceivable opposition or any different intellectual reminiscence. (Some say that this kind of secret society is still in existence today under names like Opus Dei and the Masons). This event in history constituted a major setback to the advancement of science, which remains present in our society today, as religion still induces fear or guilt to promote faith. In our existing political context, this very doctrine is still practiced. Under George W.'s administration, for example, the very same doctrine of fear and the reproduction of a given manufactured knowledge are reenacted in the following contexts:

- Under the standardization movement, students are forced to absorb an institutionalized and previously conceived knowledge that oppresses them. They are strained to undertake tests on a one-size-fits-all model and fear punishment, rather than catering to improve education. Children have multiple forms of intelligence; therefore, we should have multiple forms of assessment rather than one only. Teachers, in turn, are forced to teach to the test, making the learning experience very sterile. Ultimately, both teachers and students find themselves stressed out, which also hinders the advancement of science since students and teachers miss the opportunity to produce new knowledge or to be creative and innovative, because very few students make it over the hurdles they have to clear.
- The masses of people are educated to fear a possible "terrorist attack," legitimizing the devastating massacre and invasion of Iraq via George W.'s War on Terror. On the one hand, the attack was legitimate because a born-again Christian U.S. president was said to have prayed for the outcome, and people thought the decision was carried out with God's hand; on the other hand, of course, it was carried out also in the name of a promised democratic paradise for the "other" (the Iraqis), who were perceived as incapable to create their own government system. Evidently undermined and motivated by fear, people do anything, and in this case, they supported this destructive war; this was a major contradiction, because how can a person be "prolife" and then be in favor of

a war that kills more than abortion? Whose lives are valued? And whose lives are worthless?

- Initiatives like the U.S. Patriot Act are attempts to silence intellectuals or others who dare challenge the system, a surveillance system that enacts a kind of McCarthyist renaissance (Rossatto 2004). During these repressive times, "democracy" is promised in lieu of "heaven," much as a similar pledge was offered during the Inquisition. Michael Moore's movie *Fahrenheit 9/11* vividly depicts the war in Iraq as instigated via false assumptions and based on false evidence.

WIDENING THE CIRCLE AGAINST WHITE PATRIARCHAL CAPITALIST RELIGIOUS STRUCTURES

In the task of widening the circle of anti-oppression education, critical pedagogy has never had a greater need to be reinvented and to recommit itself to social justice roots than today, especially to confront the historical white patriarchal capitalist oppressive hegemonic religious structures. The reinvention sought out, in the context of this chapter, is to assist educators, religious leaders, and affiliated practitioners to critically analyze deeply rooted institutionalized oppressive ideologies embedded in religious practices (Boff 2002; Cone 1997; Williams 1993; West 2002; Saramago 2004; West and Glaude 2003).

When one analyzes established discourses in the world of religions, the internalization of capital and labor are intertwined with indoctrinated beliefs inherited from white, patriarchal, capitalist, religious structures, such as Catholicism (which I was part of for so long), indicating that these unleashed hegemonic systems function together to maintain some in positions of privilege at the expense of others who are subjugated. Therefore, the need to widen the circle of anti–white supremacist, patriarchal, capitalist, oppressive religious structures is a call to consciousness from the various educational sectors and religious affiliations to intervene in these very powerful systems. But first, we need to deconstruct this hegemonic structure, with its oppressive composition, to then transform the harrowing reality into a sustainable unbiased and equitable society, where true compassion can move beyond tolerance and into prosperity despite differences and similarities. A strong commitment from critical educators and liberation theologians in matters of race, gender, and class is required to unveil why many nonwhites remain structurally excluded from the societal mainstream. The goal is to attempt to address these issues effectively relative to oppressed groups' struggles to "make it" in a hostile reality of hegemonic totalities.

It is easy to notice how religious leaders and, consequently, the congregation's constituency become institutionalized and unable to think "outside the box." Case in point: I have observed in the El Paso/Juárez area, as in many other places around the world, religious advisors and worshippers remaining indoctrinated into norms, language, and practices totally distant and foreign to ordinary people's real world. For instance, members are incorporated into a structured and often highly formalized system where a prescribed agenda has been rigidly set, and ordinary people have to abide by it without alternatives or understandable choices of their own. Given this context, it is explainable why the constituency of such an idealized abstract world might have difficulty understanding the applicability of liberation theology since, for them, it becomes a dull and romanticized approach to people's real-life struggles, rather than an organic social justice commitment with transformational implications. The reoccurrence of this type of pattern was part of my personal experience, as well as that of others who had also undergone the priesthood decumbency, in which I was also an authentic witness. I even remember how out of place I felt after leaving the seminary. I was living in an unrealistic, imagined, and idealized mental space totally detached from the real world of people in the mainstream.

In addition, as a result of my studies in the El Paso region, I was able to observe religious leaders catering mainly to successful Latinos, who often had to "sell out," or assimilate, in order to "make it." Some of these groups become the favorite audience for some churches because of their monetary contributions. Even though charity is done by some of these religious institutions, in such a context, it seems a cover-up, token ritual to maintain a good public image.

Many of the Christian organized religions sustain a white, Eurocentric, patriarchal, capitalist hegemonic system; for instance, because the majority of religious leaders in the Catholic Church are white males, this denomination therefore tends to attract those of similar background and thus enables them to assemble in a more comfortable manner. Examples of white hegemony within the church are quite noticeable. I observed that prior to Juan Diego's canonization, pictures depicted him as an indigenous man from Mexico, but right after his beatitude, he was portrayed as a white man with a mustache. A few years back, when I was in Los Angeles, I recall that a study revealed that if the pope were black, 30 percent of Catholic Church members would abandon their affiliation. I remember vividly people's dismayed reactions to what they perceived as an unthinkable possibility; in other words, they had not thought of that possibility prior to this study, though an African made it to the short list recently, but was passed over. I am mentioning these events to highlight how whiteness or white supremacy has been part of religion and how it has been constructed within the institution.

When Europeans colonized the Americas, they didn't identify themselves by their white skin color but by their country of origin and language. However, when whites were challenged by "those" they perceived as "red or black," who were greater in number, then whites in the Americas started to construct a new sense of identity. They constructed new forms of white supremacy, such as the eugenics movement and the Ku Klux Klan, among others, as a way to guarantee their privilege among those they considered "other," who were inferior. In Europe, being "white" was not an issue because whites were the majority; in the Americas, however, Europeans felt outnumbered, and therefore the antagonism of skin color took priority in their minds.

Evidently, religion was the main basis for justifying the belief that whites were superior. Christians would find decontextualized bible quotes to legitimize their criminally horrifying practices against people of color and feel no remorse for the crime committed, such as slavery, lynching, and the horrendous white supremacist practices of the Ku Klux Klan. Since the majority of religious leaders were white men, they provided the assurance to eliminate any signs of guilt associated with such performances (Gutierrez and Barr 1993). In a white-dominated society, those who are not white, today just as in the past, often feel impelled to assimilate whiteness. Thus, the impact of this oppressive configuration creates identity crises among people of color, leading many to resist schooling, have self doubts, and possess a lack of self-determination. And since teachers are affiliated with diverse religious groups, it is evident that many demonstrate their tendencies and predominant patterns inherited from such membership. In one instance in El Paso, a new teacher, almost naively, whispered in my ear, "I voted for Bush because if gays are allowed to get married, then we wouldn't see boys and girls entering into marriage any longer." Her religious background blinded her to the fact that the president's job description and responsibility goes way beyond trying to control gay marriage or abortion issues. Sadly, the latter provided the alleged reason for the voting.

The religious influence on public opinion is a reality; for instance, as a couple of bishops in the Chicago area voiced their opinions against John Kerry, George W.'s opponent in the last presidential election, they indicated their intention to deny him communion if he attended their churches. In other words, they were indirectly supporting George W. because they viewed Kerry as an advocate for abortion and gay marriage; in fact, this was partially a false perception. Half truths can confuse many people. It is obvious that religions in subtle ways ruthlessly defend their political agendas. Many teachers who belong to these religious institutions become complicit in associating with this type of ideology that reproduces detrimental predicaments. For example, some teachers have voiced publicly their oblivious tendency to support George W. due to their religious associations, confirming that politics and religion often go hand in hand. However, teachers' political and religious positionalities also have a classroom impact; one particular teacher even mentioned that after telling her students she voted for Bush, all her students were disheartened, confirming how teachers' positionalities exert influence on schooling. When religion misleads the public to further its political and ideological agendas, without any doubt, religion becomes the opiate of the people. And besides white complicity, the patriarchal system is another oppressive hegemonic totality that needs to be deconstructed within religions, commencing with the Bible, because, according to D. Williams (1993), the Bible is full of patriarchal language in need of rewriting, such as, God as Father, Son, and Holy Spirit, God King of Israel, Shepherd.

ALTERNATIVES FOR RELIGIOUS AND EDUCATIONAL PRAXIS

Religion in the United States is, in many ways, both different from and similar to that in Latin America, but both can learn from each other. Since I have lived in the United States almost the same amount of time I lived in Brazil, I can say that my experiences in both countries within religious contexts are very rich ones. For example, in Brazil I once was part of a liberation theology movement, *comunidades de base* (community-based religious organizations), which, together with my involvement with the workers' party, assisted in the election of Luis Inacio Lula da Silva as the best viable leftist president, as well as in bringing down the military dictatorship. In the trenches of militant critical activism, I was able to witness the unification of real committed religious leaders with the people. We were out there with the people in the favelas, with the indigenous population, and with the poor communities. Many of us, under the dictatorship (put in power in 1964 via a U.S.-sponsored coup), suffered torture and repression for being with the people in their struggle for social justice; it was a movement led by the people and for the people, as many other publications account for those initiatives (Betto 2002, 2003; Galeano 1981; Braga 2003; Borba, Faria, and Godinho 1998; Pinheiro 1984).

  In similar ways, I can say that in the El Paso area, an interreligious organization called El Paso Interreligious Sponsoring Organization does transformational work. It is a nonpartisan issues-based community organization, focused on activism to build awareness about injustices encountered in the local communities. This group became known for organizing local citizens to improve schools and communities; changing schools' administrations; transforming the inhospitable conditions in *colonias* (favelas); doing grant writing, vocational training, and job opportunities; and, lastly, promoting political consciousness for people to go out and vote and demand changes and hold political leaders accountable for their actions. Some of their rules are (1) don't do anything for people that they can do for themselves, and (2) make no permanent allies and no permanent enemies. Another organization, called Border Interface, is also trying to do similar work on the West Side of El Paso. One religious leader in the east side, whom I became close to renounced even the humble accommodations offered by the church to be able to, make a living by his own efforts, such as teaching in public places. He works with local universities and pays his own bills. He showed a tremendous commitment to activism and social transformation. He has joined us in several marches against standardized tests and in solidarity against the killings of women in Ciudad Juárez, together with other religious leaders that support similar activities.

By the same token, educators, just like religious leaders, also ought to be willing to practice what they preach and denounce injustices, then announce hopeful educational alternatives. This hope ought to be based on the struggle for evidence that sustains a new vision of decency and dignity that will never allow inequality, racism, and injustice to set in as a norm (West 1997).

In sum, institutionalized religion in many instances is allied with power (especially economic and political) in order to subexist as a powerful social organization. It is unfortunate that in order to do so, it enables oppression by remaining silent when it is called to action or by alienating masses from their ability to transform their realities. Therefore, critical pedagogy, just like liberation theology, needs to be reinvented to constantly confront systems of abomination, such as the symbiotic relationship of religion and other organized systemic structures of oppression.

REFERENCES

Betto, F. 2002. *Lula, um operario que virou presidente* [Lula, a metallurgic that became president]. São Paulo, Brazil: Casa Amarela.
———. 2003. *Sinfonia universal: A cosmovisao de Teilhard de Chardin* [Universal symphony: A cosmavision of Teilhard de Chardin]. São Paulo, Brazil: Editora Ática.
Boff, L. 1998. *O despertar da águia: O dia-bólico e o sim-bólico na construção da realidade* [The awakening of the eagle: The diabolic and the symbolic in the construction of reality]. Maryknoll, NY: Orbis Books.
———. 2000. *Tempo de Transcendência* [Time of transcendence]. Maryknoll, NY: Orbis Books.
———. 2001. *Espiritualidade: Um caminho de transformação* [Spirituality: A way of transformation]. Rio de Janeiro, Brazil: Sextante.
———. 2002. *Fundamentalismo: A globalizacao e o futuro da humanidade* [Fundamentalism: Globalization and the humanity's future]. Maryknoll, NY: Orbis Books.

Borba, A., N. Faria, and T. Godinho. 1998. Mulher e politica: Genero e feminismo no Partido dos Trabalhadores [Women and politics: Gender and feminism in the Worker's Party]. São Paulo, Brazil: Editora Fundação Perseu.

Braga, E. M. F. 2003. *América Latina: Transformações econômicas e politicas* [Latin America: Political and economic tranformations]. Fortaleza, Brazil: Editora UFC.

Chomsky, N. 2003. *Hegemony or survival: America's quest for global dominance.* New York: Metropolitan Books, Henry Holt and Company.

Cone, J. 1997. A *black theology of liberation.* Maryknoll, NY: Orbis Books.

Ferder, F. 1993. *Words made flesh: Scripture, psychology and human communication.* Notre Dame, IN: Ave Maria Press.

Freire, P. 1993. *Pedagogy of the oppressed.* New York: Continuum.

Galeano, E. 1981. *As veias abertas da América Latina* [Latin America's open veins]. Rio de Janeiro, Brazil: Editora Paz e Terra.

Gutierrez, G., and R. R. Barr. 1993. *Las casas: In search of the poor of Jesus Christ.* Maryknoll, NY: Orbis Books.

Pinheiro, P. S. 1984. *Trabalho escravo, eonomia, e sociedade* [Slave work, economy, and society]. Rio de Janeiro, Brazil: Editora Paz e Terra.

Muller, A. 2004. *Body capital: A cross cultural study.* EdD dissertation, University of Texas, El Paso.

Rabaça, C. A. 2004. *Religião e politica* [Religion and politics]. *Jornal do Brasil,* November 22, A11.

Rossatto, C. 2004. *Social justice in times of McCarthyism renaissance: Surveillance, ethics, and neoliberalism.* In *Social justice in these times,* ed. J. O'Donnell, M. Pruyn, and R. Chávez Chávez. Greenwich, CT: Information Age Publishing.

Saramago, J. 2004. *O evangelho segundo Jesus Cristo* [The gospel according to Jesus Christ]. São Paulo, Brazil: Companhia das Letras.

Waldman, S., and J. Green. 2004. It wasn't just (or even mostly) the "Religious Right," available at www.beliefnet.com/story/155/story_15598_1.html (accessed May 19, 2006).

West, C. 1997. *Restoring hope: Conversations on the future of black America.* New York: Beacon Press.

——. 2002. *Prophesy deliverance: An Afro-American revolutionary Christianity.* Philadelphia: Westminster Press.

West, C., and E. Glaude Jr. 2003. *African American religious thought: An anthology.* Philadelphia: Westminster Press.

Williams, D. 1993. *Sisters in the wilderness: The challenge of womanist God-talk.* Maryknoll, NY: Orbis Books.

Whitehurst, T. 2004. Careful not to get too much education . . . or you could turn liberal. *CommonDreams.org,* December 28, available at www.commondreams.org/views04/1228-32.htm.

Wise, T. 2005a. *White like me: Reflections on race from a privileged son.* New York: Soft Skull Press.

——. 2005b. *Affirmative Action: Racial Preference in Black and White.* New York: Routledge.

9

On Language of Possibility: Revisiting Critical Pedagogy

Seehwa Cho

INTRODUCTION

Peter McLaren, once a chief proponent of critical pedagogy, has recently declared that critical pedagogy is no longer viable in instigating social change: "Critical pedagogy and its political partner, multicultural education, no longer serve as an adequate social or pedagogical platform from which to mount a vigorous challenge to the current social division of labor and its effects on the socially reproductive function of schooling in late capitalist society" (1998, 448). According to him, critical educators' predispositions are what have led to the demise of critical pedagogy: "There has clearly been a strong movement among many critical educators infatuated by postmodern and poststructuralist perspectives to neglect or ignore profound changes in the structural nature and dynamics of late capitalism in the United States" (1998, 449).

This is a serious blow since critical pedagogy emerged in the 1980s precisely to pursue a "language of possibility." As Carmen Luke characterized it, critical pedagogy was conceptualized and constructed to "counteract the pessimism of reproduction theories, the critical pedagogy project centered in hope, liberation, and equality" (1992, 26). "In particular, critical pedagogy was conceived as a different field from the earlier critical theories of education, particularly from the neo-Marxist theories" (Bowles and Gintis 1976; Bourdieu and Passeron 1977; Willis 1977; Apple 1979). In short, critical pedagogy marked the transition from a "language of critique" to a "language of possibility" (Giroux 1997a).

Why then do we have such serious criticism that challenges the very fundamental aim and character of critical pedagogy? This chapter problematizes

the claim made by critical pedagogy as a "pedagogy of possibility." By exploring some of the common assumptions in critical pedagogy theories and critical pedagogy praxis, I examine the ways that the dominant critical pedagogists
in the field have attempted to define critical pedagogy when they invoke the
term *possibility*. Although many would argue (and I agree) that the pedagogy of
the oppressed and Freirean pedagogy were the beginning, critical pedagogy is
by no means a unified field. Individuals' definitions/identifications of critical
pedagogy (and who are critical pedagogues, for that matter) may very well vary.
In this chapter, I focus on the critical pedagogy that emerged in the 1980s, particularly in Anglo-American regions, as a subfield within general critical theories of education. To put it differently, this chapter does not focus on original
Freirean pedagogy but rather on the Anglo-Americanized version of critical
pedagogy.

I examine a few major shifts that have taken place in the mainstream field
of critical pedagogy. My intention is to locate and link these shifts and their
implications for the political climates and for the politics of theory in general. The observations in this chapter are not just based on "theoretical" debates. My focus is to connect the theoretical debates to the "field discourses" of critical pedagogues (educators committed to studying and
practicing this pedagogy at their educational settings). Although critical
pedagogy claims to impact and change society, I argue that the inherent
limitations present within the dominant discourses of critical pedagogy are
what stifle the possibility for social change. For this reason, critical pedagogy will at best modernize, rather than change, the system.

CULTURAL POLITICS

Critical pedagogy was a reaction or an alternative to the economic determinism of the orthodox Marxist theories that preceded critical pedagogy's
renaissance in the 1980s. If education and politics are primarily determined
by the economy as argued by S. Bowles and H. Gintis (1976), little can be
done to change schools or societies in any fundamental way. As a way out
of this economic determinism and aporia, the "language of possibility"
moved away from the economy to culture, shifting theories about the *infrastructure*, or economic base (the unity of the productive forces and the relations of production), to the *superstructure* (particular historical systems of
beliefs, religious, juridical, political and so on). However, the realization of
the significance of culture and the superstructure was not new. Neo-Marxist
traditions had been grappling with this issue for some time, from Antonio
Gramsci's (1971) import of the concept of hegemony to Louis Althusser's
affective theory of ideology and ideological state apparatus (1971) to Ray-
mond Williams's structure of feeling (1977). Influenced by neo-Marxism,

the educational Left had already examined the importance of culture, hegemony, and the state in the decades previous to the emergence of critical pedagogy as a disciplinary field (Willis 1977; Apple 1979, 1982; Dale et al. 1981; Carnoy and Levin 1985).

What was new in critical pedagogy was the way that culture was to be understood. Unlike previous neo-Marxist cultural theories, this new version of cultural studies, mainly due to the heavy influence of poststructuralism and postmodernism, abandoned the centrality of the material base in its discourse. In other words, the culture became autonomous and freed from the base, and this transition has been a serious contention between neo-Marxists and poststructuralists and postmodernists. While neo-Marxists argue that culture maintains some relation to the material base (e.g., Althusser's notion of relative autonomy), post-Marxists argue that culture bears no concrete relations with the material base, or at least is autonomous from it (e.g., Hindess and Hirst 1977; Laclau and Moffe 1984). In their persistent avoidance of determinisms, poststructuralists and postmodernists understand culture (language and representation) to be free-floating, fractured, indeterminate, and infinitive—detached from any basis/base that can be traced to social structures and relations: "Eager to take a wide detour around political economy, post-Marxists tend to assume that the principal political points of departure in the current 'postmodern' world must necessarily be 'cultural.' As such, most, *but not all* post-Marxists have gravitated towards a politics of 'difference' which is largely premised on uncovering relations of power that reside in the arrangement and deployment of subjectivity in cultural and ideological practices" (Scatamburlo-D'Annibale and McLaren 2004, 183). In other words, the material base is no longer fashionable to reckon with. Symbols, representations, and meanings have become the focus in the social sciences and the humanities in general. Discourse and cultural analysis have become dominant and have since displaced materialist analysis. Since the mass media are so crucial to both the shaping and manufacturing of culture, popular culture has emerged as a key area in cultural studies. The cultural studies movement has become a booming industry. Now it is a commonplace for bookstores to have a large, separate section on cultural studies, a new phenomenon since the late 1980s and early 1990s.

The influences of cultural politics on critical pedagogy are prevalent in several aspects. First of all, critical pedagogy was defined as "a form of cultural politics" (McLaren 1995, 37), or, more specifically, "as a form of cultural politics that is fundamentally concerned with student experience" (McLaren 1995, 42). With such a definition, there has been a proliferation of cultural studies and discourse analysis in literature. Concepts such as social class, alienation, ideology, bureaucracy, the division of labor, and the state are usually not found in critical pedagogy research. The influence is shown in research methodologies as well. There has been a strong inclination or gravitation toward ethnographic and anthropological studies, "a penchant for small-scale, qualitative ethnographic methods and 'cultural' concerns with discursive positioning and identity," as pointed out by R. Moore and J. Muller (1999, 191). Qualitative studies, such as interviews, life histories, case studies, and autobiographic ethnographies, are the fashion of the day. The political economy and even liberal policy studies do not carry much weight.

Culture has become not only the privileged site of epistemological standpoints but also a site of political resistance and emancipatory politics. The postmodern condition has to be understood in the cultural field and no longer in relations of production (Lyotard 1984; Baudrillard 1975, 1994). For this reason, it is within this cultural field that the counterhegemonic war must be waged and where the boundaries and limitations of "possibility" are to be found. Now, cultural/discourse analysis and deconstruction become the site for resistance and challenge to the system. However, while cultural spheres are no doubt important in counterhegemonic struggles, the problem with cultural politics is that it overestimates the power of cultural struggles and neglects the material structures of society (Ahmad 1995; Bourne 1999). As such, cultural politics neither addresses nor provides a solution for major "structural" issues of inequality that dominate the educational system and society: "in throwing out the bath water of 'economic determinism' and 'class reductionism,' [poststructuralism and deconstruction] had thrown out the baby of political struggle against capital and the state. In its stead, there was now a 'cultural politics' which challenged 'social blocs' in civil society" (Bourne 1999, 135).

That said, culturalism in critical pedagogy has been challenged and criticized, especially in recent years (i.e., McLaren 1998; Apple 2000; Scatamburlo-D'Annibale and McLaren 2004). Michael Apple argues, "Some of it [critical pedagogy] *is* disconnected from the gritty materialities of daily economic, political, cultural, and educational struggles. Some of it *does* romanticize the cultural at the expense of equally powerful traditions of analysis based in political economy and the state. And some of it *does* place so much emphasis on 'post' that it forgets the structural realities that set limits on real people in real institutions in everyday life" (2000, 253). In so doing, V. Scatamburlo-D'Annibale and McLaren contend that "culturalist arguments are deeply problematic both in terms of their penchant for de-emphasizing the totalizing (yes totalizing!) power and function of capital and for their attempts to employ culture as a construct that would diminish the centrality of class" (2004, 185).

This postmodern culturalism, according to McLaren, is the main reason why critical pedagogy can no longer provide a viable alternative for social change: "critical pedagogy has become so completely psychologized, so liberally humanized, so technologized, and so conceptually postmodernized, that its current relationship to broader liberation struggles seems severely attenuated if not fatally terminated" (1998, 448). I agree with McLaren in that the so-called ludic postmodernism (Ebert 1996) has contributed to the culturalization of critical pedagogy. However, I do not think the influence of the infatuation with postmodernism on critical pedagogy, teachers, or classroom praxis is as strong as McLaren and some others characterize it, perhaps because the postmodernist "language" is not accessible to ordinary educators (perhaps fortunately in this regard—pun intended). The overall project of social change and possibility in critical pedagogy does not mesh well with postmodernist positions (a point to which I return later). Moreover, I think that the American sensibility is too optimistic, pragmatic, and moralistic to be genuinely ludic, which is more of a Parisian chic. Furthermore, I see postmodernism not as a cause, but rather as a reflection of, or a reaction to, the legitimization crisis of the Western welfare states (Habermas 1975) and the crisis of the imperial global capitalism (Amin 2000; Hardt and Negri 2000).

IDENTITY POLITICS

The dominant topics post-1970s were "the body" and "globalization" (Harvey 2000). However, critical pedagogy has been almost exclusively influenced by the former. It has rarely incorporated the globalization literature, with only a few exceptions (e.g., Castells et al. 1999; Burbules and Torres 2000; Allman 2001). Preoccupied with the politics and signification of the body, critical pedagogy has been pushed in a certain direction. Against structural determinism, critical pedagogy shifted to rediscover human agency, which has been all but denied or woefully ignored in structural determinism since Althusser. As such, it has focused on the subject—lived experiences, voices, and resistance. Lived experiences and everyday modes of resistance are considered as evidence and rendering possibilities against the "totalizing" reproductive nature of the system (e.g., Willis 1977; Ong 1987). The voices of those who are marginalized provide "evidence for a world of alternative values and practices whose experience gives the lie to hegemonic constructions of social worlds" (Scott 1992, 24). The everyday, small, yet significant, forms of resistance are conceived and celebrated as sources of possible challenges to, and eventual transformation of, the system. Luke elucidates the importance of "experience" in critical pedagogy: "Agency and (raised) consciousness were reinstated on center stage, albeit this time with structural constraints acknowledged. Lived experience and intersubjective construction of meaning and identity formation were reauthenticated" (1992, 26). In this way, every voice is regarded as emancipatory (or at least as having the potential for emancipation), and every resistance is an evidence of a rupture of power in critical pedagogy.

This emphasis on the subject and agency in critical pedagogy is a reflection of changes in larger social movements. The move away from class-based politics has been the predominant trend in social movements during the last few decades. We have witnessed the booming of the so-called new social movements, or identity politics, starting with the 1960s civil rights movements and the women's movement, followed by the gay and lesbian and green movements and critical-race/postcolonial politics. These new social movements based on identity politics were and are a corrective against the Marxist praxis, which tended to neglect or subordinate other forms of domination, such as race, gender, sexuality, and imperialism, to class (Butler 1997; Leonardo 2003). Identity politics do not, as Judith Butler and Zeus Leonardo have rightly contended, have to be either "merely cultural" (Butler 1997) or reduced to "an individual's experience" (Leonardo 2003, 220). Indeed, there is no reason to assume that a critique of racism, sexism, or imperialism/postcolonialism cannot be a critique of social structure. Materialist analysis of other forms of power and oppression is not only possible but also crucial to our critical understanding of vital connections among race, class, gender, and imperialism (e.g., Connell 1995; Ahmad 1995; Bourne 1999).

However, problems occur when the identity politics are understood as so-called identitarian sects (Butler 1997, 265). In her critique of the treatment of race in the Centre for Cultural Studies, Jenny Bourne describes how race politics have become a personalized, identity-based politics: "The 'personal is the political' also helped to shift the centre of gravity of struggle from the community and society to the individual. 'What has to be done?' was replaced by 'who am I?' . . . Articulating one's identity changed from being a path to political action to being the political action itself" (1999, 136). In other words, the problem is not that the new social movements and leftist politics have moved to race/gender/sexuality/postcoloniality (i.e., identity politics), but rather that the identity-based movements have become dominated by culturalized and essentialized (thus personalized) praxis. It is in this sense that I see the recent call to "go back to class" as problematic, if it is to be understood as a call to prioritize class at the expense of race, gender, sexuality, or global imperialism. Rather, the call should be to transform the dominant culturalized and personalized identitarian politics into "materialist identity politics" (Leonardo 2003, 220).

The culturalization and personalization is, as I see it, the way in which the identity politics is appropriated into the mainstream critical pedagogy. In the rush to celebrate voices and differences, "experience" has become essentialized—experience now speaks for itself. Experiences and voices are treated as irreducible and the only legitimate basis for understanding (Abu-

Lughod 1990; Scott 1992). In the search for and honoring of genuine voices, their sources become more important than their content. In other words, "who speaks is what counts, not what is said" (Moore and Muller 1999, 199). In critical pedagogy classrooms, who talks in the classroom and what one can say can become a very sensitive issue, to the point that it creates an atmosphere of fear and reluctance. Nobody wants to be regarded as interrupting, let alone challenging, the genuine voices of others (especially of minorities and women). Rather than make us more open and free, this can actually create tensions and hamper honest communication and rigorous analysis. Furthermore, this essentialized voice discourse can be wrongfully used as anti-intellectualism. For instance, my students sometimes ask, "Why do we have to study dead white men's books? They have nothing to do with me." Students' suspicion of the dominance of white men in critical pedagogy theories, in tandem with their anger and resistance, is well justified. However, it is one thing to criticize the Euro, male, middle-class, heterosexual centeredness of a given theory, but it is another thing to reject theories just because they are written by middle-class, heterosexual, white men (although, I have to say, there are close relations between the two).

Opening to the voices and experiences of marginalized groups is no doubt crucial and necessary in critical pedagogy; yet, uncritical glorification of experiences is dangerous, even when the voices and experiences come from oppressed groups. First of all, as Joan Scott points out, experiences are social constructs: "experience is at once always already an interpretation and is in need of interpretation. What counts as experience is neither self-evident nor straightforward; it is always contested, always therefore political" (1992, 37). Furthermore, Ilan Gur-Ze'ev warns us that "this marginalized and repressed self-evident knowledge has no superiority over the self-evident knowledge of the oppressors. Relying on the knowledge of weak, controlled, and marginalized groups, their memories and their conscious interests, is no less naïve and dangerous than relying on hegemonic knowledge" (1998, 480). According to Gur-Ze'ev, following the late Critical Theory of the Frankfurt School (in particular, M. Horkheimer and T. Adorno), this is because the possibilities for the very existence of an autonomous subject are rendered hopeless because of the tight grip of the present Western system on the consciousness not only of the dominant, but also of the dominated (a point echoed later by Paulo Freire, who was well aware of the fractured consciousness of the oppressed).

However, realization of the social construction of experiences (antiessentialism) and the possible fraction of consciousness of oppressed groups does not mean subscribing to arbitrarism or relativism or "debunking epistemology" (Moore and Muller 1999; Young 2000): since experience speaks for itself and since there is no absolute criteria for truth, anyone's interpretation is as good as anyone else's, and anything goes. We see this relativist position especially in "ludic" postmodernism. However, rejecting the "totalizing" truth claims of modernism does mean necessarily falling into relativism. As Terry Eagleton points out, "It is perfectly possible to agree with Nietzsche and Foucault that power is everywhere, while wanting for certain practical purposes to distinguish between more and less central instances of it" (1991, 8). One can say, for example, that criminals are more likely and are in a better position to see the injustices of the legal system than the judges or law makers without resorting to an essentialist or totalizing position like "all criminals always know better." Similarly, we are not falling into essentialism or totalizing modernistic discourse when we say that "the level of food supplies in Mozambique is a weightier issue than the love life of Mickey Mouse" (Eagleton 1991, 8).

Another influence of culturalized identity politics on critical pedagogy is the emphasis on grassroots democracy and nonhierarchical form of authority. For instance, Patti Lather defines (and promotes) "participatory, dialogic and pluralistic" and "nondualistic and antihierarchical" as the form of authority and legitimate knowledge of the "postmodernism of resistance" (1991, 160). This stance is obviously an influence of the feminist construct (especially white) and environmental movements (again, dominated by whites). This nonhierarchical, participatory form of authority is very prevalent in critical pedagogy literature and praxis. There is a strong tendency to negate any structure or any possible hint of authority in critical pedagogy classrooms as a way to achieve total freedom and the elimination of domination. Dialogue and consensus are regarded as the only legitimate and desirable form of decision making. In reality, however, the idealization of total freedom and total elimination of domination are utopian and subject to naiveté. Alexander Sidorkin argues that total freedom will not eliminate domination: "we cannot change the dominating nature of education. No amount of care and justice can do that" (1997, 235). Gur-Ze'ev goes on to say that "the consensus reached by the reflective subject taking part in the dialogue offered by critical pedagogy is naïve, especially in light of its declared anti-intellectualism on the one hand and its pronounced glorification of the 'feelings,' 'experience,' and 'self-evident knowledge' of the group on the other" (1998, 480).

Identity politics and its embodiment of grassroots democracy in critical pedagogy may seem both genuine and ideal. However, if grassroots, localized, and issue-oriented politics neglects or avoids major structural issues of inequality, oppression, and exploitation, then I think it could be both dangerous and ultimately powerless. Furthermore, I do not see culturalized and self-oriented identity politics as a counterhegemonic politics but rather as a reflection of the defeated consciousness of the Western postmodern society, which believes neither in revolution nor in any other structural changes. This is indicative of what Margaret Thatcher coined the "TINA (There Is No

Alternative) Syndrome." In addition, the "personal" and the "local" cannot be viable alternatives to growing imperial globalization (Amin 2000). The politics of identity and difference are actually what flexible global capitalism endorses and promotes (Hardt and Negri 2000). Imperial global capitalism is based not only on homogenization but also on fragmentation and diversification (Castells 1996, 1999). Perhaps critical pedagogues of the North can afford to explore and celebrate identities and differences, whereas these simply do not have any relevance to many people of the South whose daily lives are severely threatened by neoliberal imperial capitalism. The fragmentation and marginalization within identity politics, which cater to the "center" while neglecting the realities on the "peripheries," simply cannot account for everyone's experiences and differences. Rather, identity politics is plagued by the same Euro-/First World–centrism as in the universalizing and totalizing claims of modernism, from which identity politics desperately sought to break away. This contradiction has corrupted the basic tenets of diversity and differences on which identity politics was initially founded: identity politics is a winner's politics based on privilege.

MORALIZED AND INDIVIDUALIZED PROJECT

Given the predominance of cultural and identity politics, where do critical pedagogues find a "language of possibility?" Not surprisingly, the main focus of critical pedagogues has been the project of re/making individuals or subjectivities: "educators play a crucial role in shaping the identities, values, and beliefs of students who impact directly upon society," says Henry Giroux (1997b, 150). The dominant versions of critical pedagogy treat the individual as the unit to be conscientized and propose allocating greater agency to individuals as the way forward. Critical pedagogues' job is to make students, as well as themselves, more aware of classism, sexism, racism, homophobia, and other forms of oppression and domination. In my classrooms, students who are themselves educators often say that "we have to educate ourselves and our students," with the belief that enlightened students and teachers will somehow make an impact on society.

Then, how do students change their ways of thinking? If we are able to change people, will that necessarily lead to changes in society? Critical pedagogy is based on the premise that emancipation can be realized when people have an adequate understanding of their own oppressive situations. In my own teaching experiences of critical pedagogy, as well as in some of the mainstream critical pedagogy literature, I often observe the tendency of critical pedagogues to fall into the so-called false consciousness thesis: individuals are more or less caught up in illusions; thus, if they are exposed to the "real truth," they will be enlightened. This simple and linear logic of the transition from illusion to enlightenment via conscientization seems to make critical pedagogues' job much easier. However, this false consciousness thesis does not adequately provide an insight into why people comply with the legitimization of an oppressive system. It may be helpful to remind ourselves of Gramsci's concept of hegemony. People conform to the system not because they do not see their "real" interests (false consciousness) but because the ruling class gains consent from dominated groups by making concessions (such as higher wages, shorter working hours, or killing Jews, Indians, and "terrorists"). This does not mean that ideology does not involve false consciousness, such as falsity, distortion, and mystification. As Eagleton points out, however, "successful ideologies must be more than imposed illusions, and for all their inconsistencies must communicate to their subjects a version of social reality which is real and recognizable enough not to be simply rejected out of hand" (1991, 15).

My students in an educational leadership doctoral program, who are school administrators or administrators-to-be, know that in the end, "money talks." Many of them readily accept that schools function to reproduce, rather than to reduce, inequalities, and some even suggest that what we need is a revolution or a fundamental change in the system. Even though many educators believe that schools should and could be "the great equalizer," they know that this is not the reality. In other words, educators are not necessarily victims of false consciousness. Yet, it is rather amazing (and frustrating at the same time) to see how seamlessly they are able not only to absorb, but also to incorporate, this "claim" into their mostly liberal perspective without much contradiction and without much effort. I believe that Peter Sloterdijk's theory on cynicism provides a better explanation for these educators' positions. Sloterdijk characterizes cynicism, the prevalent consciousness of Western societies, as an "enlightened false consciousness." People live with false values, but they are ironically aware of their falsity, according to him. For cynicism, "the ideology critique" is powerless: "this consciousness no longer feels affected by any critique of ideology: its falsity is already reflectively buffered" (Sloterdijk 1997, 5). The sensibility of Americans, especially the white middle class, is too optimistic to be as cynical as Sloterdijk portrays. Yet, I think there is a grain of truth in his characterization of cynicism. It may be that the consciousness of the conscientizer is more naive than that of the to-be-conscientized.

Not only is the individual enlightenment project naive, but it can also lead to a moralized, rather than a politicized, project. By moralization, I mean an approach of identifying a social issue as a moral problem and prescribing a moral solution. A good example would be the conservatives' approach to the family crisis. They, especially the Religious Right, conceptualize family crisis as a moral problem (decline of moral values) and propose to solve the crisis by restoring old family values (e.g., putting women back in the homes and opposing gay marriages). This moralized approach neglects the influences that political and economical changes have had on the family over the last four decades. This moralized approach fails to address the issue in broader social, political, economic, and cultural contexts and thus prohibits us from searching for practical and structural solutions. While individual conscientization is no doubt important, there is no necessary link between individual changes and structural changes. Borrowing R. W. Connell's phrase, "so much awareness is not the crumbling of the material and institutional structures" (1995, 226). Awareness does not automatically bring the collapse of the system, and resistance does not necessarily bring new social arrangements. Reforming CEOs would not have solved the problems at Enron. Moral remaking of pharmaceutical companies or the Food and Drug Administration, without material and institutional changes, could not solve drug-safety issues. Critical teachers may "implement anti-racist teaching practices but this does not, by itself, change the racist character of our educational system" (Shilling 1992, 79).

Students do not change just because they are told to. Similarly, teachers do not change just because they have encountered the "truth." Individuals do change their moralities, values, and behaviors when social structures are conducive to supporting such changes. Then, the real task of critical pedagogy is to create the social structures that will allow individuals to change and to grow. Rather than focusing on reforming individuals per se, critical pedagogy should explore alternative visions of social structures and conditions so that ordinary teachers and students can practice, experience, and live pedagogy of hope, love, equality, and social justice. If the pedagogy of hope, care, love, and social justice is only understood to be a project of re/making or re/forming teachers and students, it will limit, rather than expand, the exploration of possibilities for alternative politics. This individualized and moralized project can make critical pedagogy just another "recipe" for good teaching (a politically correct one). McLaren laments, "The conceptual net known as critical pedagogy has been cast so wide and at times so cavalierly that it has come to be associated with anything dragged up out of the troubled and infested waters of educational practice, from classroom furniture organized in a 'dialogue friendly' circle to 'feelgood' curricula designed to increase students' self-image" (1998, 448).

As a result of this domestication, critical pedagogy is prone to becoming co-opted by the liberal educational discourse. Often in my teaching, I have found that many educators and even many critical teachers fall back into the "right-based" liberalism and multiculturalism of guaranteeing equal opportunity to the underprivileged—women, gays and lesbians, people of color, and people with disabilities. The politics of critical pedagogy are often directed against the privileges of those in positions of power rather than against the system of domination. Scatamburlo-D'Annibale and McLaren argue that "much of what is called the 'politics of difference' is little more than a demand for inclusion into the club of representation—a posture which reinscribes a neo-liberal pluralist stance rooted in the ideology of free-market capitalism" (2004, 186). Certainly, cultural and identity politics contributed greatly to moving critical pedagogy into the direction of individualized and moralized projects. However, I believe that there is a more fundamental reason that has often been overlooked. This emphasis on individualized and localized project is very closely linked to the Western accent on the ego and individualism, especially of whites. Rugged individualism, one of the strongest undercurrent hegemonies of American society, is one of the main reasons why critical pedagogy comes too close to liberalism to the extent that it is hard to distinguish between the two.

I believe that critical pedagogues are indeed aware of systemic problems and desire more fundamental changes to the system. However, they are overwhelmed by the enormous tasks required for such systemic change to take place. How do we change the system? What could be possibly done? How much can an individual teacher or even a group of teachers do? Is it feasible to abolish capitalism? Is revolution even thinkable when some liberal reforms seem impossible given the current conservative directions in which society and education have been moving? This all seems simply too big for them. Here, I agree with Apple (2000) and McLaren (1998) in that the educational Left has failed to provide alternatives. However, the lack of alternatives is not a problem just for the educational Left. It has been a general problem for the Left over the last several decades: "The inability to find an 'optimism of the intellect' with which to work through alternatives has now become one of the most serious barriers to progressive politics" (Harvey 2000, 17). Unfortunately, critical pedagogy, contrary to its intention and claims, falls short in providing, or leading us into, the optimism of the intellect.

SEARCH FOR ALTERNATIVES

As I mentioned earlier, the culturalization, individualization, and moralization of critical pedagogy politics reflects shifts in larger social movements and the politics of theories. For the last several decades, not only have the broader liberation struggles become fragmented, but the finding a common front for struggles is considered to be impossible, as well as a sinful totalizing modernism. We should no longer have illusions about systemic solutions from the top down, we are told, and the only viable option left is grassroots democratic movements from the bottom up. Along with the abandonment of the system, including the state, individual and local struggles have become the main site of social change. It is in this historical context that we have witnessed the recent boom of nongovernmental organizations (Hardt and Negri 2000) and increased scholarly interests in concepts like social capital, synergy (e.g., Evans 1996), and the civil society (e.g., Putnam 1993).

As critical pedagogy in the 1980s emerged within political and theoretical contexts to counteract the structural and economic determinism of the earlier critical educational theories, it was only logical that critical pedagogy turned to culture (at the expense of economy) and agency (at the expense of system). These redirections led critical pedagogy to microlevel politics—a narrow focus on individuals, classrooms, and teachings, where educators supposedly have direct impact. By this, I do not suggest that critical pedagogy theorists have only been promoting microcentered pedagogy and politics. In fact, they have been consistently arguing for the link between pedagogy and the larger power dynamics of the society. However, it is largely the case that much of the critical pedagogy literature and praxis still tends to focus on classroom pedagogy and agency, which has had the consequences of neglecting and ignoring structural constraints.

The question becomes, Can critical pedagogy be a "change agent?" Liberal pluralism (the mainstream ideology of capitalism) says that the only possibility is to modernize the system through the promotion of equal rights and the elimination of discrimination. Postmodernism, on the other hand, says that there is no way out since power is everywhere, and there is no discourse beyond power. It is ironic that critical pedagogy (the language of possibility) has been heavily influenced by postmodernism (the discourse of impossibility). How to combine these two contradictory discourses has been a heated debate within critical pedagogy. While the so-called critical/resistant postmodernists incorporate postmodernism without giving up "possibility" as its ultimate objective, other poststructuralists and postmodernists object to the very idea of possibility as "totalizing" and "moralizing." The charge that critical pedagogy is another totalizing morality has been launched for some time, especially by feminist and postmodernist critical pedagogues (Ellsworth 1989; Luke and Gore 1992; Lather 1992, 1998; Sidorkin 1997; Gur-Ze'ev 1998; Biesta 1998). As a way to defy the totalizing morality, some postmodernists have proposed a pedagogy of negation: countereducation as a nonrepressive form of hope (Gur-Ze'ev 1998), an emancipatory ignorance (Biesta 1998), or pedagogy of carnival and of "third places" (Sidorkin 1997).

I think that the postmodern pedagogy of negation (mainly from Europe) is a useful antidote to the romantic utopianism and easy optimism prevalent within American critical pedagogy circles. I agree with the impossibility and unpredictability of the critical pedagogy of Sidorkin, Gur-Ze'ev, and Biesta in that neither care nor justice will be able to eliminate domination and bring about total freedom. Believing so is only an illusion. However, I

138 Chapter 9

am afraid that the negation theory is yet another illusion, since "nonre-pression" and "emancipatory ignorance" are not an escape from the "total-izing morality" in the strictest sense. Although we acknowledge that moral-ity is a social construct, we cannot live without morality (à la Nietzsche). Not taking a position is still taking a position. I argue that morality is in-evitable not only in critical pedagogy but in human life in general, whether one acknowledges it or not, or whether one takes a Marxist or a postmod-ernist position. That said, there is a difference between being moral and moralistic.

I do not believe that critical pedagogy is problematic because it "offers only the most abstract, decontextualized criteria for choosing one position over others, criteria such as reconstructive action or radical democracy and social justice" (Ellsworth 1992, 93) or because "in the discourse of critical pedagogy, the educational politics of emancipatory self- and social empow-erment, and of emancipatory rationality and citizenship education, have been articulated in epistemic relation to liberal conceptions of equality and participatory democracy" (Luke 1992, 29). The problem with critical peda-gogy is, to me, not its quest for utopia or possibilities per se. Dreaming of utopian alternatives is an essential part of critical pedagogy, as rightly pointed out by Leonardo (2004). Instead, I argue that critical pedagogy is in a serious crisis because the political projects of critical pedagogy have been too narrowly focused on the individualized, moralized, and cultural politics of differences. This trend, I believe, poses a grave danger, especially considering the imperialistic globalization that is rapidly happening. Rather than going back to the body, the individual, and the subject, with which Western thought has been so terribly plagued, critical pedagogy, in its search for "possibilities," needs to explore and produce real, feasible alter-natives by linking the micro to the macro, the subject to the structure, the culture to the economy, and the local to the global.

ACKNOWLEDGMENTS

This is to acknowledge with thanks the insightful comments on an earlier draft of this chapter by Zeus Leonardo and Seorim Hong.

REFERENCES

Abu-Lughod, L. 1990. The romance of resistance: Transformations of power through bedouin women. *American Ethnologist* 17 (1): 41–55.
Ahmad, A. 1995. Postcolonialism: What's in a name? In *Late Imperial Culture*, ed. R. Campa, E. Kaplan, and M. Sprinker. New York: Verso.

Allman, P. 2001. *Critical education against global capitalism.* Westport, CT: Bergin and Garvey.

Althusser, L. 1971. *Lenin and philosophy and other essays,* trans. B. Brewster. New York: Monthly Review Press.

Amin, S. 2000. *Capitalism in the age of globalization.* New York: Zed Books.

Apple, M. 1979. *Ideology and curriculum.* New York: Routledge.

———. 1982. *Education and power.* Boston: Routledge and Kegan Paul.

———. 2000. Can critical pedagogies interrupt rightist policies? *Educational Theory* 50 (2): 229–54.

Baudrillard, J. 1975. *The mirror of production.* St. Louis: Telos Press.

———. 1994. *Simulacra and simulation.* Ann Arbor: University of Michigan Press.

Biesta, G. 1998. Say you want a revolution . . . Suggestions for the impossible future of critical pedagogy. *Educational Theory* 48 (4): 499–510.

Bourdieu, P., and J. Passeron. 1977. *Reproduction in education, society and culture,* trans. R. Nice. London: Sage.

Bourne, J. 1999. Racism, postmodernism and the flight from class. In *Postmodernism in educational theory: Education and the politics of human resistance,* ed. D. Hill, P. McLaren, M. Cole, and G. Rikowski. London: Tufnell Press.

Bowles, S., and H. Gintis. 1976. *Schooling in capitalist America: Educational reform and the contradictions of economic life.* New York: Basic Books.

Burbules, N., and C. Torres. 2000. *Globalization and education: Critical perspectives.* New York: Routledge.

Butler, J. 1997. Merely cultural. *Social Text* 15 (3/4): 264–77.

Carnoy, M., and H. Levin. 1985. *Schooling and work in the democratic state.* Palo Alto, CA: Stanford University Press.

Castells, M. 1996. *The rise of the network society.* Cambridge, MA: Blackwell Publishers.

———. 1999. Flows, networks, and identities: A critical theory of the information society. In *Critical education in the new information age,* ed. M. Castells, R. Flecha, P. Freire, H. Giroux, D. Macedo, and P. Willis. Lanham, MD: Rowman & Littlefield.

Castells, M., R. Flecha, P. Freire, H. Giroux, D. Macedo, and P. Willis. 1999. *Critical education in the new information age.* Lanham, MD: Rowman & Littlefield.

Connell, R. W. 1995. *Masculinities.* Berkeley: University of California Press.

Dale, R., G. Esland, R. Fergusson, and M. MacDonald, eds. 1981. *Education and the state.* Barcombe, Sussex, UK: Falmer Press.

Eagleton, T. 1991. *Ideology.* New York: Verso.

Ebert, T. 1996. *Ludic feminism: Postmodernism, desire, and labor in late capitalism.* Ann Arbor: University of Michigan Press.

Ellsworth, E. 1992. Why doesn't this feel empowering? Working through the repressive myths of critical pedagogy. In *Feminisms and critical pedagogy,* ed. C. Luke and J. Gore. New York: Routledge.

Evans, P., ed. 1996. *State-society synergy: Government and social capital in development.* Berkeley: University of California Press.

Freire, P. 1970. *Pedagogy of the oppressed,* trans. M. Ramos. New York: Continuum.

Giroux, H. 1988. Border pedagogy on the age of postmodernism. *Journal of Education* 170 (3): 162–81.

———. 1997a. *Pedagogy and the politics of hope: Theory, culture, and schooling.* Boulder, CO: Westview Press.

————. 1997b. *Channel surfing: Race talk and the destruction of today's youth.* New York: St. Martin's Press.

Gramsci, A. 1971. *Selections form the prison notebooks,* trans. Q. Hoare and G. Smith. New York: International Publishers.

Gur-Ze'ev, I. 1998. Toward a nonrepressive critical pedagogy. *Educational theory* 48 (4): 463–86.

Habermas, J. 1975. *Legitimation crisis,* trans. T. McCarthy. Boston: Beacon Press.

Hardt, M., and A. Negri. 2000. *Empire.* Cambridge, MA: Harvard University Press.

Harvey, D. 2000. *Spaces of hope.* Berkeley: University of California Press.

Hindess, B., and P. Hirst. 1977. *Mode of production and social formation.* London: Macmillan.

Horkheimer, M., and T. Adorno. 2000. *Dialectic of enlightenment,* trans. J. Cumming. New York: Continuum.

Laclau, E., and C. Moffe. 1984. *Hegemony and socialist strategy.* New York: Routledge.

Lather, P. 1991. *Getting smart: Feminist research and pedagogy with/in the postmodern.* New York: Routledge.

————. 1992. Post-critical pedagogies: A feminist reading. In *Feminisms and Critical Pedagogy,* ed. C. Luke and J. Gore. New York: Routledge.

————. 1998. Critical pedagogy and its complicities: A praxis of stuck places. *Educational Theory* 48 (4): 487–97.

Leonardo, Z. 2003. Resisting capital: Simulationist and socialist strategies. *Critical Sociology* 29 (2): 211–36.

————. 2004. Critical social theory and transformative knowledge: The function of criticism in quality education. *Educational Researcher* 33 (6): 11–18.

Luke, C. 1992. Feminist politics in radical pedagogy. In *Feminisms and critical pedagogy,* ed. C. Luke and J. Gore. New York: Routledge.

Luke, C., and J. Gore, eds. 1992. *Feminisms and critical pedagogy.* New York: Routledge.

Lyotard, J. 1984. *The postmodern condition: A report on knowledge.* Minneapolis: University of Minnesota Press.

McLaren, P. 1988. Schooling the postmodern body: Critical pedagogy and the politics of enfleshment. *Journal of Education* 170 (3): 53–83.

————. 1995. *Critical pedagogy and predatory culture.* New York: Routledge.

————. 1998. Revolutionary pedagogy in post-revolutionary times: Rethinking the political economy of critical education. *Educational Theory* 48 (4): 431–62.

Moore, R., and J. Muller. 1999. The discourse of "voice" and the problem of knowledge and identity in the sociology of education. *British Journal of Sociology of Education* 20 (2): 189–206.

Ong, A. 1987. *Spirits of resistance and capitalist discipline: Factory women in Malaysia.* Albany: State University of New York Press.

Putnam, R. 1993. *Making democracy work: Civic traditions in modern Italy.* Princeton, NJ: Princeton University Press.

Scatamburlo-D'Annibale, V., and P. McLaren. 2004. Class dismissed? Historical materialism and the politics of difference. *Educational Philosophy and Theory* 36 (2): 183–99.

Scott, J. 1992. Experience. In *Feminists theorize the political,* ed. J. Butler and J. Scott. New York: Routledge.

Shilling, C. 1992. Reconceptualising structure and agency in the sociology of education: Structuration theory and schooling. *British Journal of Sociology of Education* 13 (1): 69–87.

Sidorkin, A. 1997. Carnival and domination: Pedagogies of neither care nor justice. *Educational Theory* 47 (2): 229–38.

Sloterdijk, P. 1997. *Critique of cynical reason,* trans. M. Eldred. Minneapolis: University of Minnesota Press.

Williams, R. 1977. *Marxism and literature.* Oxford: Oxford University Press.

Willis, P. 1977. *Learning to labor: How working class kids get working class jobs.* New York: Columbia University Press.

Young, M. 2000. Rescuing the sociology of educational knowledge from the extremes of voice discourse: Towards a new theoretical basis for the sociology of curriculum. *British Journal of Sociology of Education* 21 (4): 523–36.

10

Social Justice Requires a Revolution of Everyday Life

E. Wayne Ross and Kevin D. Vinson

The whole life of those societies in which modern conditions of production prevail presents itself as an immense accumulation of spectacles. All that once was directly lived has become mere representation.

—Guy Debord (*Thesis 1, The Society of the Spectacle*)

But now I see what they are offering me are just bigger cages and longer chains.

—The (International) Noise Conspiracy

We have a world of pleasures to win and nothing to lose but our boredom.

—Raoul Vaneigem

What does it mean to teach for "social justice"?[1] In this chapter, we attempt to problematize this issue, as well as examine some of the fundamental obstacles to achieving a more "just" society and what is necessary to overcome them.

WHAT IS SOCIAL JUSTICE?

Despite an increased focus on social justice as an important educational outcome, the meaning of the term often remains unanalyzed in our discussions of critical pedagogy. Usually, our discussions of social justice revolve around concerns with *the fair and equitable distribution of resources that contribute to an enhanced quality of life.* And, more often than not, social justice is the underlying concern in our discussions of multiculturalism, class, diversity, race, poverty, difference, equity, social change, equality, oppression, democracy, the collective good, and critical pedagogy.

The typically haphazard use of the term *social justice* allows people to use the same, or very similar, rhetoric about the goals of education in general—and critical pedagogy in particular—but with radically different meanings. Here are three example of what we mean:

1. What does it mean to pursue "equality" in the context of schooling? Many folks, particularly in the United States, think of equal "opportunity" as a key issue in creating a more just society. And U.S. laws on access to education (as well as housing, employment, borrowing, etc.) reflect a key concern for providing "equal opportunities." But what of the notion of social justice based upon the concept of "equal outcomes"? The latter conception encompasses a radically different take on social justice but is often couched in the same "social justice" rhetoric.

2. In the field of social studies, education has had a number of debates (and disputes) over the past decade regarding issues of social justice and the responsibilities of individual scholars/educators and their professional organizations. For example, two incidents with origins at the 1994 annual meeting of National Council for the Social Studies (NCSS) in Phoenix, Arizona, illustrate the contradictions of social justice within social studies education. First, a teacher working as a staff person for the Central Committee of Conscientious Objectors was arrested and prosecuted by NCSS for peacefully leafleting against the militarization of schools at the conference; secondly, the governing body of NCSS overwhelmingly—and vociferously—rejected a resolution condemning California Proposition 187 and calling for a boycott of California as a site for future meetings of the organization. These events fueled a level of political activism that the organization had rarely experienced and identified the need for organized action in support of free speech and antiracist pedagogy in the field of social studies education in general and within NCSS in particular. Moreover, these events highlighted the unwillingness and inability of the largest professional organization for social studies educators in the United States to act on principles of social justice, which are widely touted within the field.[2] Despite a wide range of ideologies and serious differences of opinion over issues such as curriculum, pedagogy and advocacy, a language of social justice in social studies education has been widely shared within the field. Few, if any, social

studies educators want to cultivate the image that they are not for social justice.

3. A third example of confused meanings surrounding "social justice" can
be found in debates over standards-based educational reform, particularly the impact of the federal No Child Left Behind (NCLB) Act. NCLB
supporters, both within the Bush administration and in state depart-
ments of education, districts, and schools, laud NCLB as a key effort in
creating greater equality in schools. Mandating increases in test scores
and spotlighting student achievement (particularly the requirement to
disaggregate test scores by race/ethnicity) are often cited as elements of
NCLB that have the potential to contribute to a more equal/equitable/
just education system. On the other hand, critics of NCLB use social justice as the foundation for their attacks on the standards-based educational reform and its deleterious effects on teaching and learning (e.g.,
state regulation of knowledge, narrowing of the curriculum, demotiva-
tion of learning, deprofessionalization of teachers).

Two examples illustrate the contradictory use of social justice rhetoric in the
context of NCLB. First, in a March 2003 newspaper column, E. Wayne Ross described research by the Harvard Civil Rights Project on the racial resegregation
of public schools in the United States and linked increasing segregation to increased use of high-stakes testing (as a result of NCLB), which has produced
disproportionate levels of retention and dropouts among minority youth. The
following week, in the same newspaper, U.S. Secretary of Education Rod Paige
took direct issue with Ross's claims, arguing that NCLB was, in fact, an important positive force for increased civil rights for African American students.

Paige writes that he is "greatly surprised to read E. Wayne Ross's recent attack on No Child Left Behind" (2003, A8). But in his retort, Paige never
mentions the resegregation of public schools, nor does he engage the evidence illustrating how high-stakes tests function to lower student academic
performance. Rather he ignores the realities of racial resegregation in
schools and redefines what counts as quality education and socially just educational policy by placing test scores at the center of socially just educational policy and practice. He says,

> There is no doubt that until now, public education has failed to deliver on the
> promise of a good-quality education for the vast majority of African Ameri-
> cans. But eliminating this achievement gap—the difference in the academic
> performance between different ethnic groups—is one of the most important
> goals of No Child Left Behind. (2003, A8)

There is no arguing with the first point, as the Harvard Report and
Ross's article make clear. The question becomes, however, what counts as

a socially just response to the failure of public education to provide a quality education to African American students? Paige says,

Having attended a segregated school and having served as the superintendent of a school district that was 35 percent African American and 54 percent Hispanic, I have firsthand experience with the tremendous effort it takes to close the achievement gap in our schools. For the first time in history, we now have a plan in place to achieve that goal. If Ross shares that vision, he should be applauding No Child Left Behind for what it is: the most important education law for African Americans in a generation. (A8)

For Paige there is only one legitimate criterion for socially just action in schools (i.e., the test score gap between African Americans, Latinos, and whites), and to disagree with him on this goal is (by his definition) to act in socially unjust ways.

Another media-based example can be found in the claims of the *Courier-Journal*, Kentucky's largest newspaper. The *Courier-Journal* has focused tremendous resources on promoting educational reform in Kentucky, a state long plagued by high illiteracy and dropout rates. The Kentucky Educational Reform Act (KERA) and its mandated statewide tests (the Commonwealth Accountability Testing System, or CATS) have been consistently promoted by the newspaper as key instruments in the campaign to reform schools. In October 2003, the *Courier-Journal* published an editorial claiming that results on the most recent CATS tests illustrated that there was no relationship between poverty and student achievement in Kentucky schools ("KERA—Restoring Hope" 2003). The paper's claim, without reference to specific evidence, contradicted the findings of research on the relationship between poverty and student achievement as measured on standardized tests, including recent research on Kentucky schools (Munoz and Dossett 2001).

Concerned that the paper's longstanding support for improved schools had crossed the line into uncritical boosterism for policies that, despite broad acceptance, are based on unsound principles and constitute educational malpractice, Ross and Mathison (2004) empirically tested the newspaper's claim. Their analysis of test-score data (as published in the *Courier-Journal*) and poverty rates in Kentucky schools (from data provided by the Kentucky Department of Education) illustrated extremely high correlations between these two factors.[3] This example illustrates how there can be agreement among parties on the importance of social justice considerations in education but oppositional views of exactly what constitutes a socially just stance.

There is no doubt that maintaining the image of social justice is an important part of our work as educators and, in fact, one of the primary aims claimed for current educational reform efforts. Agreement on the importance of education that contributes to a more socially just society does not, however, guarantee agreement on aims, practices, or outcomes. Critical educators must carefully consider what we mean by "social justice" and examine how we construct our image/ideal of socially just educational practices and outcomes.

IMAGES AND EVERYDAY LIFE

In our recent book, *Image and Education: Teaching in the Face of the New Disciplinarity* (2003), we argue that images play a dominant role in everyday life. In our everyday lives, we are continuously confronted by physical images, and we necessarily make use of them in the complex processes of making sense of our world and ourselves. We create, maintain, propagate, and transform images and, in turn, are created, maintained, propagated, and transformed by images—all within the environs and performances of the everyday.

We maintain there is an intimate link between everyday life and image wherein image plays a role in the workings of everyday life and everyday life plays a role in the workings of image. Given image's ubiquity, the two, in effect, become nearly indistinguishable as each ceaselessly and intentionally pervades the other's domain. Moreover, the two share significant and troubling characteristics and mechanisms, such that the effects of everyday life can be just as oppressive, antidemocratic, anti–collective good, disciplinary, and inauthentic as can the effects of image.

We presume a fundamental and mutual set of relationships between schooling and everyday life whereby each influences and is part of the other. Accordingly, we hold that *there is an everyday life of schooling* and *a schooling of everyday life*. We suggest that image mediates the dynamic of school/everyday life interplay, that the social image works and is worked against within the confines of schooling, and that the pedagogical image works and is worked against in the confines of society. Our underlying question is, simply, How do we understand and transform the conditions, mechanisms, and practices of everyday life so that the potential consequences of dominant/dominating pedagogical images might be counteracted, transcended, or superseded?

In the following sections we examine (1) the reproduction of everyday life, (2) the perspective of power and social justice, and (3) the necessity of a revolution of everyday life.

THE REPRODUCTION OF EVERYDAY LIFE

In *The Reproduction of Daily Life*, Fredy Perlman argues, "Through their daily activities, 'modern men [and women]' . . . reproduce" their social situations, "the inhabitants, the social relations and the ideas of the society; they reproduce the social form of daily life" (1969, 2).

Perlman argues that "the capitalist system is neither the natural nor the final form of human society." Rather, like earlier social forms, capitalism is a response to specific material and historical conditions. But, unlike earlier forms of social activity, Perlman argues, everyday life in a capitalist society systematically transforms the material conditions to which capitalism originally responded. In considering everyday life, Perlman argues that we must analyze "not only how practical activity in capitalist society reproduces capitalistic society, but also how this activity itself eliminates the material conditions to which capitalism is a response." "The aim of the process," according to Perlman, "is the reproduction of the relation between the worker and the capitalist" (1969).

In short, within a capitalist system, people reproduce capitalism and the conditions of their own oppression. For Perlman, this is in part because the individual members of a capitalist society unknowingly "carry out two processes: [1] they reproduce the form of their activities, and [2] they eliminate the material conditions to which this form of activity initially responded" (1969, 3). That they don't see this and continue to participate relates in Perlman's view to what represents perhaps the two most dominant features of modern everyday life: "alienation" and "fetish worship."

With regard to alienation, Perlman argues that "academic sociologists," who take the sale of labor for granted, understand the alienation of labor of as a "feeling." "However, any worker can explain to the academic sociologist that the alienation is neither a feeling nor an idea in the worker's head, but a real fact about the worker's daily life. The sold activity is in fact alien to the worker; his [or her] labor is in fact controlled by its buyer" (Perlman 1969).

When people sell their labor, an alienating activity, "they daily reproduce the personifications of the dominant forms of activity under capitalism, they reproduce the wage-laborer and the capitalist" (Perlman 1969). Perlman argues that the process of selling labor reproduces physically, as well as socially, "individuals who are sellers of labor–power, and individuals who are owners of means of production; they reproduce the individuals as well as the specific activities, the sale as well as the ownership."

Perlman argues, as a result, that "every time people perform an activity they have not themselves defined and do not control, every time they pay for goods they produced with money they received in exchange for their alienated activity, every time they passively admire the products of their own activity as alien objects procured by their money, they give new life to Capital and annihilate their own lives."

Alienation implies that today the "work" of "laborers" is no longer authentically their own but instead exists under the control of someone else—

its "buyer." To paraphrase Perlman, workers alienate their lives in order to preserve their lives. If people did not sell their living activity, they could not get a wage and could not survive. "However, it is not the wage that makes alienation the condition for survival. . . . It is people's disposition to continue selling their labor, and not the things for which they sell it, that makes the alienation of living activity necessary for the preservation of life."

Perlman argues that the mystification of one's daily activities, or what he called "the religion of everyday life," attributes living activity to inanimate things. This mystification is the result of social relations under capitalism. People relate to each other through things, and through things they reproduce their activity. But, importantly, it is not the fetish that performs the activity. It is not capital that transforms raw materials, nor capital that produces goods.

For Perlman, fetish worship suggests that labor (the efforts of individuals) is a thing and that "things live."

> Economics (and capitalist ideology in general) treats land, money, and the products of labor, as things which have the power to produce, to create value, to work for their owners, to transform the world. This is what Marx called the fetishism, which characterizes people's everyday conceptions, and which is raised to the level of dogma by Economics. For the economist, living people are things . . . and things live. . . . The fetish worshipper attributes the product of his [or her] own activity to his [or her] fetish. As a result, he [or she] ceases to exert his [or her] own [power] (the power to transform nature, the power to determine the form and content of daily life); he [or she] exerts only those "powers" which he [or she] attributes to his [or her] fetish (the "power" to buy commodities). In other words, the fetish worshipper emasculates himself [or herself] and attributes virility to his [or her] fetish.

Under a fetishistic system, such as contemporary capitalism, people attribute their own power to things, inanimate things, and thus deactualize their own roles, their own real power, in the (re)constitution of society. Perlman put it this way:

> In other words, people are bought with the products of their own activity, yet they se[e] their own activity as the activity of Capital, and their own products as the products of Capital. By attributing creative power to Capital and not to their own activity, they renounce their living activity, their everyday life, to Capital, which means that people give themselves daily, to the personification of Capital, the capitalist.

To make use of Perlman's work within the context of image, education, and everyday life, it helps first to locate schooling—classroom life, if not necessarily schooling as a social institution—within the setting of contemporary global capitalism. We must consider (1) that a product, a thing, is produced, distributed, consumed, bought, and sold (ostensibly "education" or "achievement"), and (2) that the major actors in the processes of schooling represent distinctive social classes—say, the capitalist (or ruling, or powerful, or oppressor) class (e.g., school boards, politicians, bureaucratic management, corporations) and the working (or laboring, or teaching–learning, or oppressed) class (e.g., teachers, students, and parents). (Of course, we recognize here the risks of reductionism, oversimplification, and overgeneralization).

Perlman's work implies, to the extent that schooling is a part of everyday life and, in turn, everyday life is a part of schooling, contemporary education is reproductive—it doesn't work to transform or even "improve" society. It works to maintain it, to rationalize and mystify it, and to present it (and therefore schooling itself) as right, natural, and neutral, but not as a means to promote, for example, social justice or radical democracy. Moreover, contemporary schooling and society work to reduce, if not eliminate, the conditions that brought about current pedagogical practices; yet, current pedagogical practices continue to grow. The recent move toward standards-based educational reform (as embodied in NCLB), for example, stems from the alarm initially raised two decades ago by *A Nation at Risk* (National Commission on Excellence in Education 1983), which argued that schooling must change because the United States was "losing out" in terms of international economic competition—especially with respect to Japan and Germany—and that U.S. schoolchildren were not performing as well as their European and Asian peers. Although both of these arguments have now been effectively debunked, standards-based educational reform continues forward (see, for example, Berliner and Biddle 1995; compare current Japanese and German economic woes against the global hegemony of U.S. megacorporations).

These circumstances extend and reinforce alienation and the worship of fetishes. As we argue, this primarily occurs around pedagogical image(s), images that in many ways link everyday classroom life and everyday social life, so that teachers and students (and to some degree many parents) no longer "control" the images of their work, but the images of their work are now (and increasingly) controlled by their "buyers," according to the rules of a system that those buyers create and that privilege their dominant/dominating situations. These images are treated as things and credited with power—think test scores, as if simply having tests and curriculum standards makes schools better instead of their quality being derived from the work of individual classroom participants. As we have frequently seen when test scores increase, those who sanctioned the tests take credit (superintendents, managers, legislators, etc.). When they decrease, teachers, students, and parents take the blame (i.e., are held "accountable"), thus reinforcing current divisions.

The relationship between the reproduction of daily life and alienation entails teachers and students doing the system's work—that is performing tasks designed, developed, more or less implemented, and evaluated by the buyers of its results (the powerful, for example, school officials and political and corporate leaders). The link between the reproduction of daily life and fetishism involves the worship represented in certain images of particular ideologies, scores-as-things, and specific disciplinary characteristics depicting the good/effective (or bad/ineffective) teacher, student, principal, parent, and/or school (e.g., as depicted in popular films).

THE PERSPECTIVE OF POWER AND SOCIAL JUSTICE

In *The Revolution of Everyday Life*, Raoul Vaneigem ([1968]2001), a former Situationist International (SI) colleague of Guy Debord's, argues that it is the dominant perspective of power—"power's perspective"—that undergirds all alienation in terms of modern everyday life. Although engaging in many ways in a fundamentally Marxist critique, Vaneigem contends that no longer can the oppression of workers (as a class) be understood in isolation from the oppression that occurs throughout the totality of human existence, especially to the extent that capitalist economics, continuous consumption capitalism, has extended its reach even into the ostensibly private, or "subjective," aspects of contemporary experience.

For Vaneigem, the alienating, oppressive, and exploitative "power of power" rests in its capacity to make the authentic—"really living"—impossible by prohibiting the ability of individuals to relate to one another, to connect, to escape boredom, and to construct the situations of themselves qua selves. In fact, power perpetuates, and perpetuates itself by way of, an interlocking threefold problematic (i.e., "power's perspective"):

1. The impossibility of participation: power as the sum of constraints, which Vaneigem identifies with five "mechanisms of attrition and destruction: humiliation . . . isolation . . . suffering . . . [the decline and fall of] work . . . [and] decompression," where "Decompression is the permanent control of . . . antagonists by the ruling class"; think of today's U.S. Democratic and Republican parties ([1968]2001, 27, 57).
2. The impossibility of communication: power as universal mediation, that is, "the false necessity wherein people learn to lose themselves rationally . . . by the dictatorship of consumption . . . by the predominance of exchange over gift . . . [and] by the reign of the quantitative" (65).
3. The impossibility of realization: power as sum of seductions (105).

On this third point, arguably the most important and complex, Vaneigem is worth quoting at length:

Where constraint breaks people, and mediation makes fools of them, the seduction of power is what makes them love their oppression. Because of it people give up their real riches: for a cause that mutilates them . . . for an imaginary unity that fragments them . . . for an appearance that reifies them . . . for roles that wrest them from authentic life . . . for a time whose passage defines and confines them. (105)

In sum, power (i.e., "the rulers") alienates, oppresses, and exploits by demolishing any opportunity for participation, communication, and self-realization. It denies individuals the chance to build communities, to connect to one another, and to become who and what they might become. It isolates and fragments, passes off false relationships as human (i.e., as "real"), and defines subjective persons objectively—all in large measure as everyday life becomes less about joyous, creative, loving, and playful inter-human experiences and more about the capitalistic imperative always to consume (if not also eventually to be consumed).

We argue that the discourse of social justice in education (whether based on "liberal" or "conservative" ideologies) has been framed almost completely within the "perspective of power" and, as a result, offers little or no opportunity for transcending the deleterious effects of the power perspective with regard to the "idealism" of social justice. (In addition, we would argue that "mainstream/liberal" conceptions of critical pedagogy are constructed from the power perspective and thus suffer from the same problems).[4]

People may perceive differences among "liberal" or "conservative" visions of social justice, but there is in fact more similarity than difference in our discussion of multiculturalism, class, diversity, race, poverty, difference, equity, social change, equality, oppression, democracy, the collective good, and so forth; that is, almost all these views are constructed from the perspective of power whether they represent "liberal" or "conservative" politics. To paraphrase Marx on wage labor,[5] one form of critical pedagogy may correct the abuses of another, but no form of critical pedagogy constructed from the perspective of power can correct the abuses of the perspective of power itself; a critical pedagogy constructed from the perspective of power may, in fact, assist in the construction of "bigger cages and longer chains."

SOCIAL JUSTICE REQUIRES A
REVOLUTION OF EVERYDAY LIFE

Perhaps obviously, then, Vaneigem's "revolution of everyday life" calls for a "reversal of perspective," one opposed to the hierarchical workings of power, one he designates "the unitary triad: self–realization, communication, [and] participation," one incompatible with what he calls "survival sickness" and "spurious forms of opposition." As he states,

> The repressive unity of Power is threefold: constraint, seduction and mediation are its three functions. This unity is merely the reflection of an equally tripartite, unitary project, its form inverted and perverted by the techniques of dissociation. In its chaotic, underground developments, the new society tends to find practical expression as a transparency in human relationships which promotes the participation of everyone in the self-realization of everyone else. Creativity, love and play are to life what the needs for nourishment and shelter are to survival. . . . The project of self-realization is grounded in the passion to create . . . ; the project of communication is grounded in the passion of love . . . ; the project of participation is grounded in the passion for play. . . . Wherever these three projects are separated, Power's repressive unity is reinforced. Radical subjectivity is the pressure—discernible in practically everyone at the present time—of an individual will to build a passion-filled life. . . . The erotic is the spontaneous coherence which gives practical unity to attempts to enrich lived experience. (236)

And,

> The project of self-realization is born of the passion for creation, in the moment when subjectivity wells up and aspires to reign universally. The project of communication is born of the passion for love, whenever people discover that they share the same desire for amorous conquest. The project of participation is born of the passion for playing, whenever group activity facilitates the self-realization of each individual. (237)

But for Vaneigem, these three passions must be connected in a meaningful totality, for

> Isolated, the three passions are perverted. Dissociated, the three projects are falsified. The will to self-realization is turned into the will to power; sacrificed to status and role-playing, it reigns in a world of restrictions and illusions. The will to communication becomes objective dishonesty; based on relationships between objects, it provides the semiologists with signs to dress up in human guise. The will to participation serves to organize the loneliness of everyone in the crowd; it creates the tyranny of the illusion of community. (238)

Thus, in order to combat the alienation, oppression, and exploitation inherent in everyday life, created and promoted by power, we must explore the possibilities of self-realization (creation), communication (love), and participation (playing). It is only through these passions that the everyday can transcend the banalities—the threats—of power-based consumer capitalism and fragmented disconnection.

With respect to education for social justice, a revolution of everyday life requires that we consider schooling and its various representations according to their complicity in reinforcing the effects and techniques of power and their limitations on the actualizations of creativity, love, and playfulness. Do test scores, for example, restrict or promote the deadness of isolation, or do they instead promote its opposite (i.e., self-realization, communication, and participation). Are such imaginary depictions designed to liberate, to maximize subjectivity, or to extend the consequences of consumption further into the realm of schooling? And, finally, to what degree does (or can) critical pedagogy contradict the effects of images via the everyday, and to what degree does (or can) the everyday contradict the effects of images via critical pedagogy?

Ultimately, it seems to us that social justice can only be achieved via the struggle to overcome alienation.[6]

The revolution of everyday life comes with our ability to understand and transform our world—for us the fundamental goal of critical pedagogy. As Vaneigem closed his treatise on the *Revolution of Everyday Life:* "We have a world of pleasure to win and nothing to lose but our boredom" (279). And wherever passionate acts of refusal and passionate consciousness of the necessity of resistance trigger stoppages in the factories of collective illusion—whether those factories be schools that only offer students alienation, spectacle, surveillance, and training for consumption or a corporate media that offers us fear and perpetual war—there the revolution of everyday life is under way.

NOTES

1. An earlier version of this chapter was delivered by Ross as a keynote address at the Second International Conference on Education, Labor and Emancipation in El Paso, TX/Ciudad Juárez, Mexico, in October 2004. The chapter draws on the collaborative work of Vinson and Ross, particularly parts of chapter 6 in *Image and Education: Teaching in the Face of the New Disciplinarity* (2003), which more fully examines the notion of everyday life by analyzing not only the work of Vaneigem, but also Perlman (1969), de Certeau (1984), Brown (1973), and Lefebvre (1947).

2. For more details on these and subsequent events, see Queen, Ross, Gibson, Vinson (2003) and Ross (1997, 1999).

3. The analysis included every school in Jefferson County Public Schools (JCPS) (Louisville) and all schools *The Courier-Journal* reported as "top 10" and "bottom 10" achievers from across the state. We found very strong correlations between wealth and CATS scores across JCPS schools at all levels: JCPS elementary schools (r = 0.72), JCPS middle schools (r = 0.89), and JCPS high schools (r = 0.91). The correlations between wealth and CATS scores for the reported top and bottom 10

achieving schools in Kentucky were as follows: elementary schools (r = 0.81), middle schools (r = 0.71), and high schools (r = 0.93).

4. See, for example, Peter McLaren (2000) on the "domestication" of critical pedagogy.

5. The quote from Marx is, "One form of wage labour may correct the abuses of another, but no form of wage labour can correct the abuse of wage labour itself" ([1856]1973, 123).

6. Ross (2004) examines "dialectical" thinking as a practical strategy for educators to use in constructing educational experiences that reveal and work against the perspective of power.

REFERENCES

Berliner, D. C., and B. J. Biddle. 1995. *The manufactured crisis*. Reading, MA: Addison-Wesley.

Brown, B. 1973. *Marx, Freud, and the critique of everyday life: Toward a permanent cultural revolution*. New York: Monthly Review Press.

de Certeau, M. 1984. *The practice of everyday life*, trans. S. Rendall. Berkeley, CA: University of California Press.

KERA—restoring hope. 2003. *The Courier-Journal* (Louisville, KY), October 10, A10.

Lefebvre, H. [1968]1971. *Everyday life in the modern world*, trans. S. Rabinovitch. London: Allen Lane/The Penguin Press.

——. [1947] 1992. *Critique of everyday life*, vol. 1. trans. J. Moore. New York: Verso.

Marx, K. [1856]1973. *Grundrisse: Foundations of the critique of political economy (rough draft)*. New York: Penguin.

McLaren, P. 2000. *Che Guevara, Paulo Freire, and the pedagogy of revolution*. Lanham, MD: Rowman & Littlefield.

Munoz, M. A., and D. Dossett. 2001. Equity and excellence: The effect of school and sociodemographic variables on student achievement. *Journal of School Leadership* 11 (2): 120–34.

National Commission on Excellence in Education. 1983. *A Nation at Risk*. Washington, DC: U.S. Government Printing Office.

Paige, P. 2003. Bush education law will help black students. *Lexington (Kentucky) Herald-Leader*, March 17, A8.

Perlman, F. 1969. *The reproduction of everyday life*. Detroit, MI: Black and Red, available at www.pipeline.com/~rgibson/repro-daily-life.html (accessed June 7, 2006).

Queen, G., E. W. Ross, R. Gibson, and K. D. Vinson. 2003. "I participate, you participate, we participate . . . they profit, but let's change things": Building a K–16 movement for progressive educational reform. *Workplace: The Journal for Academic Labor* 5 (2) (July), available at www.louisville.edu/journal/workplace/issue5p2/rougeforum.html.

Ross, E. W. 1997. A lesson in democracy? CUFA, Proposition 187, and the boycott of California. *Theory and Research in Social Education* 25 (3): 256–58, 390–93.

——. 1999. What is to be done in the aftermath of Proposition 187? *Theory and Research in Social Education* 27 (3): 292–95.

————. 2000. Redrawing the lines: The case against traditional social studies instruction. In *Democratic social education: Social studies for social change,* ed. D. W. Hursh and E. W. Ross, 43–63. New York: Routledge Falmer.

————. 2003. Segregation returning to public education. *Lexington (Kentucky) Herald-Leader,* March, 10, A11.

————. 2004. Critical thinking in social studies. In *Critical thinking and learning,* ed. J. L. Kincheloe and D. Weil. Westport, CT: Greenwood.

Ross, E. W., and S. Mathison. 2004. Response to *The Courier-Journal*'s "KERA—restoring hope." Unpublished manuscript, October 13, Louisville, KY, University of Louisville.

Vaneigem, R. [1968]2001. *The revolution of everyday life,* trans. D. Nicholson-Smith. London: Rebel Press.

Vinson, K. D., and E. W. Ross. 2003. *Image and education: Teaching in the face of the new disciplinarity.* New York: Peter Lang.

III

APPLICATIONS, EXTENSIONS, AND EMPIRICAL STUDIES

11

Mathematical Power: Exploring Critical Pedagogy in Mathematics and Statistics

Lawrence M. Lesser and Sally Blake

Always remember that the use of algebra is to free people from bondage.

—Mary Everest Boole, *Philosophy and Fun of Algebra* (1909)

It no longer suffices to know how things are constituted: we need to seek how things should be constituted so that this world of ours may present less suffering and destitution.

—Nineteenth-century French statistician Eugene Burét

Though traditionally viewed as value-free, mathematics is actually one of the most powerful, yet underutilized, venues for working toward the goals of critical pedagogy—social, political, and economic justice for all. This emerging awareness is due to how critical mathematics educators, such as M. Frankenstein, O. Skovsmose, and E. Gutstein, have applied the work of Paulo Freire. Freire's argument that critical education involves problem posing that challenges all to reconsider and recreate prior knowledge reads like a progressive definition of mathematical thinking. Frankenstein (1990) supports the idea that critical mathematics should involve the ability to ask basic statistical questions in order to deepen one's appreciation of particular issues and should not be taught as isolated formulas with little relevance to individual experiences.

At first, mathematics seems an unlikely vehicle for liberation. As S. E. Anderson asserts, "By junior high school, the overwhelming majority of our youth are convinced that mathematics teachers are their enemies and, even worse, that mathematics is some sort of poison or mind controlling drug that teachers try to force upon them" (1997, 295). Anderson's quote is not as extreme as it may sound in light of accounts of math abuse (e.g., Fiore 1999). Also, many citizens (and teachers) seem to have "a pervasive societal belief in North America that only some students are capable of learning mathematics [as opposed to learning to read and write]" (NCTM 2000, 12). Mathematics classes are therefore viewed as gatekeepers to keep the intellectually "less gifted" from joining an exclusive club, thus creating a perpetual lower class of citizen. This is connected to the reality that mathematics qualifications continue to be an admission ticket for most high-paying jobs. Furthermore, Frankenstein explains how "politically, people can be more easily oppressed when they cannot break through the numerical lies and obfuscations thrown at them on a daily basis" (1983, 12). Frankenstein (1987) and Skovsmose (1994) assert that knowing mathematics and statistics is a key part of moving toward more democratic economic, political, and social structures in society.

Freire (1970) describes "self-depreciation" as a condition derived from the internalization of the oppressors' opinions. Schools reinforce the idea that students are not capable of learning mathematics, and this becomes reality. Studies on self-efficacy (e.g., Bandura 1994) further support the effect of the internalization of perceived influences of authority figures on abilities to perform tasks successfully. This continued labeling of individuals as failures and the accompanying alienation that many continue to experience are due, in large part, to the interactions among social, political, and economic structures of the U.S. political economy, functioning both as a determining factor and a social filter in the phenomenon of unrealized potential and alienation (Frankenstein and Powell 1989).

Because of the importance of the relationship between individual belief in ability to perform tasks and actual performance, it is crucial to confront false negative internalizations. Perhaps one of the most powerful ways is to have the instructor make it a point to join sides with the student in a revolution (using mathematical thinking as a tool) against social inequities and the "culture of silence" that conceals them. Freire (1970) criticized as "the banking model of education" the traditional view of students as receptacles filled passively by teachers. We support an ideology that responds to this critique, similar to the "public educator" (Ernest 1991, 202). Critical understanding of data prompts students to make decisions about how a society is structured and enables them to act from a more informed position on societal structures and processes (Frankenstein and Powell 1989).

Traditional mathematics instruction also rarely makes connections between applications and theory and even fewer connections to culturally relevant issues in students' lives. Anderson describes how mathematics is one of the few subjects typically presented with "little or no historical, cultural, or political references," an approach that "reinforces the institutionalization of Eurocentrism, class elitism and sexism" and results in censorship of mathematical knowledge of certain cultures as "childlike and primitive" (1997, 296). The recent emergence of mathematics curricula that include mathematics history and multiculturalism (Bidwell 1993; Lumpkin 1997) has started to help students see mathematics as an ongoing creative and cultural (indeed, multicultural) process rather than a received fixed set of rules and abstractions. This is important but does not always actively empower students or get them to grapple deeply with equity issues or cultural or political biases or assumptions. For example, it is unlikely that a class would discuss why a piece of mathematics is sometimes associated with a person who followed the non-Western originators by centuries (e.g., Pascal's triangle and Gaussian elimination were discovered centuries earlier by Chinese) or the role that nonstatistical considerations played in deciding not to adjust the 2000 Census.

M. M. Hatfield et al. wrote an elementary/middle school methods book whose "culturally relevant mathematics" chapter includes not only multiculturalism (e.g., connections with African Americans, Native Americans, Hispanic Americans, and Asian Americans) but also "the effect of mathematics on any culture and its people; the right for *all* people to acquire the mathematical power for success in today's world, that is, *equity*" (2000, 19). This is consistent with "the Equity Principle," the first of the six unifying principles of the National Council of Teachers of Mathematics (NCTM) (2000). This principle includes some discussion of technology equity and the roles of learning style, speed, competition, culture, and language. Culturally relevant pedagogy has certainly been explored in great depth (e.g., Ladson-Billings 1995), but the application to mathematics has been done by only a few (e.g., Gutstein et al. 1997).

"READING THE WORLD" WITH MATHEMATICS

As Gutstein applies the work of Freire, "reading the world with mathematics means to use mathematics to understand relations of power, resource inequities and disparate opportunities between different social groups and to understand explicit discrimination based on race, class, gender, language and other differences" (2003b, 45). We see the explicit mathematical connections by raising three questions: How can people recognize, analyze, or fight against social inequalities without the tools to analyze mathematics inequalities? How can people talk about what is unfair without tools such as proportional reasoning to calculate what would be expected as a fair share and how much statistical deviation from that might be tolerated as innocuous? How can people produce or interpret depictions of quantitative information without awareness of pitfalls (e.g., Huff 1993; Paulos 1988)?

Use of mathematics' analytical reasoning and tools (e.g., data analysis, graphing, and modeling) to explore several specific, concrete, real-life scenarios that stimulate a sense of social justice could influence student empowerment. As E. Lee asks, "In mathematics, instead of studying statistics with sports and weather numbers, why not look at employment in light of ethnicity?" (1995, 11). Datasets that are not merely simulated or taken from "safe" areas of life but that take on important social issues have the potential for (unexpectedly) sustained engagement with mathematics as students encounter deep relevance to their lives. Activities and resources have been articulated by Frankenstein (1990), Gutstein and B. Peterson (2005), and so forth. Also, Lawrence Lesser (2006) found roughly 10 percent of datasets in major dataset repositories to be readily suitable for social justice teaching.

EXAMPLES OF APPLYING MATHEMATICS TO SOCIAL JUSTICE

Let us now share specific examples of social justice topics to which instructors have applied mathematics in the classroom. Critical pedagogy in mathematics has been used with students of a variety of grade levels, even as young as upper elementary school. When R. S. Kitchen and J. M. Lear (2000) offered fourth- and fifth-grade Latinas neutral-appearing body-measurement activities of various women and of the (disproportionate) Barbie doll, the girls' analyses prompted them "to question their views of themselves, which were largely based on their body type." Other educators have extended the activity to male superhero action figures, as well as to discussion of the sweatshop labor and multiculturalism of the dolls (Mukhopadhyay 2005).

Also, a root cause of prejudice is overgeneralizing (i.e., stereotyping), and this might be initially confronted through an algebra activity such as that described by Lesser (2000) in which high school students generate diverse lists of functions (e.g., constant, linear, square, cubic, radical, absolute value, rational, exponential, or log) and possible traits [e.g., even, odd, increasing, decreasing, continuous, one-to-one, or $f(a + b) = f(a) + f(b)$]. This shows how hard it is to find one trait that fits all functions and how hard it is to describe a function fully from just one of its traits. This could also be done with a collection of shapes and geometric traits, such as equilateral, equiangular, convex, having a pair of parallel sides, having a right angle, having line symmetry, and so forth.

Lesser contributed the following problem to an algebra textbook (Mayes and Lesser 1998, 156):

Objectification objection: In popular usage, the phrase "treating as an object" has negative connotations, because it implies an entity as rich as a human being can be reduced to a single dimension, such as gender, a physical characteristic, ethnicity, perceived sexual appeal, financial status, sexual orientation, religion, or occupation. Would it be just as foolish to say that we know everything about a function or its behavior from one particular classification of it (e.g., whether or not it is an even function)? Explain.

Tellingly, this problem was one of several critical pedagogy–type problems that were deleted from the subsequent edition of the textbook (against Lesser's wishes). On a larger scale, the choice of what books are adopted for a state's public schools is usually made by an appointed board. The social, political, and educational composition of such boards may not always be fully supportive of student emancipation. This could be particularly critical in states such as Texas, California, New Mexico, Hawaii, and the District of Columbia, where there are more minorities than Anglos.

Peterson (1995) and Gutstein (2003b) have explored classroom activities to simulate distribution of wealth (between continents and within the United States), a topic that often appears in the news. C. K. Wilson (2004) reports that median Hispanic and black households in the United States have less than 10 percent of the wealth typical Anglo households have. Algebra verifies that even if all salaries rise at the same rate, the dollar gap between any two people's salaries will simply increase at that rate, too. Students can discuss the Census Bureau's Gini index of income inequality.

In one activity, fifth-graders used data to produce their own conclusions about federal spending, such as that one stealth bomber could pay the annual compensation packages of thirty-eight thousand teachers (Peterson 2003). To supplement such concrete examples and ground them in a more general abstract framework, instructors in introductory college courses have shown how the concepts of mathematics and statistics can be applied explicitly to philosophical normative ethics as a way to explore or critique a particular perspective of judging when society is better off. For example, Lesser and E. Nordenhaug explore pitfalls of the rule-utilitarian concept of "greatest good for the greatest number" (2004).

Gutstein (2003b) had middle school students discuss a newspaper article about racial disparities in mortgage loan approvals, allowing them the opportunity to differentiate between "individual racism" (e.g., a white loan officer rejecting an applicant of color because of her race) and "structural racism" (e.g., why African Americans have less collateral). Gutstein (2002) also had his middle school students explore racial profiling (applying simulation, expected value, and proportion to see if stops and searches are racially fair) and socioeconomic and racial patterns in SAT scores (e.g., scores highly positively correlated with family income).

Another real-life topic is random drug testing. Statistical reasoning shows that when the drug tested for is rare in the population, a significant fraction (even the majority) of positives can be false positives (e.g., Lyublinskaya

2005). Students can simulate this quite informally by filling in a 2×2 table of "actual user status" versus "what the drug test says." For example, if a test that is 95 percent accurate is given to a population containing 3 percent drug users, then a positive drug test result means there is a 63 percent chance that person is really a nonuser! J. A. Paulos asserts, "To subject people who test positive to stigmas, especially when most of them may be false positives, is counterproductive and wrong" (1988, 66–67). On a more critical note, it is not uncommon for "random" drug testing to include a disproportionately high percentage of minorities.

Lesser explored with high school and university students the implausibility implicit in the claim made by some (e.g., Pambianco 2000) that no innocent person has ever been falsely executed by civil authority under the death penalty (Lesser and Nordenhaug 2004). The classes were asked for estimates of the probability that a typical death penalty case resulting in execution is indeed "the correct decision," and students typically volunteered numbers ranging from 0.70 to 0.98. It was suggested that we see what happens by giving the judicial system more benefit of the doubt and use 0.995. The 2004 *Statistical Abstract of the United States* says that there were 4,744 executions performed by U.S. civil authorities between 1930 and 2003. Raising 0.995 to the power 4,744 suggests that the probability that all 4,744 executions were correct decisions is about 1 in 21 billion! We then explored the fairness of the death penalty, such as what roles the race of the defendant or of the murder victim play in whether the defendant is sentenced to death. Classes tracked down primary-source data themselves or, when time was limited, worked from a textbook exercise such as that in D. S. Moore and G. P. McCabe (1989, 232–33), whose three-way table classifies 326 actual murder cases. This exercise is mathematically quite rich because of a paradoxical result: "a higher percent of white defendants are sentenced to death overall, but for both black and white victims, a higher percent of black defendants are sentenced to death." This reversal generated animated discussion in the classroom and illustrates how a statistical claim can depend on the human or political choice of how data are disaggregated. Mathematics education researchers have long documented the power of conflict or paradox to motivate student learning (e.g., Shaughnessy 1977; Movshovitz-Hadar and Hadass 1990; Wilensky 1995; Lesser 1998). Lesser (2001a) offered preservice secondary teachers a similar opportunity to look for possible inequities in hiring and salary datasets.

Lesser team-taught a field-based integrated block set of elementary preservice courses during the fall 2004 semester at an elementary school in an unincorporated community in the southwestern United States. Of the 90 percent Hispanic population in that community, 75 percent speak Spanish in the home. Of the district's elementary school students, 100 percent receive free or reduced lunch. Ongoing work there includes developing a culturally relevant set of school-based programs within a service-learning framework, such as a Mayan math project and Parent Power Nights with parents, children, and preservice teachers working together on mathematically and culturally rich activities (e.g., Munter 2004).

A mathematics and social studies connection made with those preservice elementary teachers was the making of flat maps. A three-dimensional curved surface cannot be perfectly projected onto a two-dimensional plane without some kind of distortion, so each projection will have trade-offs. For example, the traditional Mercator projection preserves shapes and angles, but exaggerates the size of countries (e.g., Greenland) farther from the equator. The more recent Peters projection preserves sizes, but somewhat distorts shapes. Even students who had heard of more than one map projection were generally shocked to realize what a difference the choice of projection can make. Adapting an activity from Gutstein (2001), Lesser showed the preservice teachers two maps published by Rand McNally and asked, How many times larger than Greenland does Africa look? For one map projection (Miller Cylindrical), teachers' estimates clustered around two times, but for another (Goode's Homolosine Equal Area), estimates clustered around eight or nine (the true answer is about fourteen). From one map, all thirty teachers said (incorrectly) that Alaska was bigger than Mexico, but drew the opposite conclusion from the second map. When reflecting on this activity, some had to work through the idea that no one projection was inherently more "correct," but each reflected what was being asked for. For example, while we want an equal-area projection to compare areas, we would prefer an azimuthal equidistant projection if we were airplane pilots and a conformal projection (e.g., Mercator) if we were navigators or surveyors, and so on. It does not take great imagination to discuss how someone might make a map choice for political reasons, to make his country appear larger or more central in the world. A general lesson learned by one preservice teacher was "how teacher's [sic] really need to be careful of where they get their information and how they present it to their students." This is just another example of what Frankenstein (2005) calls the "politics of mathematical knowledge," in which seemingly neutral procedures or summaries depend highly on choice of average, choice of a variable's definition, choice of disaggregation, and so forth.

While this type of teaching has its own inherent value and goal, educators are starting to find empirical evidence that suggests students will be more engaged in learning in this environment. Gutstein (2003b) found far more student engagement when his middle school students made a scatterplot of SAT scores and income than when they made a much more conventional "real-world" scatterplot of heights of children and same-sex parents. Investigating a course for preservice teachers designed to develop understanding of equity through data-based statistical inquiry, K. M. Makar

(2004) found a significant correlation between prospective teachers' degree of engagement with their topic of inquiry and the depth of statistical evidence they used, particularly for minority students.

As S. Derry, J. R. Levin, and L. Schauble (1995) explain, statistics represent controversial knowledge [even among expert statisticians whose different positions on probabilistic foundations (e.g., frequentist or Bayesian) have immediate impact on their practice] and therefore should not be thought of as something for the teacher to hand down as fixed, universally accepted concepts. Instead, students should participate in the statistics controversy and gain the tools to construct evidential arguments that many adolescents and adults struggle to construct (Kuhn 1991). Such a teaching approach has been successfully used as an intervention for at-risk seventh graders (Osana, Leath, and Thompson 2004). D. W. Johnson and R. T. Johnson (1992) found that controversy tends to yield many benefits that might ease the mind of an instructor wanting to use a more critical approach, such as greater mastery and retention of subject matter, greater ability to generalize, higher-quality decisions and solutions to complex problems, and more frequent creative insights. Seeing that mathematics is fallible or can generate conflicting answers should be a powerful experience for students, one that may help them imagine that much more readily the possibility of such experiences involving far less abstract social constructions and institutions.

ADDRESSING PEDAGOGICAL PITFALLS

In an introductory college statistics lesson about scatterplots a few weeks before the 2004 presidential election, a University of Texas, El Paso, faculty member illustrated the tool of scatterplots by facilitating discussion of the sequence of plots that strongly suggest that the butterfly ballot of Florida's Palm Beach County confused many voters in the 2000 presidential election (Adams 2001). Students were very engaged, though this untenured faculty member wondered if it was potentially perilous to introduce an example so connected to political controversy. We affirm that the psychological implications of equity demand many views, more understanding of the election process, and critical analysis of policies that impact the future of all students.

However, Gutstein (2003b) cautions that classroom teachers must take care in introducing potentially volatile or normally undiscussed topics to make sure that students have already learned "to take seriously their roles as learners and knowledge creators" and that students will not be unduly demoralized or paralyzed by the bleakness of some data that they "see themselves in." Many students view their situations as personal rather than as problems woven into the institutional fabric of society. Most often, individual disadvantages are not unique and not the result of individual failure but due to the failure of society to ensure equality and justice for all (Frankenstein 1990).

The key is not to presume you are reaching definitive answers to all questions, but to nurture the students' overall spirit of critical inquiry as they gain mathematical power in general, while empowering themselves to understand more deeply a meaningful situation (and thereby making mathematics itself unexpectedly meaningful to them). P. Ernest suggests that students of many backgrounds may not be used to controversy, conflict, and rational argument in the classroom, especially younger learners. He adds that public educators will have to address powerful contradictions such as "personal empowerment versus examination success" and "ethnomathematics versus abstract mathematics" (1991, 213–14). Ernest also warns that the public educator "is at risk of being seen as attempting to subvert mathematics education into a propagandist activity" (1991, 212) and must anticipate the opposition of conservative critiques (e.g., Ravitch 2005).

Another tension is that Freirean pedagogy calls for teachers to be explicit in their opinions while creating space for students to develop their own views apart from what they might think the teacher wants. What may help support this balance is the reality that with such a wide variety of issues and areas, the mathematics teacher cannot possibly answer all of the questions students will raise, empowering the students to share the role of "expert" and search for the information to answer their own questions.

Another perception that needs to be addressed by a critical educator is whether the time devoted to social justice issues might keep the required "purely mathematical" goals of the course from being met. Gutstein (2003b) addressed this by making it a point to have a well-respected, rigorous, rich curriculum aligned with NCTM (2000) in place as the "main curriculum" so that the social justice projects he added to the course would not be seen as interfering with normative goals.

Perhaps critical pedagogy in mathematics instruction is best or most naturally implemented in stages, not unlike the stages of multicultural, antiracist education articulated to Barbara Miner by Lee (1995): surface stage (one-shot events and signs), transitional stage (self-contained one-to-three week units of study), structural change stage (elements of the unit integrated into existing units), and social change stage (curriculum leads to changes outside school). Most attempts at implementation rarely go past the surface stage. One-time events like parents' night, guest speakers, and posters may touch the surface of the problem, but they do not deal with the social, economic, and political roots of the situation. Letting change stop at this superficial level gives credibility to discrimination by treating ethnic and minority students as interesting oddities rather than as accepted stakeholders in education. And traditional parents' nights place the teachers as the masters who determine what is important in mathematical understanding with little awareness of how concepts really apply to local environments.

Other instructors integrate critical pedagogy goals with occasional activities dressed in more conventional trappings. For example, by discussing song lyrics containing mathematical language, Lesser (2001b) found a simple means to encourage reflection on popular culture along with mathematics. C. Aceves (2004) teaches his first- and second-graders culturally rich mathematics (from counting to algebra) using "mythic pedagogy," which could safely pass for a multicultural, holistic approach to a conventional observer's eye. But it goes deeper, allowing his elementary students to experience their culture as something that is dynamic, empowering, and interdisciplinary with a nurturing and egalitarian worldview that places "their history within a universal context where being part of an ethnic group is a reflection—not a separation—of their humanity" (Aceves 2004, 275). Preservice teachers in Lesser's course had the opportunity to observe, discuss, and reflect upon Aceves's teaching. One wrote, "If there is one thing I learned from watching Mr. Aceves teach it is that it's okay to teach by another way just as long as it is used to teach the basics of the class."

Some pitfalls may hit hardest some of the very groups who are underserved. As Y. De La Cruz relates, "Teachers are finding that reform-based mathematics instruction places more demands on facility with oral and written English. They do not have the strategies, however, that enable them to work more effectively with their limited-English-language students" (2000, 22). The cultural and political aspects of critical pedagogy may take extra work to communicate effectively, taking care that the questions are posed in straightforward language that is not unduly technical or biased. Some instructors have found it helpful to give students a reading guide with discussion questions to prepare them for facilitating the ensuing class discussion. Mathematics instructors new to critical pedagogy may benefit from starting slowly, using focus groups of students or community members to learn about their lives, hardships, and interests. All instructors should prepare to persevere and not expect overnight success.

IMPLICATIONS FOR MATHEMATICS TEACHERS

Ernest (1991) includes very specific traits about how a public educator should teach, assess, and use resources. Suggestions include not only creating a community of learners, using cooperative group work and projects for engagement and mastery, but also autonomous projects to give students the chance to pursue personally meaningful directions. It is no small thing for a mathematics instructor to reach, experience, or respond to the realization that his or her very pedagogical practices may inadvertently or implicitly portray mathematics as an absolute, authoritarian discipline that contributes to students' feeling excluded and disempowered. Many students and teachers have the same conception of mathematics that their previous teachers and texts presented. They have internalized the "reified typification of mathematics" and have been unsuccessful in learning or re-membering mathematics (Frankenstein 1990). Awareness of this influence and reflection on how to change this powerful chain of intellectual neglect is important.

One aspect of hope from Freire's work is teachers' and students' development of critical consciousness, which he maintains can emerge only through dialogical, problem-posing education that moves past reflection toward action. Teachers must show students that they can understand how mathematics works and how to use it in their own interest. Teachers must also engage in this understanding themselves for change to occur.

Teachers hopefully already know that curricula need not be neutral, as dramatically demonstrated by some of the "how much poison gas needed to kill" problems used in Nazi-era German textbooks (Cohen 1953; Shulman 2002). While today's books generally avoid such grossly blatant evils, they still require critical examination by mathematics teachers for less blatant evils (e.g., gender stereotypes in word-problem scenarios) that unduly or uncritically reinforce an oppressive or unhealthy social hierarchy or worldview. For example, teachers should note whether the "real-life" application problems in the textbook are simply focused on maximizing profit, while ignoring the human or environmental dimension, such as a typical offshore oil pipeline cost-minimization problem (e.g., Swokowski 1988, 171). Frankenstein maintains that even the most trivial math applications are biased (such as a grocery bill calculation presupposing the naturalness of everyone having to buy food from grocery stores) and that even a problem with no real-life data has "the non-neutral hidden message that learning math must be divorced from helping real people understand and control the real world" (1983, 12).

There are clearly degrees of criticalness in curricula. For example, on global human survival issues, P. C. Kenschaft (2002) clearly goes further than C. Schaufele and N. Zumoff (1993) toward raising questions from a critical perspective. Many solid reform curricula that include higher-order thinking might be used as a foundation for the instructor to add that next critical element as desired. Even if a teacher cannot choose her textbook, she can and should insert additional examples, such as those in this chapter. Social justice is more meaningful and lasting when classes seek out examples that speak strongest to their locality, lives, and times rather than wait for a fixed collection someone else has compiled.

A mathematics instructor employing critical pedagogy should consider critical methods to analyze his or her philosophy of assessing students. Perhaps he or she will recognize, as did L. Romagnano (2001), that subjectivity is inherent in mathematics assessment, whether it is a teacher-made test or an SAT or an Advanced Placement test.

DIRECTIONS FOR FUTURE INVESTIGATIONS

On a global level, it will be interesting to follow the emergence of relevant organizations (e.g., the Critical Mathematics Education Group and the Radical Statistics Group), classes (e.g., the University of Georgia's "Rethinking Mathematics Education from a Critical Pedagogy Perspective"), resources (e.g., Gutstein and Peterson 2005), and conferences (e.g., Mathematics Education and Society). As the aims of the 2005 Mathematics Education and Society Conference declare,

> There is a need for discussing widely the social, cultural and political dimensions of mathematics education; for disseminating research that explores those dimensions; for addressing methodological issues of that type of research; for planning international co-operation in the area; and for developing a strong research community interested in this view on mathematics education.

It would be interesting to observe and interview teachers to see if the nature and magnitude of transitioning from traditional "transmission" teaching to an active-learning approach differs from transitioning from an active-learning approach to critical pedagogy. And, are there mathematics teachers who had a critical pedagogy approach from the outset, and what might they have in common?

REFERENCES

Aceves, C. 2004. The Xinachtli project: Transforming whiteness through mythic pedagogy. In *Identifying race and transforming whiteness in the classroom*, ed. V. Lea and J. Helfand, 257–77. New York: Peter Lang.

Adams, G. 2001. Voting irregularities in Palm Beach, Florida. *Chance* 14 (1): 22–24.

Anderson, S. E. 1997. Worldmath curriculum: Fighting Eurocentrism in mathematics. In *Ethnomathematics: Challenging Eurocentrism in mathematics education*, ed. A. B. Powell and M. Frankenstein, 291–306. Albany: State University of New York Press.

Bandura, A. 1994. Self-efficacy. In *Encyclopedia of human behavior*, ed. V. S. Ramachaudran, 71–81. Vol. 4. New York: Academic Press.

Bidwell, J. 1993. Humanize your classroom with the history of mathematics. *Mathematics Teacher* 86 (6): 461–64.

Cohen, E. A. 1953. *Human behavior in the concentration camp*. Westport, CT: Greenwood Press.

De La Cruz, Y. 2000. Reversing the trend: Latino families in real partnerships with schools. In *Involving families in school mathematics*, ed. D. Edge, 21–24. Reston, VA: National Council of Teachers of Mathematics.

Derry, S., J. R. Levin, and L. Schauble. 1995. Stimulating statistical thinking through situated simulations. *Teaching of Psychology* 22 (1): 51–57.

Ernest, P. 1991. *The philosophy of mathematics education*. London: Falmer Press.

Fiore, G. 1999. Math-abused students: Are we prepared to teach them? *Mathematics Teacher* 92 (5): 403–406.

Frankenstein, M. 1983. Taking the numb out of numbers: Teaching radical math. *Science for the People* 15: 12–17.

———. 1987. Critical mathematics education: An application of Paulo Freire's epistemology. In *Freire for the classroom: A sourcebook for liberatory teaching*, ed. I. Shor. Portsmouth, NH: Heinemann Educational Books.

———. 1990. Incorporating race, gender, and class issues into a critical mathematics literacy curriculum. *Journal of Negro Education* 59 (3): 336–47.

———. 2005. Reading the world with math: Goals for a critical mathematical literacy curriculum. In *Rethinking mathematics: Teaching social justice by the numbers*, ed. E. Gutstein and B. Peterson, 19–28. Milwaukee, WI: Rethinking Schools.

Frankenstein, M., and A. B. Powell. 1989. Empowering non-traditional college students: On social ideology and mathematics education. *Science and Nature* (9/10): 100–12.

Freire, P. 1970. *Pedagogy of the oppressed*. New York: Continuum.

Gutstein, E., P. Lipman, P. Hernandez, and R. de los Reyes. 1997. Culturally relevant mathematics teaching in a Mexican American context. *Journal for Research in Mathematics Education* 28 (6): 709–37.

Gutstein, E. 2001. Math, maps, and misrepresentation. *Rethinking Schools* 15 (3): 6–7.

———. 2002. Math, SATs, and racial profiling. *Rethinking Schools* 16 (4): 18–19.

———. 2003a. Home buying while brown or black: Teaching mathematics for social justice. *Rethinking Schools* 18 (1): 35–37.

———. 2003b. Teaching and learning mathematics for social justice in an urban, Latino school. *Journal for Research in Mathematics Education* 34 (1): 37–73.

Gutstein, E., and Peterson, B., eds., 2005. *Rethinking mathematics: Teaching social justice by the numbers*. Milwaukee, WI: Rethinking Schools.

Hatfield, M. M., N. T. Edwards, G. G. Bitter, and J. Morrow. 2000. *Mathematics methods for elementary and middle school teachers*. 4th ed. New York: Wiley.

Huff, D. 1993. *How to lie with statistics*. New York: W. W. Norton.

Johnson, D. W., and R. T. Johnson. 1992. Encouraging thinking through constructive controversy. In *Enhancing thinking through cooperative learning*, ed. N. Davidson and T. Worsham, 120–37. New York: Teachers College Press.

Kenschaft, P. C. 2002. *Mathematics for human survival*. Island Park, NY: Whittier Publications.

Kitchen, R. S., and J. M. Lear. 2000. Mathematizing Barbie: Using measurement as a means for girls to analyze their sense of body image. In *Changing the faces of mathematics*, ed. W. G. Secada, 67–73. Reston, VA: National Council of Teachers of Mathematics.

Kuhn, D. 1991. *The skills of argument.* Cambridge: Cambridge University Press.

Ladson-Billings, G. 1995. Toward a theory of culturally relevant pedagogy. *American Educational Research Journal* 32:465–91.

Lee, E. 1995. Taking multicultural, anti-racist education seriously. In *Rethinking schools: An agenda for change,* ed. D. Levine, R. Lowe, B. Peterson, and R. Tenorio, 9–16. New York: New Press.

Lesser, L. 1998. Countering indifference using counterintuitive examples. *Teaching Statistics* 20 (1): 10–12.

——. 2000. Reunion of broken parts: Experiencing diversity in algebra. *Mathematics Teacher* 93 (1): 62–67.

——. 2001a. Representations of reversal: An exploration of Simpson's paradox. In *The roles of representation in school mathematics,* ed. A. A. Cuoco and F. R. Curcio, 129–45. Reston, VA: National Council of Teachers of Mathematics.

——. 2001b. Musical means: Using songs to teach statistics. *Teaching Statistics* 23 (3): 81–85.

——. 2006. Critical values and transforming data: Toward a framework for teaching statistics for social justice. Manuscript submitted for publication.

Lesser, L., and E. Nordenhaug. 2004. Ethical statistics and statistical ethics: Making an interdisciplinary module. *Journal of Statistics* 12 (3), available at www.amstat.org/publications/jse/v12n3/lesser.html (accessed June 17, 2006).

Lumpkin, B. 1997. *Algebra activities from many cultures.* Portland, ME: J. Weston Walch.

Lyublinskaya, I. 2005. How fair is the drug test? *Mathematics Teacher* 98 (8): 536–43.

Makar, K. M. 2004. *Developing statistical inquiry: Prospective secondary math and science teachers' investigations of equity and fairness through analysis of accountability data.* Doctoral dissertation, University of Texas, Austin.

Mathematics Education and Society Conference. 2005. Website: www.griffith.edu.au/text/conference/mes2005 (accessed June 17, 2006).

Mayes, R., and L. Lesser. 1998. *ACT in algebra: Applications, concepts and technology in learning algebra.* Preliminary ed. Burr Ridge, IL: McGraw-Hill.

Moore, D. S., and G. P. McCabe. 1989. *Introduction to the practice of statistics.* New York: W. H. Freeman.

Movshovitz-Hadar, N., and R. Hadass. 1990. Preservice education of math teachers using paradoxes. *Educational Studies in Mathematics* 21:265–87.

Mukhopadhyay, S. 2005. Deconstructing Barbie: Math and popular culture. In *Rethinking mathematics: Teaching social justice by the numbers,* ed. E. Gutstein and B. Peterson, 122–23. Milwaukee, WI: Rethinking Schools.

Munter, J. 2004. Tomorrow's teachers re-envisioning the roles of parents in schools: Lessons learned on the U.S./Mexico border. *Thresholds in Education* 30 (2): 19–29.

National Council of Teachers of Mathematics. 2000. *Principles and standards for school mathematics.* Reston, VA: NCTM.

Osana, H. P., E. P. Leath, and S. E. Thompson. 2004. Improving evidential argumentation through statistical sampling: Evaluating the effects of a classroom intervention for at-risk 7th-graders. *Journal of Mathematical Behavior* 23:351–70.

Pambianco, R. V. 2000. Innocents are being executed? Name one. *Savannah Morning News,* June 23, 17A.

Paulos, J. A. 1988. *Innumeracy: Mathematical illiteracy and its consequences*. New York: Hill and Wang.

Peterson, B. 1995. Teaching math across the curriculum: A fifth grade teacher battles "number numbness." *Rethinking Schools* 10 (1): 1, 4–5.

———. 2003. Understanding large numbers: A useful purpose for the military budget. *Rethinking Schools* 18 (1): 33–34.

Ravitch D. 2005. Ethnomathematics. *Wall Street Journal*, June 20, A14.

Romagnano, L. 2001. Implementing the assessment standards: The myth of objectivity in mathematics assessment 94 (1): 31–37.

Schaufele, C., and N. Zumoff. 1993. *Earth algebra: College algebra with applications to environmental issues*. Preliminary ed. New York: HarperCollins.

Shaughnessy, M. 1977. Misconceptions of probability: An experiment with a small-group, activity-based, model building approach to introductory probability at the college level. *Educational Studies in Mathematics* 8: 295–316.

Shulman, B. 2002. Is there enough poison gas to kill the city? The teaching of ethics in mathematics classes. *College Mathematics Journal* 33 (2): 118–25.

Skovsmose, O. 1994. *Towards a philosophy of critical mathematics education*. Dordrecht: Kluwer.

Swokowski, E. 1988. *Calculus with analytic geometry*. 4th ed. Boston: PWS Kent.

Wilensky, U. 1995. Paradox, programming and learning probability: A case study in a connected mathematics framework. *Journal of Mathematical Behavior* 14: 253–80.

Wilson, C. K. 2004. Minority wealth gap gets wider. *El Paso Times*, October 18, A1–A2.

12

Teaching Ecocide: Junk Science and the Myth of Premature Extinction in Environmental Science Textbooks

David K. Goodin

The benchmark of environmental science textbooks for high school and first-year college students is arguably the series prepared under the direction of G. Tyler Miller Jr. It has long been the standard for introductory environmental science education, and the primary text, *Environmental Science: Working with the Earth*, is in its tenth edition. But a most curious change in terminology has crept into its pages and has thus far gone unnoticed within the critical pedagogy and environmental science communities.

A striking example of this subtle alteration is found in a particular graphic used to augment the textual narrative on endangered species. In the 1995 version (fifth edition), the caption for Figure 17–6 on page 453 reads, "Some species that have become extinct largely because of human activities, mostly habitat destruction and overhunting." The accompanying picture depicts various animals, such as the dodo bird and the passenger pigeon (see also Miller 1996, 639, and Miller 1997, 433). The same graphic also appears in the 2004 version (tenth edition), this time denoted as Figure 18–2 and appearing on page 449. This recycled drawing from the earlier editions appears in only slightly different form, updated with more vibrant colors and the addition of some landscape features. The real change is in the underlying text, which now announces, "Some animal species that have become *prematurely* extinct largely because of human activities, mostly habitat destruction and overhunting" (emphasis added). This is a most peculiar caveat to add because the modifier "prematurely" is unscientific.

At face value, the adverb "prematurely" implies that these animals were somehow predestined to die out, that humankind only hastened their removal from the evolutionary stage. And so, rather than portraying their extinction as something tragic and preventable, the phrase "prematurely extinct" instead insinuates that their deaths were inevitable. This is a substantial change from the earlier editions. Now, the shocking reality of entire species being exterminated by human capriciousness has been rationalized away as an inescapable naturalistic outcome. This one added word threatens to undermine the entire debate over protecting critical habitats needed for endangered species, as they too are portrayed in these textbooks as being threatened with only *premature* extinction (e.g., Miller 2004b, 564–65).

This recent alteration in textbook terminology has nothing to do with normative science. The phrase is wholly subjective, and its aim appears to be to manipulate classroom values. Curricula are at the forefront of society's effort to educate students as fully functional and conscientious citizens. This change therefore has to be interpreted either as an attempt to influence public discourse and societal values as a whole or as a terrible and poorly thought-out editorial comment missed during quality-assurance reviews. It is noteworthy that the lesser-known environmental science textbooks, competitors to the preeminent G. Tyler Miller Jr. series, do not include the phrase "premature extinction." These texts faithfully present only the normative science (see, for example, Kaufman and Franz 2000; Marsh and Grossa 2002; Botkin and Keller 2003). Accordingly, whether this alteration is intentional or just an editorial oversight, it is now necessary to present an analysis of the science and potential politics behind this new textbook terminology.

EVOLUTIONARY SCIENCE AND EXTINCTION

Mark Sagoff (1999) claims that over 99 percent of all life that has ever existed is now extinct. Any natural history museum will testify to this truth. There, you can find bizarre experiments in evolution on display. Crude prehistoric anatomies in skeletal abstract form colonnades along the museum walls, and chandeliers of bone hang from the ceiling on wire. Each exhibit corresponds to an evolutionary failure. These bygone monstrosities were all outcompeted (in the Darwinian sense) by more advanced, better-adapted, or just plain luckier creatures in the slow procession of time that leads to the present day. In the words of Holmes Rolston III, "Life is advanced not only by thought and action, but by suffering, not only by logic but by pathos" (1987, 144). The natural history museum is a fitting memorial to this cruel truth. From such empirical evidence, it is easy to conclude that humankind is at the spearhead of evolution, the pinnacle of adaptation and perfection. Such displays of fossilized bone and petrified wood could very well be perceived as trophy cases testifying to our evolutionary success. Extinction, it would seem, is both inevitable and natural. At least, that is what certain environmental-policy analysts, such as Sagoff, would have us believe.

The figure cited above, that over 99 percent of all life that has ever existed is now extinct (the percentage most often cited is 99.9 percent), is badly misleading. Global biodiversity has remained relatively constant for the last 570 million years (excepting, of course, during the Cretaceous, Permian, Devonian, Ordovician, and Cambrian mass-extinction and subsequent re-speciation events). The cyclic return to a stasis of comparable species richness across the surviving taxa, versus the total biodiversity that existed before, is referred to as the phenomenon of macroevolutionary punctuated equilibrium (for further discussion, see Eldredge 1985, 176–77).[1] Simply stated, throughout geologic time, biodiversity has remained relatively constant; yet, at the same time, only 0.1 percent of that life remains. But how can both statements be true? First, it must be realized that evolution is not a game of elimination. Billions of different types of creatures did not emerge from the primordial ooze with only the top tenth of a percent still surviving today. Rather, the 99.9 percent of life forms that no longer exist did not in fact all become *fully* extinct. Here is the key to this puzzle: many of these ancient creatures disappeared from the evolutionary stage by evolving into something new.

This is the first important distinction to be made. Germline extinction (also known as clade extinction) is the death of the entire genetic legacy of a species. In contrast, in the phenomena of directional selection (also known as pseudoextinction, or chronospecies extinction), a creature becomes a new species as a result of environmental or inter- or intraspecies pressure. In both cases, the original plant or animal disappears from the face of the earth and can be said to be extinct. Germline extinction, however, represents the death of that species' evolutionary history—that particular genetic lineage has come to an end. In the case of directional selection, the lineage of the progenitors lives on in the newly emerged species, the successors to their ongoing epigenetic heritage.

To fully convey this distinction to a nonscientific audience, an analogy is often helpful. So, imagine a family tree. Now, if all the male descendents of a certain founding patriarch die due to some tragedy before another male heir is born, that family name will also die out (germline extinction). There will be, let us say, no more Billingtons of New England to carry on that family's rich history and tradition dating back, let us also say, to the time of the Pilgrims. That great family name will disappear into history, and the Billingtons will never more play a part in the unfolding history of New England. However, let us imagine that a Billington daughter (the first to be born to a Billington) survives to marry an orphan, who was given a new surname by the state. Her children will inherit a new family name. There will still be no more Billingtons, but the genetic legacy from her side of the family will live on in her children (directional selection). Likewise, if two daughters survive to marry and have children, two new family trees will be created through their husbands, who will be the founding patriarchs of new germlines. Though rudimentary and somewhat problematic with respect to representing the complex biology of evolution (not to mention its chauvinist overtones!), the scientific laity can think of the extinction and establishment of new family names as a good proxy for the distinction between germline extinction and directional selection.

For a better and specific biological example, we have to look no further than to Charles Darwin. His fame comes from observing that the finches of the Galapagos Islands were somehow related to a particular South American finch species (*Volatinia jacarina* or a close relative), yet no South American finches remained in the Galapagos. This mystery helped spawn the theory of descent with modification. Looking back on his findings, it can now be said that the South American finches had become extirpated (a geographically localized extinction) from the Galapagos. But they were not actually gone. Again, this is the key distinction. While there were no more South American finches left after an unknown number of generations once they became stranded on the islands, the descendents of these finches survived. Through directional selection, the progenitor finches became thirteen new species of finch, all different from one another and all distinct from the original South American finch. This is how evolution works to maintain biodiversity. Because of this phenomenon, it is also true to say that the dinosaurs never really became extinct. Their distinct anatomical homologies are preserved in all modern bird species. An American bald eagle is a *Tyrannosaurus rex* in feathered miniature (both share a distant blood relative as a common ancestor). Likewise, the Galapagos finches have the epigenetic heritage of dinosaur DNA at their disposal. (Perhaps this helps explain why they are such consummate survivors!) The point is, again, that extinction may not really be extinction at all, but evolution producing a new form of life from a less well-adapted predecessor.

And so, to reiterate the key points, if 99.9 percent of all life forms that ever existed were truly extinct, then the earth would have very few species indeed. But there are around ten million, and possibly as many as fifty million, different kinds of species alive today—roughly the same in geologic ages past. This signifies that with each germline extinction, there has been a directional selection to take the species' place, either occupying its predecessor's former environmental niche or finding a new niche that has emerged in response to changing environmental conditions. Now we arrive at the final thrust of this line of argument. The extinctions caused by humankind, such as with the aforementioned dodo bird and the passenger pigeon, are all germline extinctions. Their deaths did not result in natural directional selection in response to changing environmental conditions. This was instead the indiscriminate elimination of entire genetic lineages based merely upon economic expedience. By way of another rough analogy, the historical human impact on nature has been comparable to a Mafia "hit" that executes every last man, woman, and child at a family reunion, leaving no heirs to that family name. Such was the fate of the dodo bird and the passenger pigeon.[2] Nothing natural (i.e., in accord with the evolutionary history of the planet prior to human dominance) can be claimed to explain away these species' capricious and complete extermination from the face of the earth. To contend that these were somehow "premature extinctions" seriously misrepresents the true science. Such unsupportable and disreputable rhetoric has no place in environmental education. It is junk science at its worst.

ANTHROPOCENTRIC IMPACTS UPON THE BACKGROUND EXTINCTION RATE

Stuart Pimm et al. (1995) determined that species have lasted, on average, one to ten million years before becoming extinct (0.1 to 1 extinction per million species years) by examining the geological record. Of course, there are examples of species that long outlive this average species lifetime, such as Devonian-age sturgeons and the primordial blue-green algae, which is at least 3.5 billion years old (and very well may have been the directional-selection source for all life on the planet today). These incredibly ancient creatures refute the widely held, nonscientific belief that evolution always favors anatomical and cognitive advancement over comparatively more primitive species. Even in archaic physiology, evolution has perfected species' ecological adaptations. Despite being in the midst of more complex and sophisticated species, the older were not rendered obsolete. These so-called ancient relicts (Holdgate 1996, 415) disprove the unsupportable idea that germline extinction equates with evolutionary progress.

In terms of the overall average for all lifetimes, considering species that have not (and may never) become extinct[3] and those that disappeared quickly, Pimm et al. arrived at an estimate that one species per million (using the highest rate) naturally becomes extinct each year. The probable total number of species is far higher than the documented number, and the current estimates, as mentioned above, range from ten million to fifty million (May 1988; Wilson 1992), with as much as 80 percent of all species possibly being insects (Erwin 1997). So, multiplying the average against the total, this equates to approximately ten to fifty species that naturally become extinct each year. Using the more conservative estimate, about eight insects plus another two species from the collective plant and animal kingdoms become extinct annually. This is called the "background rate" of extinction, which is the natural rate before considering human impacts to ecosystems. Again, the term *background rate of extinction* implies that these species either died out completely or became something new. The ten annual species extinctions must also be measured against the ten million species in existence at any given time. Natural extinction is an exceedingly rare and improbable event—literally, it is (at most) a one-in-a-million chance.

Despite these nearly impossible odds against natural species death, the current rate of extinction is now one thousand to ten thousand times the background rate (Miller 2004a, 453; cf. Pimm et al. 1995, 348–49).[4] This translates to a figure of between ten thousand and five hundred thousand species per year that are now becoming extinct, instead of the ten to fifty species that become extinct naturally. What is worse, these anthropocentrically induced extinctions are all of the germline variety. Worse still, plant and animal species (particularly top predators) are being disproportionately killed off by humankind's usurping of terrestrial ecosystems for short-term economic benefit. The combined effect is that overall global biodiversity is declining drastically. It is estimated that 20 percent of the life forms on the planet will become germline extinct by 2030, and half of the global biodiversity will be gone by 2100 (Miller 2004a, 453).[5]

The phrase "premature extinction" conceals these tragic realities behind a facade of naturalistic inevitability.[6] But the harsh truth is ecocide, the capricious destruction of life forms throughout the biosphere by humankind.[7] One has to wonder how such a peculiar and nonscientific term entered the academic vernacular.

POLITICAL TRENDS IN CONSERVATION BIOLOGY

A recent paper discussing the ecological significance of biodiversity by Holdgate (1996) defines the value of species in terms of ecosystem function, suggesting that the loss of biodiversity can in some cases be absorbed by the functional redundancy of species. Holdgate further contends that it is "scientifically untenable" to claim that all species must be saved from extinction for resource policy to be considered sustainable (1996, 415). Such conclusions reveal a utilitarian bias that has emerged in the now ironically named science of conservation biology. Species tend to be seen only in terms of their potential value in ecosystem services for the benefit of humankind, not their intrinsic or existence values. This is one consequence of the New Perspectives ecosystem approach used by federal agencies for the management of public lands and endangered species (see Kessler et al. 1992; Salwasser 1999). The New Perspectives program is cloaked in New Age buzzwords that seek to quiet environmental concerns, such as the phrase "holistic resource management" (Salwasser 1999, 88). Yet, this holism is not really meant as a means to ensure a particular ecosystem's overall health (as may be inferred from the connotations of this word) but rather to ensure that humankind's economic stakeholders are to be included in all decisions involving natural resource policy, including whether to designate critical habitats for endangered species. Wilderness preservation, biodiversity, and economic gain have become competing anthropocentric values to be balanced by resource managers for areas without the protected habitats needed by at-risk species. Alarmingly, this balance is not being maintained, and endangered species under the New Perspectives program are four times more likely to exhibit a declining status and to be headed for germline extinction than species under traditional "nonholistic" approaches (Boersma et al. 2001). The carefully crafted nomenclature hides the true reality.[8] In a battle of words, no one could possibly be against the idea of holistic ecosystem management. Only later is it revealed that the outcome is something different. It is with the tools of rhetoric that public opinion can be swayed, and this is exactly how the New Perspectives program came to be adopted by federal agencies.

Conservation biology, in seeking to preserve its status as a normative science, has embraced an economic and utilitarian ethic for the valuation of endangered species. But strict reliance on economic analyses introduces a bias in favor of development and, indeed, necessitates environmentally sensitive areas' undergoing economic improvement (Sagoff 2000). Sagoff (1999) has also challenged the seemingly self-evident principle that protecting native species is an environmental good. Instead, Sagoff argues that invasions of exotic species into pristine ecosystems caused by humankind are just as natural as our excursions into these areas. Though he admits invasive exotics may lead to the extinction of native endemics, he is quick to mention (as already discussed) that over 99 percent of species that have ever existed are now extinct. For Sagoff, extinction is a natural consequence of healthy evolutionary competition (see also Fitzsimmons 1999, 129). He even goes as far as to suggest that if society wants to control invasive exotic fauna populations, such as the European green shore crabs (*Carcinus maenas*) and the Asian rapa whelks (*Rapana venosa*) infesting North American waterways, "executive orders may be less effective than [distributing] recipes" and a better use of public funds. This strange environmental philosophy embraces an unconstrained capitalistic ethic that even denies the legitimacy of environmental preservation performed for the public good (see also Sagoff 2002).[9]

While Sagoff is perhaps unparalleled in his ability to twist environmentalist logic to support the anthropocentric agenda, what is most fascinating, and disturbing, is that such obviously prejudiced arguments against environmental causes are taken more seriously in the public forum than the preservationist counterarguments proffered by environmental philosophers and deep ecologists. Those producing mainstream scientific, economic, and policy analysis studies have deliberately circumvented any mention of intrinsic value or biotic rights in their published papers, either out of disdain for such perceived sentimentalism or fear of being summarily discounted by their critics (see Herrick and Jamieson 2001). Yet, this is clearly a bias. The public debate has not been resolved, and important stakeholders are now being increasingly excluded. Bill Devall, for example, has urged that natural areas be set aside for "future generations of all creatures, rocks, and trees," not for anthropocentric uses. Likewise, deep ecologists Arne Naess and George Sessions have argued that natural areas must be considered "independent of the usefulness of the non-human world for human purposes" (Nash 1989, 149–50). Yet, none of these counterarguments are being represented in the scientific papers submitted to policy makers and legislators. Instead, policy analysts and conservation biologists are tacitly, and at times explicitly, advocating further ecological degradation under the current guise of holistic ecosystem management.[10]

CONCLUSIONS AND RECOMMENDATIONS

This chapter does not argue that philosophical opinion ought to be taught in science classrooms. The above comments are intended to illustrate how the phrase "premature extinction" now appears to be at the apex of the political debate between two opposing camps, just as the related phrase "holistic resource management" was beforehand. The G. Tyler Miller Jr. textbooks are now clearly showing partiality to one side of the debate while marginalizing the other. The textbook *Living in the Environment* (Miller 2004b), for example, contains a chapter entitled "Sustaining Wild Species," which is pervaded with the phrase "premature extinction" to contextualize improperly the information therein, but it only provides brief mention of deep ecology and environmental philosophy in the very last chapter of an eight-hundred-page textbook. Educators know very well that that the last chapter is seldom reached in any given semester. The alarmingly scant information relegated to these back pages may just as well have been left out entirely.

   Environmental science education must be restored to its proper expression as an unbiased agency of normative instruction. To do this, the phrase "premature extinction" needs only to be eliminated from textbooks and curricula. The real science will speak for itself. With regard to the larger debate being waged between deep ecologists and those who argue for unconstrained anthropocentric entitlement, these issues can be addressed in a liberal studies colloquium, an environmental philosophy class, or any other elective directed to such aims. The point is, again, that a science course must be free of hidden prejudice and political agendas, especially those passed off as scientific fact. Action should therefore be taken to eliminate any science textbook that includes the scientifically unsupportable phrase "premature extinction" from the classroom. Miller should move quickly to correct this quality-assurance breakdown.

POSTSCRIPT FOR ENVIRONMENTAL PHILOSOPHY EDUCATORS

Conservation biologists tend to ignore the existence values of nonhuman species, focusing instead on their utility in terms of ecosystem services for humankind. Animal-liberation activists would characterize this as symptomatic of a culture of oppression, a sociological pathology extended to the sphere of nonhuman life. An ideologically similar argument is found with Nobel laureate Albert Schweitzer, who declared that a reverence for all life is necessary for humankind to truly claim its humanity.[11] To augment these philosophical arguments, educators can highlight the underappreciated potential of ecotheology in the endangered-species debate. A very brief overview of three Christian perspectives is provided in the space remaining for this chapter.

St. Maximos the Confessor of the Orthodox Church proclaimed that all life in creation contains the mark of the Creator, in that Jesus as the Word (*Logos*; cf. John 1:1–3) "ineffably hid Himself in the principles (*logoi*) of created beings for our sake, [for] He indicates Himself proportionally through each visible thing, as through certain letters, present in His utter fullness in the universe" (cited from Blowers 1991, 120). For St. Maximos, species are the "words" to the Word, and a source of divine revelation that can be "read" through contemplation (see also Edwards 1999, 715). Catholicism has a similar tradition. St. Thomas Aquinas, in confirming the doctrines of St. Augustine, declared that nature possessed intrinsic value, for "in all creatures there is found the trace of the Trinity" (*Summa Theologiae*, Part 1, Q.45, Art. 7). St. Aquinas also pronounced that "creatures lead us to the knowledge of God, as effects do to their cause" (*Summa Theologiae*, Part 1, Q.32, Art. 1). Protestantism professes this same truth. Yet, because of the influence of sin on the common man, John Calvin believed that "in vain for us, therefore, does Creation exhibit so many bright lamps lighted up to show forth the glory of its Author" (*Institutes*, First Book, Ch. 5, Sec. 14). This brief overview of historical Christian doctrine can be used as counterpoint to the famous 1967 essay of Lynn White Jr. The blame for the modern ecological crisis, he wrote, lay squarely with Christianity's misconstrued sense of entitlement to the earth's resources, unconstrained by either humility or common sense, resulting from specious reading of historical doctrines and biblical scripture (see Goodin 2005). But, what Christianity became in facilitating environmental degradation does not prevent the church from becoming the agent of its restoration.

The Delhi Sands flower-loving fly (*Rhaphiomidas terminatus abdominalis*) and the deltoid spurge (*Chamaesyce deltoidea deltoidea*) may never provide a cure for cancer, be appreciated for their beauty, or be of any other utility to the general public. This would seem to be a death sentence. Yet, each species and subspecies exist as words to the Word in the book of nature; to destroy these creations erases the words and defaces the natural testament that makes known the Creator (cf. Psalms 104). Anthropocentrically induced germline extinctions obliterate the presence of God in the created order and intercede against God's will for creation to be restored from the corruption caused by humankind (cf. Romans 8:21; St. Irenæus *A.H.* 5.32.1). Current environmental policy has rationalized and facilitated this ongoing desecration. But there is still time for change.

NOTES

1. Punctuated equilibrium also refers to cladogenesis, the sudden emergence of new species without transitional phases. It should also be noted that some estimates indicate global biodiversity steadily increasing over the last five hundred million years despite periodic mass-extinction events (e.g., see McMenamin and McMenamin 1994, 17).

2. Some contend that overhunting simply led to a decrease in the population of these species to a level below the "minimum viable population" needed for survival, whereupon the coup de grâce came from disease, insufficient genetic diversity, invasive exotics overtaking their niches, or a combination thereof. Such nuanced distinctions, however, do not counter or mitigate the true precipitating cause for their germline extinctions: the needless killing of entire populations for short-term benefit to humankind.

3. The continuing existence of ancient life forms, like six-gill sharks and cypress trees, reveals the fallacy of assuming that all species are destined someday to die out. This fact alone refutes the concept of premature extinction because no species necessarily ever has to become extinct.

4. This chapter is careful to include the very G. Tyler Miller Jr. textbook being critically reviewed as a source of this central figure. The Miller series, in this author's opinion, was deservedly a leader in environmental science textbooks for its thoroughness, clarity, and conscientious presentation of oftentimes complex scientific findings. And so, while the relevant information is still present in the Miller texts for educators and students, the science is superseded by the caveat "premature extinction," which denotes an opposite conclusion to that which would logically be induced from the objective data. The phrase "premature extinction" functions as a rhetorical trope aimed squarely at the preservationist movement. Although it is unstated in the textbooks, this new phrase effectively undermines the effort to preserve

endangered species, as this would necessarily have to be perceived by students as an irrational attempt at trying to prevent the inevitable and a fight against nature itself.

5. Thomas et al. (2004) report extinction rates ranging from 18 percent (best case) to 35 percent (worst case) by 2050 from climate change alone.

6. Such a position is philosophically inconsistent. First, the phrase "premature extinction," to be scientifically legitimate, must differentiate a known phenomenon. So, what could this phrase distinguish from other extinctions? Are there, for instance, overdue extinctions or timely extinctions that science can identify? Horseshoe crabs (*Limulus spp.*) have been around for five hundred million years and would seem to be long overdue for extinction. Does the presence of such anachronisms point to an evolutionary oversight requiring correction by human intervention, a counterpoint to the premature extinctions? Facetiousness aside, there is obviously no such phenomenon of overdue extinction; consequently, there are no premature extinctions either. There is only the average for all species lifetimes identified by Pimm et al. in 1995. This normative fact also helps to reveal a second philosophical flaw. The phrase premature extinction necessarily places humans outside nature. The only extinction that could be premature (i.e., not in accord with the natural rate) would have to be caused by an external agent. To wit, all extinctions occurring within nature would be neither premature nor overdue: they would simply be extinctions in accord with the overall average. The concept of premature extinction is therefore self-refuting. To digress further into environmental philosophy would not be germane here. The point is to show both the scientific and philosophical incoherence of this phrase, not to offer a full treatment of the question of whether the human species is still an integral member of the biotic community, even though we are virtually immune to the environmental constraints that shape the population dynamics of all other life forms in nature.

7. A flawed counterargument is that humankind's impact upon the biosphere is comparable to the comet/meteor impacts believed to have caused previous mass-extinction events; thus, the argument continues, the anthropocentrically caused extinctions are somehow mitigated by precedent. In reality, the astrological object impacts had the result of changing environmental conditions uniformly for all species (e.g., sunlight levels, ambient temperature, turbidity in aquatic systems): when these conditions exceeded the inherent "range of tolerance" for each species, extinction occurred. In contrast, the germline extinctions caused by humankind have not been the result of changing environmental conditions. In many cases, the species' niches have been taken over by invasive exotics introduced by humankind or obliterated entirely when lands have been economically developed. Other species were hunted to extinction. Accordingly, there is no legitimate basis to claim the comparably even-handed Permian mass extinction (i.e., the same changed conditions challenged all species equally, forcing them to adapt or perish) as naturalistic precedent for humankind's capricious ecocide. Likewise, on account of the unique impacts and changes caused by humankind, there is no precedent to claim that adaptive radiations will restore biodiversity in the future.

8. Several recent studies have examined the factors involved in endangered-species recovery-plan implementation and found that the "holistic" multispecies plans had a lower level of task implementation (Lundquist et al. 2002) and were actually a less effective management tool than single-species plans (Boersma et al.

2001; Lundquist et al. 2002). In addition, Clark and Harvey (2002) criticized multispecies plans for lacking a threat similarity analysis to determine appropriate species for concurrent management. Multispecies plans also appear to be biased toward certain types of species (Lundquist et al. 2002). Still, proponents would argue that the potential for initial imperfections is accounted for with multispecies plans and that these problems are to be addressed through adaptive management. However, Clark and Harvey (2002) concluded that adaptive management, in practice, has not been more flexible to changing conditions or new information. It must also be recognized that the most critical problem affecting both single species plans and holistic plans is the severe underfunding of the species recovery programs under the Endangered Species Act (ESA). Miller et al. (2002) examined historical recovery-plan funding versus recovery-plan costs and found that overall recovery program funding was only 18 percent of the requested levels for all species on average—an inexcusably severe underfunding of the recovery programs that has lead to the erroneous conclusion that the ESA is ineffectual legislation (cf. Miller et al. 1994). Even so, the traditional nonholistic plans still outperform the holistic management plans. In addition, the New Perspectives program denies the legitimacy of individual geographic areas as ecosystems, instead claiming this designation is a matter of "our convenience" (Salwasser 1999, 86), and further calls for "opening the [land use] decision-making process" to economic interests (95). This has resulted in the disfavoring of new critical habitats under the ESA despite the fact that critical habitat designation is positively correlated with species recovery-plan task implementation (Lundquist et al. 2002). The good intentions on the part of those developing this new policy initiative have not translated into greater species protection. Thus, it appears that the emergent de facto consequence of the New Perspectives program is that it has served as a "Trojan horse" to facilitate further economic encroachment into habitats needed by at-risk species, pushing these species closer to germline extinction. Demonstrating the power of rhetoric to create erroneous impressions of the underlying reality, such as with the examples of holistic ecosystem management and premature extinction, is one aim of this analysis.

9. Sagoff (2002) offers a flawed counterargument against preserving undeveloped natural areas for ecosystem services. He ignores nonpoint source pollution, such as volatile organic hydrocarbons and dissolved toxic metals associated with suburban and urban runoff (pollutants that are subject to bioremediation/sequestration), pretreatment of agricultural runoff (gray-water wetland concept), as well as the quantifiable recreational and existence values of restored natural areas. Sagoff narrowly focuses on only the biogenic pathogens that would be addressed by mandatory filtration and disinfection required for surface water treatment plants. He thus creates an erroneous economic argument against the planned safeguarding of the Catskill drainage basin.

10. Policy analysts marginalize preservation ethics by considering species existence values as just another anthropocentric interest to be balanced against economic interests, using political consensus among the recognized (human) stakeholders as a proxy for measuring policy efficacy. Such methodology is inherently flawed if it does not explicitly recognize the priority of the philosophical questions concerning extinction—just like the ethics of euthanasia supersede cost-benefit

analyses on patient care. Some conservation biologists, however, go further by dismissing the existence values of "functionally redundant" and "relict" species from the onset in their position papers, which represents both a reprehensible bias and a shocking nullification of the stated goals of the ESA.

11. Schweitzer (1923), a preeminent scholar of religion and philosopher, stated that "the world is indeed the grisly drama of will-to-live at variance with itself. One existence survives at the expense of another of which it yet knows nothing. But in me the will-to-live has become cognizant of the existence of other will-to-live" (148). From this, Schweitzer concluded that "a man [sic] is really ethical only when he obeys the constraint laid on him to help all life which he is able to succor, and when he goes out of his way to avoid injuring anything living" (146).

REFERENCES

Ante-Nicene Fathers. [1885]1993. Irenæus: Against Heresies. In *The Ante-Nicene Fathers*, ed. Alexander Roberts and James Donaldson. Vol. 1. Grand Rapids, MI: William B. Eerdmans Publishing Company.

Aquinas, Thomas. 2003. *The summa theologica of St. Thomas Aquinas*, trans. Fathers of the English Dominican Province. 2nd rev. ed., available at www.newadvent.org/summa (accessed June 18, 2006).

Blowers, Paul M. 1991. *Exegesis and Spiritual Pedagogy in Maximus the Confessor: An Investigation of the* Quaestiones ad Thalassium. Notre Dame, IN: University of Notre Dame Press.

Boersma, P. D., P. Kareiva, W. F. Fagan, J. A. Clark, and J. M. Hoekstra. 2001. How good are endangered species plans? *BioScience* 51: 643–50.

Botkin, Daniel B., and Edward A. Keller. 2003. *Environmental science: Earth as a living planet.* 4th ed. New York: John Wiley & Sons.

Calvin, John. 1997. *Institutes of the Christian religion*, trans. Henry Beveridge. Albany, OR: AGES Software (CD-ROM).

Clark, J. Alan, and Erik Harvey. 2002. Assessing multi-species recovery plans under the Endangered Species Act. *Ecological Applications* 12 (3): 655–62.

Edwards, Denis. 1999. The ecological significance of God-language. *Theological Studies* 1 (December): 708–22.

Eldredge, Niles. 1985. *Time frames: The rethinking of Darwinian evolution and the theory of punctuated equilibria.* New York: Simon and Schuster.

Erwin, Terry L. 1997. Biodiversity at its utmost: Tropical forest beetles. *Biodiversity II: Understanding and protecting our biological resources*, ed. Majorie L. Reaka-Kudla, Don E. Wilson, and Edward O. Wilson. Washington, DC: Joseph Henry Press.

Fitzsimmons, Alan K. 1999. *Defending illusions: Federal protection of ecosystems.* Lanham, MD: Rowman & Littlefield.

Goodin, David K. 2005. *Understanding humankind's role in creation: Alternate exegeses on the Hebrew word kabash, and the command to subdue the earth*, ed. Hubert Meisinger, Willem B. Drees, and Zbigniew Liana. Studies in Science and Theology (SSTh) 10: Yearbook of the European Society for the Study of Science and Theology. Lund, Sweden: Lund University Press.

Herrick, Charles N., and D. Jamieson. 2001. Junk science and environmental policy: Obscuring public debate with misleading discourse. *Philosophy and Public Policy Quarterly* 21 (2/3) (Spring/Summer): 11–16.

Holdgate, Martin. 1996. The ecological significance of biological diversity. *Ambio* 25 (6): 409–16.

Kaufman, Donald G., and Cecilia M. Franz. 2000. *Biosphere 2000: Protecting our global environment.* 3rd. ed. Dubuque, IA: Kendall/Hunt Publishing Company.

Kessler, Winifred, Hal Salwasser, Charles W. Cartwright Jr., and James A. Caplan. 1992. New Perspectives for Sustainable Natural Resources Management. *Ecological Applications* 2 (3): 221–25.

Lundquist, Carolyn J., Jennifer M. Diehl, Erik Harvey, and Louis W. Botsford. 2002. Factors affecting implementation of recovery plans. *Ecological Applications* 12 (3): 713–18.

Marsh, William M., and John M. Grossa Jr. 2002. *Environmental geography: Science, land use, and earth systems.* 2nd ed. New York: John Wiley & Sons.

May, Robert M. 1988. How many species are there on earth? *Science* 241:1441–49.

McMenamin, Mark, and Dianna McMenamin. 1994. *Hypersea: Life on land.* New York: Columbia University Press.

Miller, Brian, Richard Reading, Courtney Conway, Jerome A. Jackson, Michael Huchings, Noel Snyder, Steve Forrest, Jack Frazier, and Scott Derrickson. 1994. A model for improving endangered species recovery programs. *Environmental Management* 18:637–45.

Miller, George Tyler, Jr. 1995. *Environmental science: Working with the earth.* 5th ed. Belmont, CA: Wadsworth Publishing Company.

——. 1996. *Living in the environment: Principles, connections, and solutions.* 9th ed. Belmont, CA: Wadsworth Publishing Company.

——. 1997. *Environmental science: Working with the earth.* 6th ed. Belmont, CA: Wadsworth Publishing Company.

——. 2004a. *Environmental science: Working with the earth.* 10th ed. Belmont, CA: Wadsworth Publishing Company.

——. 2004b. *Living in the environment: Principles, connections, and solutions.* 13th ed. Belmont, CA: Wadsworth Publishing Company.

Miller, Julie K., J. Michael Scott, Craig R. Miller, and Lisette P. Waits. 2002. The Endangered Species Act: Dollars and sense. *BioScience* 52 (2): 163–69.

Nash, Roderick Frazier. 1989. *The rights of nature: A history of environmental ethics.* Madison: University of Wisconsin Press.

Pimm, Stuart L., Gareth J. Russell, John L. Gittleman, and Thomas M. Brooks. 1995. The future of biodiversity. *Science.* 269: 347–50.

Rolston, Holmes, III. 1987. *Science and religion: A critical survey.* Philadelphia: Temple University Press.

Sagoff, Mark. 1999. What's wrong with exotic species? *Report from the Institute for Philosophy and Public Policy* 19 (4) (Fall): 16–23.

——. 2000. Environmental economics and the conflation of value and benefit. *Environmental Science and Technology* 34 (8): 1426–32.

——. 2002. On the value of natural ecosystems: The Catskill parable. *Philosophy and Public Policy Quarterly* 22 (1/2) (Winter/Spring): 10–16.

Salwasser, Hal. 1999. Ecosystem management: A new perspective for national forests and grasslands. In *Ecosystem Management*, ed. W. Burch, J. Aley, B. Conover, and D. Field. Philadelphia: Taylor and Francis.

Schweitzer, Albert. [1923]1999. *Ethical vegetarianism: From Pythagoras to Peter Singer*, ed. Kerry Walters and Lisa Portmess. New York: State University of New York Press.

Thomas, Chris D., et al. 2004. Extinction risk from climate change. *Nature* 427 (January 8): 145–48.

White, Lynn, Jr. 1967. The historical roots of our ecological crisis. *Science* 155 (March 10): 1203–1207.

Wilson, Edward O. 1992. *The diversity of life*. Cambridge, MA: Harvard University Press.

13

Hooters Pedagogy: Gender in Late Capitalism

Nathalia Jaramillo

Gender in late capitalism is often considered outmoded, unfashionable, or "anti-chic"; in other words, it is irrelevant to the main social problematic of the era (following Karl Marx), namely, the fundamental social relation of labor in capitalism. But by ignoring the integral concept of gender in late capitalism, educators in the main fail to understand the ways in which capital, as the most preponderant and rapacious economic, social, and political system on a global scale, offers new form and content to understanding the culture of empire and the politics of imperialism. Our profound ignorance with respect to matters of gender is not unanticipated or that revealing. From capitalism's primordial age, women have participated as active producing agents in the domestic sphere, but their work has been disregarded, devalued, and discarded as a manifestation of a woman's genetic differences from men. And we have the embarrassing, yet illustrative example, of Harvard University president Lawrence Summers, who posited the genetics hypothesis to a private conference on economics (Hemel 2005). According to Summers, marked discrepancies between men and women on achievement tests in math and science can emerge from "innate" genetic differences between the sexes (rather than institutional and social frameworks that condition men and women into different fields of study). Comments like those of Summers remind critical educators that the need for feminist critique can no longer be considered a sidebar issue and that we must continue to respond to the moment by addressing the "gender question."

It was not until the 1970s that feminists broke the silence around the taboo concept of gender by activating a social movement that could no longer overlook or deny a woman's place as a deserving citizen worthy of the human rights often restricted to their biological counterpart. Feminist theory made great strides and contributions in articulating a politics of liberation and developing a language of critique that included and held central the lives of women, but it also fell prey to essentialist Western-based conceptions of feminism, or gender. While the work of women of color, such as Gloria Anzaldúa, Cherrie Moraga, and bell hooks, added necessary complexity to the concept of gender in late capitalism by theorizing the importance of race and other material factors, it often remains, to this day, a theoretical aside or conceptual add-on to our understanding of broader social phenomena. Gender's relevance to the social condition of the era should be self-evident, especially as it unequivocally threads through the red, white, and blue fabric of the imperialist doctrine of U.S.-led warfare. Female interrogators at the U.S. military prison at Guantánamo Bay feign menstruation on male Muslim inmates prior to prayer because "Muslims believe that if a woman touches him prior to prayer, then he's dirty and can't pray" (Tate 2005), and working-class white women "pussy whip" Muslim men in the prison chamber of Abu Ghraib (Eisenstein 2004) as a sign of U.S. virility and dominance. As Zillah Eisenstein notes,

> Gender differentiation will be mobilized for war and peace. This is the ugly side of the rewired patriarchy or war-capitalism. Bush's war of/on terror masks its realpolitik—that of a racist capitalist misogyny operating in drag for unilateral empire building. Abu Ghraib showed us that humanity and inhumanity comes in all colors and genders. (2004)

The social relations of capitalism have profound consequences on people, on nation-states, on ecology, and on the future of humanity in general, which should caution and compel us to unearth the hidden complexities in how we understand *gendered* social relations or activity. However, the transnational capitalist class would like to convince people around the globe that the processes and seemingly uncontested spread of capital (i.e., globalization) is a humanizing project (albeit through the barrel of a gun) that provides the world's poor with gold card opportunities toward self-sustenance. In particular, the introduction of women into the public sphere of production has been regarded as a welcome and necessary shift for alleviating chronic poverty, rupturing traditional roles between the sexes, and ushering in an era of unbeknownst equity and democracy. But the mere introduction of women into the strata of paid labor does not erase or eliminate gendered hierarchies and forms of exploitation. On the contrary, we can look to the femicide of women in the *maquilas* of Juárez as a daunting example of the ways in which gender serves as a "marker of worker brands" (Wright 2001). As Melissa Wright pointedly asserts, the tale of turnover in the maquilas demonstrates how women take the shape of variable capital "whose worth fluctuates from a status of value to one of waste" (2001, 126).

The purpose of this chapter is to explore further our conceptions and engagements with gender through the lives of working women. This is not the only point from which to articulate gender in late capitalism, but it does provide a necessary lens for understanding otherwise hidden, neglected, or "benign" forms of being in the world that hinder our progress toward more egalitarian forms of sociability. One of the central arguments posited here is that a study of gender cannot be delinked from the social relations of capitalism, specifically at the level of production.

This chapter represents the culmination of an ethnographic journey into a growing U.S.-based conglomerate, Hooters, Inc. Ranked as one of the most successful and fastest-growing restaurant chains in the United States and abroad, with an estimated $750 million in annual revenues, Hooters, Inc., unabashedly asserts that "it was the girls that gave Hooters legs that other theme restaurants lacked" (Heylar 2003). Because of the restaurant's unabashed marketing of the female body and because of its motto that "sex sells," Hooters served as a prime site to focus on the interplay between gendered identities and capital.

It is important to note that while I embarked on this study centering on women as the unit of analysis, my lens for understanding women was paired with an analysis of men and the ways in which the material environment mediated the relations between and within the sexes. Methodologically, it was necessary to execute a dialectical mode of analysis that would capture the web of relations that mutually informed the constitution of gender. In other words, I began to consider how men and women mutually spoke to each others' gendered formations and the ways in which the built environment worked to sustain and perpetuate them with the sole purpose of extracting surplus value from its workers. Further, I made the methodological decision to focus on the co-construction of heterosexual gendered identities since both the built environment and the restaurant's social practices signified heterosexual relations. Although Hooters, Inc., does not shy away from the motto "sex sells," I became more interested in how "sex" came into being and how those social relations were informed by the restaurant's built environment. Like any ethnographic project, a flurry of ethical considerations impacted this research project. As feminist scholars have documented previously, a researcher cannot evade the problematic of power, of position, and of place between the object and subject of analysis. And yet, on the other side, this project is one about challenging assumptions and letting go of the moral *oeuvre* that often plagues how we view gendered behavior and relations. It is a project rooted in critique that does not fail to consider the profit motives of Hooters, Inc., in shaping and informing the co-construction of gendered identities but that nonetheless seeks to make a small contribution to how social scientists view gender and to understanding how gender shifts and changes in this heightened era of capitalist accumulation. Hooters pedagogy ultimately speaks to the economies of sex that school men and women in relating to their surroundings and to each other in contextually specific ways. It captures the pervasive logic of production and consumption that allows us to consider gender in relation to capitalism. Following Fredric Jameson (1991), late capitalism designates an era marked by the cultural logic of capitalism. This does not cast Marxist theory into the proverbial dustbin of history, but it does propel us to examine capital and its attendant cultural factors in historically and materially specific ways.

UNPACKING GENDER: CRITICAL FEMINIST THEORY

The last several decades have witnessed a renewed focus on the female body as the site, or origin, of experience. Western feminist-standpoint theorists (Haraway 1991; Harding 2004; Hartsock 2004; Smith 1974) have advocated for a return to the "body" to understand women's position in existing social structures. Using a Marxist framework as a starting point, the feminist standpoint emerged with a focus on the concrete, bodily, and gendered experiences of women as a source from which to articulate localized and different understandings of the dominant social structure. The underlying premise is that "starting off research from women's lives will generate less partial and distorted accounts not only of women's lives but also of men's lives and the whole social order" (Harding 2004). For feminist-standpoint theorists, women's bodily experiences offer creative sites of exploration and meaning making that will ultimately undress dominant social structures and expose multifarious forms of oppression. Through standpoint, the woman is viewed within a broader social framework where not only is her body implicated in labor's sphere of production but she is also concerned in the reproductive sphere of production, or what Nancy Hartsock has termed the "sexual division of labor." Based on the collective and gendered lives of women, the feminist standpoint calls upon researchers to move beyond individual understandings and experiences into what Dorothy Smith describes as an "exploration" past one's tacit knowledge and into that "of what passes beyond it and is deeply implicated in how it is" (1974, 29). Although a feminist standpoint implies causality between the "local" and the "social whole" rather than viewing social phenomena as linear, standpoint claims a dialectical lens of analysis where the specificity of oppression considered is interlocked in a web of broader social relations. Standpoint does not diffuse the problematic of class, race, culture, or sexuality (to name a few), but it is in the process of abstracting knowledge from the singular unit of the concrete and understanding the complex unit of the whole that multiple and shared awareness is developed. Within these conceptual frameworks, research attempts to work with, and not for, women who live on the margin. The object of research is twofold. The process of generating knowledge from "below" to describe social structures from "above" is seen as the first step of the project. But "awareness" must be followed by an act of collective "agency," in which women subvert dominant patriarchal structures and change things from the way they have been done to the way that they could be. The challenge for standpoint theorists remains, however, in deconceptualizing women as an all-encompassing category and in recognizing that women, depending on where they are situated across class, race, and sexual planes, experience varying degrees of marginality.

Feminists along a similar, yet different, continuum have become increasingly concerned with an aesthetic or cultural focus on the body to expose the ways in which gender, sexuality, or both are constructed. Judith Butler's thesis on performativity has led to a focus on how the body serves as a site of performance, where gender "is manufactured through a sustained set of acts, posited through the gendered stylization of the body" (Butler 1999, xv). A thesis of performativity can erroneously lead to fetishized and cosmetic notions of gender that neglect to consider the full spectrum of social life. It was not until Butler's subsequent work that the notion of performativity has been reconceptualized within a material framework. Normalizing sex implies that gender becomes "natural" or "usual" vis-à-vis material surroundings that inform and sustain gendered identities. A project that views gender as both a performative and material register theoretically captures, to a greater extent, the essence of gender.

Clearly, "feminists" do not share a unified perspective on how to approach feminist theory. Some speak in terms of gender (as a social construct or performance), whereas others advocate for measuring degrees of difference based on sexual distinction alone. But just as "criticalists" merge in sharing a particular value orientation in their work, feminist theorists (or theorists who advocate feminism) share an agreement that an analysis of women—articulated through discourses of identity formations, productive lives, and gendered constructions—must serve as a necessary unit of analysis when considering relations of exploitation and oppression.

Feminist theory's limitations are framed along two main axes of critique. Within the academy, a certain feminism has evolved that has been criticized as essentialist and Western and as disseminating predominantly white views of women's struggle. The debates that emerge from this work are typically associated with "equal representation, equal voice"; unsurprisingly, their political struggles are short-lived. They end when new policies have been implemented to secure a woman's placement in positions of high officio, when women are depicted as powerful objects in control of their sexuality through mainstream media, or when the history books assert that women have contributed to the development of society. In education, a "feminist success story" includes the removal of gendered stereotypes from the curriculum or the equal representation of boys and girls in the YMCA-led after-school math club. While these are important and necessary accomplishments, they remain limited and neglect the continued marginalization and exploitation that women experience on a wider, indeed global, scale. Further, they assume that feminist theory and methodology are no longer useful because "gender equity" has been achieved along certain dimensions. In the second axis of feminist theory, feminist inquiry is acknowledged for its "contributions" to critical thought but faulted for its purported failure to address the ways in which women occupy different spaces according to an overall economy of structural hierarchies. Engaged in the "primacy paradox," some strands of feminist thought claim the centrality of the female subject at the expense of broader materialist understandings of social experience.

HOOTERS PEDAGOGY

Examining how gender is constructed and normalized in sites such as Hooters requires multiple levels of analysis. Gendered culture in Hooters is both informed and determined by existing phenomena in and out of the restaurant's physical structure. Outside the restaurant, adult men and women are socially situated within an existing class and gender hierarchy, and they presumably take with them preexisting notions of gender that influence their actions inside the restaurant. Inside Hooters, a predetermined configuration of social practices, physical structures, and artifacts conveys meaning, literally and symbolically, about what gender and gender relations are. Life-sized posters of voluptuous females and an assortment of signs that emphasize "Size Matters" occupy most of the available spaces on the restaurant's walls. While this study explicitly examined interactions within the restaurant, understanding the depth and implications of Hooters requires broadening the purview and recognizing that Hooters, because of its politics of signification, fosters a space for men and women to co-construct and normalize, in part, existing gendered inclinations and tendencies. When capital and the production and exchange of money enter the equation, then it is necessary to view the construction and normalization of gendered behavior in all of its iterations. Gender, in this case, cannot be misunderstood as an instance of biological determinism—where men fancy women because they are rendered powerless by genetics or because women simply embrace their "hooters." Rather, gender is informed by its historic specificity, rooted materially in the body, in the physical structure, in the exchange of money/capital, and in society's class and gender social structures that define privilege, power, womanness, and manness. A look into Hooters is a look into the restaurant's built environment—the physical structure and its material artifacts—and its social practices. It is a place where the female body becomes the central focus and where interactions between men and women mutually define gender. Taken together, this material configuration outlines how gender was and is performed and idealized.

The female body served as a conduit for gendered identity within the restaurant. For both female patrons and female waitresses, racialized degrees of "womanness" were established implicitly, depending on how close a woman came to resembling the archetypal "Hooters girl." This was made clear across multiple scenarios. The life-sized posters hanging from the front windows displayed large busted, small-waisted, light-skinned, and light-eyed women bearing a welcoming smile, while bright yellow warning signs suggested that a woman's physical assets might come at the expense of "cautionary" intellect. Signs that read "Caution Blondes on Duty," "High Levels of Hydrogen Peroxide in the Air," "Hooters at Play," and "Double Curves" suggested that, outside of the physical realm, women were mentally vacuous. Their worth, presumably, existed in their body, to the extent that they were able to satiate the observer. The varied heights and positioning of tables further entrenched these belief systems. With a "Hooters Aid" station conveniently placed in the center, men, women, boys, and girls could cock their heads back from any location in the restaurant to receive a full view of a woman's body, from head to toe, and side to side. But the working women never ceased to work. Their bodies would freely associate at the center of the station as they filled drinks and placed food orders.

> I start looking around and my eyes lock on a table across the way. Three children, two young boys and one girl with two older men. . . . Their heads are cocked back, looking at the women standing directly behind them. A "Hooters Aid Station" stands in the middle of the restaurant, where the women go to refill drinks. It is an open station, so the children and men are looking at the women at the station. More precisely, they are eyes are fixed at their rear ends. I continue to look around and watch the women as they walk to and fro. Men gaze incessantly at their rear ends.

Interestingly, I did not note any reaction from the waitresses at that moment. Presumably, they were unaware that the patrons at the table directly behind them were grossly entrenched with the rear-side view of their bodies. And further, they were preoccupied with their tasks—filling/refilling drinks and sending food orders to the kitchen. Alternatively, the degree and extent to which their bodies are on continuous display suggest that at a certain point, the prolonged gazes become normalized. No one place exists for women to escape viewing—it is part of the restaurant's normal practices. The arrangement and varied heights of tables secure a customer's gaze down her breasts as she places the drink on the table or straight up her "ass" as she bends over to pick up a fallen napkin. And it is expected that all women appreciate and seek the same level of exposure. As one of the restaurant's bouncers indicated when I refused to sit at a small table behind a tall wooden pillar that would have obstructed my view, "You want to move because you can't be seen there, huh?" Perhaps he was correct. In fact, during my initial visits, I felt myself "gazing" at the women's bodies for prolonged periods of time, but after several weeks, exposed breasts and bare rear ends hardly caused a twitch, and neither did the sustained gazes I received as a woman in a predominately male environment. What did not cease to amaze me, however, were the ways in which the restaurant exhausted every opportunity to construct, sustain, and normalize gendered identities. This was accomplished through the use of a marquee to deliver messages to the customers, through the use of paintings, drawings, and message blurbs on most, if not all, of the available wall space, and through the practice of daily rituals (i.e., birthday celebrations).

The marquee—large and brightly lit—hung on the main restaurant wall. It was often used to advertise an event (i.e., "Reserve Your Superbowl Seats Today"), but it also conveyed messages of male-female relations. Close to Valentine's Day, the sign read, "Buy a Calendar, Get a Kiss," and on another occasion, the letters spelled out, "No Man Is Happy Until a Woman Makes Him Miserable." According to Sol, one of the waitresses, the messages conveyed on the marquee were "all corporate." She elaborated: "They [corporate office] send these lists with catchy phrases or promos. . . . Its for the guys, you know, catchy phrases for the guys." It was not difficult to prove Sol's hypothesis correct, especially with oversized and brightly colored stickers that read "Falling in Love Is Hard on the Knees" plastered all over the large, stainless steel grill covering in the kitchen. But not all of the messages conveyed were truly "for the guys." Images of the virile male and the lithe female and several of the restaurant's message blurbs were directly tailored to women's "interests." A mural painting of an oversized, iron-clad, and large-groined Superman figure wrapped in a latex superhero suit greeted every woman in the bathroom stall (not to mention that when a woman pulled the paper dispenser, she was implicitly pulling at his groin). Next to him, a "Hooters Girl" maiden with feeble and supple arms draped over his overpowering physique mouthed the phrase "Every Woman Deserves Her Superhero." In the men's restroom, three bosom-heavy "Hooters girls" were strategically painted over the urinals with a ruler in hand, a sucker in mouth, and a magnifying lens conspicuously pointed toward the area that would expose men's genitals. Therefore, not only does the built environment give meaning to the archetypal "woman," but it also supports dominant notions of the archetypal "man" that defined men as virile objects bounded by the size of their genitals. Through a configuration of varied table heights and positioning, marquees, posters, signs, and mural paintings, both men and women were implicated in the construction of gendered identities. The built environment further enabled the performance of highly heterosexual and differentiated gender roles that placed women in the role of servitude (bodily and mentally through their labor) and men in a position of power over their female counterparts. However, these relations were not static or uniform across all interactions. Consider, for example, the daily ritual of celebrating customers' birthdays.

> A loud siren sounds in the restaurant. I look to where it is coming from and see a young-looking Asian male wearing a light blue shirt and khaki pants standing up on one of the tables. There are two to three waitresses standing next to him, and one of them cries out "hooter girls to the front," and another one chimes in louder "hooter girls to the front." The man has balloons tucked under his shirt to simulate breasts and two females and one male companion are seated diagonally from where he is standing, preparing to take a photograph. Roughly five Hooter girls encircle the male, and one of the girls yells out "its Andrew's birthday, and if he doesn't dance while we sing to him, then he has to buy everyone a beer in the restaurant." Andrew shakes his hips back and forth and swings his arms in the air. They sing two songs, clap, and Andrew's friends take a picture. One of the girls then jumps up and punctures the balloons through Andrew's shirt, popping both of them. In an instant, Andrew's breasts are gone, and he rejoins his table of friends.

Conversely, Sol viewed the birthday ritual as a way to undermine dominant gendered relations. She viewed birthdays as a way "of degrading them [men] for a chance, since they always get to degrade us [Hooters girls]. We see birthdays as our way to make fun and degrade them."

It is unlikely, in my view, that male customers viewed the birthday ritual as a form of ridicule, but according to Sol, it served as an opportunity for women to redefine relations between themselves and men. In fact, however, women had little to no say over the practice; it, too, was a directive from the corporate office. The built environment and the established rituals were clearly linked to an overall corporate profile designed to induce sensationalism over the female body and to support hypermasculinity by stroking men's insecurities, in an overall project of extracting and accumulating profit from women's laboring bodies and men's blinkered consumption. The gendered identities that took form and that were made manifest given these material conditions were complex, insidious, and varied widely.

John, a long-time regular and one of the waitresses, Kristie's, fiancée, spoke at length about the confluence between virility and the Hooters experience. He defined masculinity in terms of wealth, status, and prestige as a group of smirking middle-aged men dressed in Ralph Lauren polo shirts and Haggard slacks glided across the restaurant to a tabletop next to the bar while several waitresses hugged them along the way. John commented,

> Sons of a bitches. No, they're perverts. These guys know that Kristie is engaged but they like to brag, and they think that money is everything. They are merger-and-acquisition attorneys. They get shit faced drunk when they come in here so I don't know when they work. But they come in and they hit on all the girls here. But with Kristie, they come in and say they saw me sitting at the bar, and they comment to Kristie, I bet if I give him my Porsche and my country club membership he'll let me go out on a date with you.

Even though Kristie has never seriously entertained the men's advances, John became offended over the men's attempts to secure material power over his "woman." John, an attorney himself with an $80,000 salary and a BMW parked in the adjacent parking lot, presumably did not take the threat too seriously. The question then becomes, would John react differently if he did not view himself in parallel masculine terms with these men? Degrees of masculinity were clearly measured across multiple planes (appearance, wealth, and status) as various types of men frequented the establishment. The managers and waitresses described older men that entered the restaurant alone as "definitely weirder" and at times ascribed them nicknames, such as "Poltergeist," "Shrimp" and "Pussy Pouch," based on the men's physical appearances. Consider the following description by Kristie when a tall and slumped-back male, unattractive, unkempt, and wearing inexpensive clothing, in his late fifties to early sixties entered the restaurant at approximately 1 p.m. on a Saturday:

> Oh, there's pussy pouch. Yes, pussy pouch. He has this fat that just hangs from this area right here [she motions to the area below her belly button], so the girls have named him pussy pouch. We have a bunch of names for them.

She continued,

> Every time he is here, he'll only order one cup of coffee, and that's it. One time, we didn't have coffee ready, so he got up and left. He's cheap, too. He'll only tip a dollar. He is such a pervert. I'm like, why don't you go to Starbucks and buy a coffee? Ours tastes like shit.

Initially, "Pussy Pouch" sat toward the front of the restaurant, which brought Kristie sought-after relief because he avoided her section. But as the minutes ticked away and not one waitress approached him with his routine cup of coffee, he decided to move toward the back of the restaurant where other people were seated. When Kristie returned to my table, she noticed that he was seated at one of her tables, and she deliberately blurted out, "Oh shit, damn, damn, damn." For the following five minutes, several waitresses approached Kristie and offered their "condolences" for having to serve "pussy pouch." "Pussy Pouch" became a lively spectacle of ridicule. As an observer, I became increasingly confused over this customer. Indeed, he sat at his low-to-the-ground table for over an hour, sipping a cup of mass-produced, stale coffee with his eyes fixed on the young and firm female bodies that grazed his view, which made him a "pervert" from the women's perspective. Yet, at the same time, I was well aware that if the provisions of masculinity (i.e., wealth, status, physical attractiveness) applied to "Pussy Pouch," he would be subject to less vapid service and less loathsome reactions from the waitresses. The oscillation between the "ideal" and the "actual," in this case directly related to notions of masculinity. This, consequently lead to the question, What difference do the interactions between men and women make for how they construct their gendered and class identities given the conditions of Hooters? The point to be made is not so much one of change on an individual level, but, in effect, these observations lend themselves to an understanding of how gender is mediated through the production and exchange of money and the dominant and idealized forms of "maleness" and "womanness" that are the subject of this study. To capture the various iterations of these co-constructions, it is instructive here to contrast customers in the vein of "Pussy Pouch" with other regulars that frequented the restaurant. Consider the case, once again, of the mergers-and-acquisitions attorneys that arrogantly taunted John and attempted to seduce Kristie with material indulgence.

As I was sitting at the bar with Mona and Kristie, the women spoke of the various pitfalls associated with their labor. Mona articulated the multiple forms of verbal and physical harassment that the environment exposed her to as a result of her corporeal assets and the normalized belief systems associated with Hooters. Men often asked, "Jesus Christ, your tits real or fake?" and she objected to the fact that others would "start rubbing" her and "grabbing around my ass." According to Mona, Hooters "gives them a license to ask [about her breasts]." As she noted,

> If I were on the street they wouldn't ask that. It's just the environment and the stigma of Hooters, and it's unfortunate that, you know, some guys come here and think that's the green light for them. Honestly, there are a lot of guys that come in here that couldn't score these bitches seriously.

Soon thereafter, Kristie and Mona moved the conversation to the beer-drinking, boisterous group of merger-and-acquisition attorneys seated two tables behind us that had their eyes focused with particular sharpness in our direction. Kristie motioned to the regulars behind us, saying "they can get out of line." Apparently, the men had been in recently for Halloween. Mona describes the outfit she wore that day: "a gangsta outfit, and it had a little garter and a little pistol and stuff." She flips her mane back and points to one of the men in the group. "He," she remarked, "said something really rude—like, he had been drinking, he's married, and he has a baby on the way, but he was so out of line. . . . He was looking at my outfit and he was like, 'Jesus Christ, where are there cum stains on that?'" Mona continued, "all his friends and I was like 'hey . . . you are out of line.' Even Kristie looked at me, and she was like, 'oh no.'" But the conversation soon ended as Kristie remarked, "and they're really good tippers so a lot of girls will give them a lot of attention and stuff, deal with them." In a way, we dealt with them, too, as they sent over a waitress to pay for our dinner and drinks shortly thereafter.

Outside the built precincts of Hooters, the production, consumption, and exchange of capital in both the domestic and public spheres shaped power relations between men and women and informed how gender is ultimately performed. In Hooters, the women's dependence on capital influenced both her outer and inner body. For the average waitress, male patrons demonstrated their pleasure or satisfaction with her bodily assets and, secondarily, her personality via a monetary equivalent. Waitresses frequently expressed an acute understanding of their perceived value—vis-à-vis their bodily worth. As Mona and Kristie noted, their capacity to gain wages varied according to how well their personalities suited the client.

Mona: That's just the thing too. . . . I've been here so long, and I've lasted so long, and I still [have] been able to pay my bills off. There's some little girls that are like, "I don't make any money." It's like, you have to know how to work it. You have to know how to interact with people and have fun.

For Mona, "working it" went beyond frivolous or superficial flirting. She commented on the need to "educate yourself," to "be up with it and be able to carry a conversation . . . whether its politics or sports." "Education," as both Mona and Kristie alluded to, referred to a set of characteristics outside the traditional realm of degrees, diplomas, or certificates. It referred to the women's self-perceptions of intelligence and mental worth as measured by her "personality." Put plainly, a "ditsy" woman was classified as "dumb," while all others were viewed as "intelligent" or "educated." But as Kristie subsequently stated, "even the ditsy girls get good tips because they are tipsy, but some guys like that. Some guys don't like the fact that we are like we are. It's like we're on to them." As Kristie remarked, she would tell the client, "Don't bullshit me, don't give me any shit, sometimes they're like, 'uh, uh,' you know. It's like, what do you want, it's a restaurant. I'll joke around with them and stuff, but I'm not prepared to be like, 'Oh my god.'" Our conversation comes to an end as Mona remarks, "There are a lot of girls that are young, the ones that do act like that way or act that they're very young, like eighteen, nineteen, or twenty years old."

Hooters thrived on female competition for tips. The women often compared themselves to one another based on their physiques, ages, personalities, and behavior (often sexual in nature). In a setting that seeks to erase individuality and develop a homogenous "Hooters girl," women at times distinguished themselves from one another based on their perceived differences in personality and intellect. But all women shared certain things in common. From the moment they stepped foot on the freshly waxed laminate hardwood floors to fill out an application, their bodies were judged first and their personalities second. Even "regular" customers would participate in the decision-making process by giving women a "thumbs up" or a "thumbs down," while an all-male management crew interviewed the five to ten women that sought employment on a daily basis. Sol suggested that the fixed focus on the female body often led women to "change." According Sol, "Women get a lot of implants and then they start wearing a lot of makeup" as a result of being in close contact with one another in Hooters. She elaborated, "You start looking around at other people's bodies, and you want to look like that. But the girls are just getting younger. Seventeen, eighteen, nineteen, it's like looking at a magazine. You need to get what you see."

This study attempted to reveal the various ways that gendered identities emerged between the sexes and within a built environment designed to exploit and sustain highly heterosexual gendered identities. Clearly, Hooters represents an exaggerated environment that targets urban working men and seeks women to fulfill the image of the archetypal "Hooters girl"—an image predicated on working notions of "American" or "white" beauty. While one of the limitations of this study was a failure to delve into the racial dynamics present among the women and the clients, capital served as a constant mediator in the construction of gendered identities. To study, in essence, Hooters culture was to delve into the multiple threads that constructed gender. This involved an examination of the restaurant's built environment and of interactions between women and men. It is not uncommon for the lay observer to question the validity or importance of such a project. At times, male customers and female waitresses did not hesitate to question the relevance of my study. Harry, Ben, Kristie, Sol, John, and Mona all asked at least once, "What is the big deal anyway? This is just a restaurant." In fact, social researchers in the main may very well argue that Hooters is a place that releases modern women from the confines of puritan conceptions of sexuality and gendered behavior. Further, it does so at the monetary expense of men willing to pay to have their egos stroked—visually, not physically—for a short time. One male client put it thusly: "You think of Hooters as a stripbar or something, but it's just a restaurant. I mean, don't get me wrong, I like to have my fun, but not while I'm eating chicken wings." Ultimately, given this logic, women subsume and strip men of their power, leaving at the end of the workday as the ultimate benefactors, with a stash of sweat-drenched dollar bills tucked tightly inside their Diesel brand jean pockets. But this narrative, I argue, neglects to consider the material basis underlying gender relations, and it fails to capture the cunning corporate motives behind the construction of these identities and performances.

At the current historical juncture, we must closely examine the origins of our inscrutable desires to enact womanhood and manhood fully. Our gendered identities and performances are implicated in a wide range of social and cultural phenomena that do not exclude the indurate logic of capitalist accumulation and maximization. Enacting gender takes place at every level of social life. We learn, gain, and expand our understandings of "manhood" and "womanhood" through the symbolic gestures and material conditions that impact our livelihoods. Our human bodies are not exempt from commodification—we are not only consumers of products and of images, but we ultimately produce them. This study partially examined this process of production and consumption to highlight the complex and ultimately human ways in which gender is mediated, absorbed, and lived. Ultimately, Hooters is not just a restaurant. It is a situated locale of competing discourses and overdetermined social relations that symbolically transcends the limits of enclosed space and permeates our daily lexicon and performative register as we idealize, or criticize, what it ultimately means to be a woman and a man in the social production of what we term our culture.

TOWARD A CRITICAL PEDAGOGY THAT ADVOCATES FEMINISM

Relations between gender and capitalism deserve our attention, especially as critical educators around the globe attempt to shape pedagogical movements and to develop "languages of critique" and "resistance" that will aid in moving the current world toward a more humane existence. The problem, however, remains at the point of articulation. Accustomed to the free-flowing soft politics of postmodern theory that focus on the particular and its relation to difference, some educators remain suspended in thin air without a materialist politics to anchor their projects of social struggle. And conversely, those who emphasize a materialist or Marxist framework for understanding social phenomena have a tendency to treat gender as a free dangling modifier to the class or the race-class problematic. Theoretically, our challenge remains in developing a language and a methodology that is able to capture the very material relations that undergird the systems and processes of oppression—whether we are primarily concerned with race, class, gender, or a combination thereof—in a way that does not reduce one manifestation of inequality to another but provides us with a broader understanding of social phenomena. The point is not only to name or document practices but to view the gendered social organization of learning in its entirety. A feminist critical ethnography analyzes the myriad and multi-leveled ways in which cultural and social sites not only transmit normative constructions of gender but also produce them; it also opens the space for critical dialogue around mainstream notions of enacting "manhood" or "womanhood." Feminist traditions advocate different things, but ultimately, the aim is to generate knowledges that include and begin with the lives of women, unveil how both men and women are implicated in the capitalist logic and practices of exploitation and marginalization as producers and consumers, and situate analyses of gender materially and historically as an integral part of a pedagogical project of liberation and transformation.

REFERENCES

Butler, J. 1999. *Gender trouble*. New York: Routledge.
Butler, J., P. Osborne, and L. Segal. 1994. Gender as performance: An interview with Judith Butler. *Radical Philosophy* (summer).
Eisenstein, Zillah. 2004. Sexual humiliation, gender confusions and the horrors at Abu Ghraib, June 22, available at www.zmag.org/content/showarticle.cfm?SectionID=12&ItemID=5751.
Haraway, D. 1991. Situated knowledges: The science question in feminism and the privilege of partial perspective. In *Simians, Cyborgs and Women: The Reinvention of Nature*. New York: Routledge.
Harding, S. 2004. Rethinking standpoint epistemology: What is "strong objectivity?" In *The Feminist Standpoint Reader*, ed. S. Harding. New York: Routledge.
Hartsock, N. 2004. The feminist standpoint: Developing the ground for a specifically feminist historical materialism. In *The Feminist Standpoint Reader*, ed. S. Harding. New York: Routledge.
Hemel, D. 2005. Summers' comments on women and science draw ire. *The Harvard Crimson* (January 14).
Heylar, J. 2003. Hooters: A Case Study. *Fortune* 148 (4): 140–46.
Jameson, F. 1991. *Postmodernism, or the cultural logic of late capitalism*. New York: Verso Books.
Smith, D. 1974. Women's perspective as a radical critique of sociology. *Sociological Inquiry* 44:1–13.
Tate, Julie. 2005. Detainees accuse female interrogators. *Washington Post*, February 10, available at www.msnbc.msn.com/id/6942867.
Wright, Melissa. 2001. The dialectics of still life: Murder, women and maquiladoras. In *Millennial capitalism and the culture of neoliberalism*, eds. Jean Comaroff and John Comaroff. Durham, NC: Duke University Press, 126–45.

14

The Matrix of Freirean Pedagogy: Time and Cultural Literacies

YiShan Lea

In this chapter, I will contextualize the matrix of Freirean pedagogy in relation to the Chinese metaphor for cultural critiques and multiculturalism. This chapter intends to address critical literacy (Freire and Macedo 1987) in practice through metaphor. Using the Chinese fable "The Tiger and the Sheep," I will illustrate the dialectic between the teller and the listeners, then the cultural worker and students, essentially aiming to provide experiences of meaning transformation as an example of critical education in the teacher preparation program. The thesis of the chapter moves through various generative themes and guided critiques that emerged in my classrooms, TESOL, philosophy of education, and multiculturalism in the United States. The argument will center on the power of oral tradition and cultural sustainability to address issues of diversity against the all-encompassing corporate interpretation of schooling today and the resulting unitary metaphorical colonization and loss in the global sphere. I want to advocate critical education through metaphor reading and dramatization as one version to counter hegemony.

POWER OF METAPHOR

The oral tradition embodies a pedagogy of seeing how much drama resembles reality and reality, drama. It is a process of separation of self from others, of the dimensionalization of human world consciousness. A. Delbanco argues that "a literary tradition from Goethe to Melville and Dostoevsky to Conrad expounds evil as the capacity to render invisible another human consciousness" (1995, 89). To do the opposite, using a Chinese fable, story telling will be the first pedagogical move to engage the audience.

Fables of all cultures were created to express social concerns. Fables are representative of humans' world consciousness in relation to the full understanding of their own place in the universe. The utility of impersonating animals to act or to speak has also functioned to lament or expose human frailty and flaws. The embodiment of social meanings upon other creatures is characteristic; an example can be found especially in Chinese calligraphic art. The power of metaphor resides in its simplicity, vicariousness of meaning creation, and extension. Its political value is evident as a genre of literacy to indict and, at the same time, to avoid social suppression and oppression. It can be deemed the courage to speak truth to power in the repressing of cultures of silence.

The idea of using this particular Chinese fable to teach social consciousness came from my experience in teaching the Chinese language. As F. Smith (1988) synthesizes, literacy acquisition takes place vicariously, and telling this story intends to introduce the cultural aspect encoded in the Chinese language. Language learners are often drawn to a language by the unknown. This aspect of mystery that connects the language, the learner, and the culture can be a fundamental force for language teachers to accomplish language teaching with a critical perspective. Since it is the unknown that attracts the learners at the first glance, it can be turned into a salient passage to explore as a terrain for dialectics. According to Audre Lorde, anger, fear, and chaos are sources of power and creativity (1984). The unnamed can be named. The already named can be renamed in a second language. Establishing such metalinguistic and cultural knowledge is a process for coming to a higher consciousness, a central task for cultural work. As Lorde notes, it is "only within that interdependency of different strengths, acknowledged and equal" that we can find the power "to seek new ways of being" (1984, 113).

In our times, there is more metaphorical conformity than diversity. Oral tradition faces a challenge of becoming an endangered tradition from the globalization of economic life and the resulting ontological digitization. Under the suffocating "duckling stuffing schooling" (Lea 2003a, 2003b), or "banking education" according to Paulo Freire, even the majority of Taiwanese Chinese college students are naive about their own rich cultural heritage, socialization, and discipline in cultural literacies through storytelling. Their ways of knowing have been deskilled for the sake of economics and material survival. The instigated need for a second language, especially English skills, becomes a medium for international labor and cross-continental economic oppression. Knowledge has been commodified and compartmentalized, like goods in the market. Freedom is conceptualized within the framework of need governed by the theory of scarcity. The price to pay is that Homo sapiens has been made homo needy (Illich 1999). Technology; fashion; pop cultures; standardized tests; "best practices"; local, political, and ideological alignment; and management—all are fetishisms and result in an existential numbness. Fetishism has become the center of meaning domination that leads to invisible colonialism and oppression.

A glimpse of the significance of fables tips the scale on the trivia of the literal reading programs (Bahruth 2004) and the standardization movement. Folk wisdoms are seriously underrepresented in the curriculum. When they are present, their significance has been ignored, mostly because most teachers are not aware of their metaphysical structure allowing for exploration and engagement. Neither other ways of knowing nor the essence of the ontological or the aesthetics of simplicity for political critiques are included in the public school system; most teachers are not prepared with a critical education. The trained teachers are not to break the continuity of hegemony but to sustain the present social/intellectual stratum of domination. There are many well-intentioned teachers, but "those who do not have the political clarity can best teach how to read the word, but they are not able to teach how to read the world" (Freire 1987).

Reading fables allows a personal space for interpretations. Personalization from various cultural backgrounds makes way for the emergence of multicultural manifestations in class. "Divide to conquer" is replaced with "define to empower" (Lorde 1984). The abstractness of theory in a pedagogical space is therefore enfleshed by the participants. Such uniqueness is evident in its commonality that the personal is turned into cultural inquiry; inclusiveness becomes the norm rather than a contrived relativity for tolerance. It differs from a "romantic pedagogical model," where there is no inquiry and critique. Because stories are never innocent, experiences are filtered contextually. Negotiation between the word and the world will therefore enhance the individual reflexivity in a collective effort, mediating reading the world critically.

THE FABLE

There were once two creatures in the world. One was a sheep, the other a tiger. They both lived in the mountains. The tiger loved to show off his strength, how fast he could run, how muscular he was, his gigantic sharp teeth, and so forth. The sheep, fearful of the tiger, intelligently avoided contact with the tiger at all cost. But the sheep was not meant to be left alone by the tiger. Without the sheep, how could it be possible for the tiger to display his own power? Without bullying the sheep, how could the tiger know if he caused fear and could wound?

The sheep reached its limit of tolerance one day. It did not take long for her to figure out how to stop her suffering. The sheep revealed a piece of information to the tiger. "I met another tiger in the forest. He is not as humble a giant as you are. He actually ordered me to tell you that you are nothing compared to him, like a dwarf to a giant."

"Where did you meet this liar? Take me to him."

As the tiger ordered the sheep, his fist fell on her as usual. The sheep obediently led the way, and finally they came to a well. Eyeing to the bottom of the well, the sheep spoke: "Oh, mercy, Tiger, I beg you to run with your tail between your legs. This tiger is nothing like what you know; he is more determined, stronger. . .eh. . ."

Provoked to the competition, the tiger looked into the well. Instantly, he was shocked to see a really mean looking and physically superior creature in the well. First, he tried his growls, attempting to sound as frightening as he could. But the one in the well was not intimidated. The growls from the one in the well created earth-shaking echoes that almost deafened the tiger. After several matches, the tiger was drawn by the one in the well, who tried to charge him and claw at him with his powerful paws. The tiger matched as he was provoked. The claw from the well was getting closer and closer to the tiger. The tiger was getting angrier and angrier. To end the match, to defeat the one in the well, the tiger jumped into the well. Thus ended the match.

The sheep went home.

I usually tell the fable in Mandarin Chinese in the United States or in English in the context of TESOL. Telling the story, including dramatization, usually takes about five minutes. Pedagogy can provide a critical experience in knowledge production via a genre such as the fable. Using such a genre, short and sweet, as well as thought provoking, the rest of class time is saved for longer inquiries and dialogues. The dramatization of the fable, told in a foreign language, engages the students in comprehending the story. The content is made comprehensible in the discourse level. The whole of the fable will be preserved through layers of contextualizations. Conversely, traditional foreign-language instruction often puts students in a defensive learning posture, raising the affective filter as language is due to a skill and drill orientation.

Natural curiosity is provoked through the dramatization or telling of the fable. The dynamism between the reader and the author should be further made rigorous. The teacher can work toward transforming natural curiosity into epistemological curiosity through the lens of multiple readings (Freire 1998). When a reader meets a writer via a text, a critical reader becomes a writer who rewrites the text. Comprehension of a text entails going through several literacy acts, which the reader experiences with the writer's text, such as "transaction," "composition," and "creation." These are the temporary products of reading, rereading, and rewriting. The important act of reading through the fable is substantiated when the students experience the dialogical interaction. Knowledge emerges generatively.

After the story, told in Chinese, it usually takes a few seconds to move back into the mother tongue of the students and to realize what just happened. To further the process of comprehending the fable, I will ask, "Tell me what you understand about the story." The American adult students have no problem in identifying the main characters as the tiger and the sheep. "What do they look like?" The students will begin to name their sense of the characters from my dramatization. From identifying the surface features of the characters, the students begin to name the elements or events in the fable. "What happened between the tiger and the sheep?" The students usually make tentative guesses as they try to make sense of the whole fable, cause and effect, and the connections between events and characters. Going through this process, the students who are foreign to the language of the storytelling usually feel a sense of accomplishment in reading the fable through my gestural and their collective effort, gathering information from the readings of others. The students find cooperative learning to be experiential, contextualized, and meaningful.

At first, using this fable in a culture circle, I used the following questions:

- What might the tiger and the sheep represent?
- How do you relate this fable to your life?
- How did the tiger die?
- What might "the tiger" and "the sheep" symbolize?
- What was in the well?
- What is the relationship between the tiger and the sheep?

I began to put the questions on the board since this fable actually does not need too many guiding questions. Later, I began by asking one question at a time, for example, "Tell me about how you understand the fable?" The whole process, from questions to responses to dialogues to inquiry, takes its own course. Questions generate more questions in a cultural circle. Responses provoke dialogues. Dialogue pushes the epistemological productivity among the participants.

The dialectic flows in cultural circles that guide the process of decoding the codification of a fable, wherein the readers read the word in connection with their world. The words begin to live as the readers bring in their experiences to decode the fable and make it meaningful. The readers will be invited to interpret the fable by naming their world to uncover the situationality wherein they find that they themselves are limited and can be transformed. In cultural circles, the named generative themes are interconnected and constructed through reflection and dialogue, whereby reality can be perceived, and critical perceptions emerge among the investigators/students/teacher. The abstractness of a fable is rendered concrete with people's named "limit situations" (Freire 1970). The association of a fable with a concrete situation marks the dimensionalization of the reality wherein the subject recognizes itself and wherein the self is also found (Freire 1970).

In working with teachers on this fable, I have found that they come to reflect on the use of power in relation to authority in classrooms. The character of the tiger often gives the teachers some discomfort about their practice of constantly asserting the need to maintain control over their students. However, the sheep character is equally entrenched in the teacher identity in relation to the administrators, the overall expectations of society, and the political/intellectual censorship of teachers by others. The generative themes usually surround inquiries into teacher praxis, dehumanization, humanization, authoritarianism, authority, and technicism/banking education as opposed to pedagogy. The generative themes become intertwined and expand like a fan from the interrogation of teacher praxis to overall social practices/invisible colonialism. There are various "isms" named in cultural circles that govern the structure of social hierarchies and that divide human relationships—monolingualism, monoculturalism, ethnocentrism, sexism/patriarchy, scientism, egocentrism, materialism, capitalism, racism, and so forth. That is cultural domination.

THE ONE-EYED GIANT

"The white man," says Laurens Van Der Post, came into Africa (and Asia and America for that matter) "like a one-eyed giant, bringing with him the characteristic split and blindness which were at once his strength, his torment, and his ruin" (Merton 1964, 1). The pedagogy of the oppressed has been a real practice in societies across cultures because oppression and domination are as real as the exercises of power in the span of historical moments. The signification in the matrix of the historical, geographical, and existential is measured against time. The advancing of civilization moves forward against our time. The pedagogy of the oppressed is a pedagogy of power with time.

As we examine history, we will find economic exploitation in imperial colonization and the consequent oppressions. Imperialism can be first identified as the tiger to the sheep or the one-eyed giant to the invaded indigenous cultures. A. Phizacklea analogizes the imperial colonizer to the "pastoral" (Gabbard 2000) "global master" (Chomsky 2000):

> Colonization meant the enrichment of the European nation-states at the expense of the colonized economy and population, often the latter's destruction and its substitution with imported slave labour. . . . In many cases the colonized, dispossessed of their land either through compulsory acquisition or changes in communal land holding, were forced to work on estates or in mines producing food and raw materials for export. . . . The same countries continued to be economically dependent on their ex-colonizers and other affluent developed countries through the presence of multinational companies, external debt and a dependence on export-led growth. (2001, 321)

On imperialism and colonialism across the span of time to world industrial development, Noam Chomsky (1994) points out that "Japan is the one area of the Third World that [is] developed. That's striking. The one part of the Third World that wasn't colonized is the one part that's part of the industrialized world. That's not by accident." The oppression of today is interconnected with the imperial conquests of yesterday. The most effective method of control is economic control. To control the world is to control the resources. The anthropocentric division between cultural economics and nature overdetermines today's economic cultural behavior patterns of development while dismissing organic needs. Today's merging and expanding of the market operates on the paradigm of the dichotomy of human and nature in which humans are dominators, whereas nature is an object for exploitation.

The ramifications of the Chinese Opium Wars for the British Empire provide a good example for bringing historical and economic connections to the fable. The contact between these two powerful empires of the 1800s can illustrate the inception of awakening in the modernization, the defeats, and the conquest in cultures, economics, and technologies. The erosion and collapse of ancient civilizations were accompanied by misery, tragedy, and impoverished human conditions among the indigenous cultures. A brief introduction to the history will help.

> By the 1830s . . . the English had become the major drug-trafficking criminal organization in the world; Growing opium in India, the East India Company shipped *tons* of opium into Canton, which it traded for Chinese manufactured goods and for tea. This trade had produced, quite literally, a country filled with drug addicts, as opium parlors proliferated all throughout China in the early part of the nineteenth century. In an effort to stem the tragedy, the imperial government made opium illegal in 1836 and began to aggressively close down the opium dens. The English . . . refused to back down from the opium trade. In response, [China] threatened to cut off all trade with England and expel all English from China. Thus began the Opium War. The Chinese were equally unprepared for the technological superiority of the British. (Hines 1999, 1–2)

As the result of the defeat of the proud ancient empire by the British, Chinese coastal regions and major seaports were granted treaties for economic favors to the British, and later to the French; the United States also later followed these examples (Hines 1999). Colonialism creates a structure to exploit and dominate in the economic life of indigenous cultures.

What about another ancient civilization, the neighbor of China, India?

> [The British] first destroyed the agricultural economy and then turned dearth into a famine. One way they did this was by taking the agricultural lands and turning them into poppy production (since opium was the only thing Britain could sell to China). Then there was mass starvation in Bengal. (Chomsky 1994, ¶17)

To come back to the theme of the tiger and the sheep, the immediate example in history is Gandhi versus the British Empire, leading India to break away from the imperial colonial domination. He was fighting not only for political independence for his nation but also against the version of civilization based on development and Eurocentrism. And in the early 1900s, Gandhi responded to a reporter's question in the following way:

> *Reporter:* Mr. Gandhi, what do you think of modern civilization?
>
> *Gandhi:* I think that would be a good idea.

Gandhi knew enough to see the split psyche of the one-eyed giant: A colonizer in a suit of a civilizer, "that to be 'civilized' by force was in reality to reduce oneself to barbarism, while the 'civilizer' himself was barbarized" (Merton 1964, 3). What needs to be noted here is the exported culture from Europe to the indigenous cultures.

INDIGENOUS EPISTEMOLOGIES

> He who knows glory but keeps to disgrace becomes the valley of the world
> Being the valley of the world
> He finds contentment in constant virtue,
> He returns to the uncarved block.
> The cutting up of the uncarved block results in vessels,
> Which in the hands of the sage become officers,
> Truly, "a great cutter does not cut . . ."
>
> (Chuang Tzu, cited in Chang 1963, 65)

According to Taoism and Zen Buddhism, needs are shaped through an awareness of the coexistence between the relation of humans and nature. The concept of needs is existentially congruent with the ontological recognition of humans' integral place in the metaphysical structure of being. Needs and decisions about resources are determined with the vision of generations and consideration of community survival. Names are safeguarded or faces are saved through consideration of how clean the smell one leaves behind is. The means to meet needs draws from conservation and balance between needs and fulfillment in light of being. In the words of Zen Buddhism to needy men, "There are no byroads, and no crossroads here; the mountains are all the year round fresh and green; east or west, in whichever direction, you may have a fine walk" (Suzuki 1959, 113). The epistemology in Zen expounds the "sudden enlightenment" accomplished in a leap from one cliff to the other. The preservation of the whole of being is manifested in the act of knowing. The theology of liberation provided here is "seeing is being, being is acting." The at-oneness is central to maintaining a balanced life to live in the present.

An ontologically centered epistemology is congruent with a philosophy of abundance. It is community-centered, person-oriented existence. Time gives the meaning of being. Time mediates the metaphysical structure construed in either well-being or well-having. The interdependence and coexistence signifies the evolution of civilization rather than dominance. Power is released in the ontological interfusion of subjectivity and objectivity. The former is timed by sustainability, the latter by comsumability to deplete. Humans are dwellers in the former, and part of nature, rather than dominators of nature, in the latter.

Freire (1970) stresses that the global theme in the modern world is domination. Humans become the means for the prize of development. The division and split of modernization epistemology blind the minds, which Chuang Tzu actually expounds in alignment with Zen Buddhism. Explaining the concept of "having too many minds," Chuang Tzu draws an analogy to the discipline of archery:

> If [the archer] shoots for a prize of gold, [the archer] goes blind
> Or sees two targets—
> [The archer] is out of mind. (Chuang Tzu, cited in Merton 1969, 107)

The forces for modernization and development are like the forces possessed by the tiger of the fable. They are forces to conquer. It is an unbalanced world and schizoid culture. The world is a resource to live off of rather than to live with. The ontological structure is conceptualized as a relation between the consumer and the market. It is timed by speed to locate sites for resources and labor. The frontier of the market is the beginning of species extinction and the erosion of being to a quantified, empirical, exaggerated ego. The one-eyed giant lives in the moment of uninhibited perversions of technical power for a brief period of dominance. In the paradigm of modernization, advancement is conceptualized in key words such as "progress," "development," "resources," "economics," "digitization," "technology," "speed," "GB," and so forth. The one-eyed giant and the unconscious tiger of the fable have "science without wisdom." As opposed to destruction racing against the hand of the stopwatch for economization, the indigenous epistemology in which meaning is conceptualized in continuity and sustainability transcends.

D. Gabbard contends that "myth," "ritual," and "ceremony" "[help] to maintain certain social conditions from which people in rich nations can learn in order to both diagnose and recover from the social and environmental illnesses generated by economization" (2000, xix). The act of simplicity of life in relation to nature and heaven in Taoism is reflected by I. Illich in that "All known traditional cultures . . . can be conceived as meaningful configurations that have as their principal purpose the repression of those conditions under which scarcity could become dominant in social relations" (1992, 117). The ontological structure in Taoism for liberation through *wu-wei*, an active engaging in self-so-ness with the world, places power in action, which can be interpreted as Freire's praxis, theory in practice through active reflection and contemplation. Both philosophies engage humans as subjects that construct a world based on biocentric concepts rather than through a corporate developmental model of domination, which places all living things and biodiversity as expendable objects for consumption. T. Merton explains the middle way/wu-wei as a human-world-engaged epistemology guided by an ontological understanding: "It is a wisdom which transcends and unites, wisdom which dwells in body and soul together and which, more by means of myth, of rite, of contemplation, than by scientific experiment, opens the door to a life in which the individual is not lost in the cosmos and in society but found in them" (Merton 1964, 1).

In the epistemology of sustainability, through myth, ritual, stories, and ceremonies in maintaining world and human harmony, personalism is not sacrificed but interconnected in social existential meaning construction. It constructs a communal self within a personal community. Conversely, an alienated self-aggrandized ego impoverishes community in its aimless flight in space; a community is destroyed, a self-seeking ego only becomes a lost kite trampled by the traffic of insignificance, annihilation, and noise in a constantly expanding and decaying overcrowded metropolis. Without community and the dynamism of self and others, we live in isolation unfulfilled in our humanity. Community and personhood mutually complete one another in a dialectic. Without community, a person cannot truly develop. Because the character of the tiger over-asserts its own strength and tramples upon others, it fails to recognize its own reflection, which leads to its own self-destruction. Chuang Tzu characterizes the divorce of subjectivity and objectivity, the privileging of the quantitative over qualitative, as follows: "to lose one's life is to save it, and to seek to save it for one's own sake is to lose it" (Merton 1964, 12). It is ominous that the one-eyed giant seeks its own destruction when it thinks of assertion as liberation.

The rebirth from cultural contact, the unity of ontological structures with the cosmos, and the generative productivity of metaphor have been replaced with the conformity of metaphors through the forces of domination in economization and development in nature and humans alike. The global masters, or the one-eyed giant, become the producers of metaphors for the masses. The arguments made by Chomsky, Illich, Gabbard, and G. Berthoud place a parallel between colonialism and modern schooling and are valid as we make cultural inquiries into social oppression and meaning domination. What used to be abundance has been commodified with limited means to meet the unlimited wants and needs for industrial development and economic consumption. In a world where the word "conservation" has become a buzz word, we know that a whole lot more of what was "pristine" has been burned down, cleared, developed, farmed, built, destroyed and rebuilt, and abandoned. As market capitalism has evolved/invaded, economic growth and development have presupposed "overcoming symbolic and moral obstacles . . . disposing of various inhibiting ideas and practices such as myths, ceremonies, rituals, mutual aid, networks of solidarity and the like" (Berthoud 1992, 72).

Decoding metaphors is an organic process, like establishing community. The reading of metaphors has been named in various ways. For Freire, it is "reading the word and the world" (Freire and Macedo 1987). For Maxine Greene, it provokes "social imagination" in our minds to reach the "as if" to the "not yet" and to "the might be" (1995). To Virginia Woolf (Greene 1995), it brings the severed parts into a whole. Freire conceptualizes it as establishing "the unity within diversity" (Freire 1997), and A. Schutz calls it "making music together" (1964, 159–78). In contrast to the artificial technicality of isolation and exclusion of meaning, the "epistemological encircling" (Freire 1997, 92) investigates a "web of relationships" (Arendt 1958, 18) in people's reality. "The generative theme cannot be found in people, divorced from reality; nor yet in reality, divorced from people. . . . It can only be apprehended in the human-world relationship" (Freire 1970, 106).

Perceiving the ontological connection in our being is integral to our ways of knowing. A metaphysical structure that affirms creativity is interdependent with an organic view of epistemology. Curiosity, our way of coming to know, grows on love of life, and vice versa. Only does a community survive when epistemology is structured in life, in oriented ways of knowing, which is creativity. Control of meaning leads to oppression, while the dialectic between reflection and change liberates in action. The relationship between liberation and conscientization is organic, creative, and life centered, which recognizes being in relation to a cosmic ecological family. "Modern science speaks to us of an extraordinary range of interrelations" (Rinpoche 2002).

Ecologists know that a tree burning in the Amazon rain forest alters in some way the air breathed by a citizen of Paris, and that the trembling of a butterfly's wing in the Yucatán affects the life of a fern in the Hebrides. Biologists are beginning to uncover the fantastic and complex dance of genes that creates personality and identity, a dance that stretches far into the past and shows that each so-called identity is composed of a swirl of different influences. Physicists have introduced us to the world of the quantum particle: all particles exist potentially as different combinations of other particles.

A necrophilic view of life operates on unlimited wants without a long-term vision of life. The ideology of free trade pushing for development in the frontier manifests "ontological sterility" (Purpel 1999), "demolishing, poisoning, destroying all life-systems on the planet. We are signing IOUs our children will not be able to pay. . . . We are acting as if we were the last generation on the planet" (Rinpoche 2002, 8). Therefore, the reading of metaphors is the central vehicle to juxtapose, announcing the praxis of humanization while denouncing dehumanization. The former is generative, creative, and subsistence oriented; the latter is destructive, short-sighted, and ephemeral. Essentially, the pedagogy implemented in this chapter endeavors to approach a state of consciousness-raising because the reading of metaphor is "one of the chief agents of our moral nature" (Greene 1995, 99) that calls for intrinsic meaning making and our aspiration to humanize. It is founded on solidarity of "relationality, reciprocity, and mutuality" (Greene, 99). "Only through this constant mutual release from what [we humans] remain free agents, only by [our] constant willingness to change [our] minds and start again can [we] be trusted with so great a power as that to begin anew" (Arendt 1958, 18).

Therefore, in light of indigenous epistemologies through the historical journey, a pedagogy of liberation is a pedagogy of time, with time, against time, and in time all at once. It is present in the Taoist thought and practiced in critical pedagogy. Recalled and illustrated in the words of Chuang Tzu that "a great cutter does not cut," cultural works are acts of solidarity in theory and practice. It is the fluidity "to appreciate the theoretical elements within movements' practices" and "to discover the theoretical elements rooted in practice" (Freire in Freire and Macedo 1987, 62). When theory unites with practice, there is the sense of Taoist nondifferentiation, of the interfusion of things. There is transformation that unites subjectivity and objectivity, self and others, artist and medium. Historical wisdom and folk memories perceive and resist the world contextually/tacitly. An organic intellectual (Gramsci 1971) or a mandala master, slid his stork-shaped scissors from a type of sheath hanging about his neck on a leather strap, revealing the long beak that opened and closed as his hands interpreted what his eyes had already perceived. The paper twisted and turned between the beaked blades with an ease that announced the many years of subtle grace evolved from time and patience.

To follow Freire's pedagogy is to not follow him. "A great cutter does not cut," but creates, which is the Taoist sense of the ontological experience of the release of power. Mortal humans who reside in the city, "Truth or Consequences," are mortal because they are limited by time; yet, paradoxically, for the very limitation, they are immortal and explosive in power through creativity engaging in the act of world making and transformation.

COLLEGES OF EDUCATION

Colleges of education are sites of colonization by the one-eyed giant. Colleges of education overrepresent classroom management in place of education. Expensive textbooks and long lists of readings perform as tokens of doing the time for those teacher "wannabes." Words disconnected from the world are normalized as teaching disconnects from learning. Fragmented teacher identities find solace in their mediocrity at securing "an iron rice bowl" (Lea 2003a, 2003b) and satisfaction at teaching the word without the world. The dichotomization of the oppressed and the oppressor endangers the use of power in the name of liberation. In reflecting on historical advocacies of liberation intersecting the interrogation of geographical, economic, and cultural epistemologies, the dialectic of freedom and oppression should be comprehended simultaneously as internal contradictions of a site of struggle.

In the model of economization and development, there is more metaphorical conformity than diversity. Our ways of knowing are commodified, compartmentalized, exported, and imported. There are cries of need for information for economization and demand for techniques and methodologies in schooling. Reinvention of a pedagogy has been a rare find. There have been too many teacher imposters, armed with methodologies, teaching with a script of "repeat after me." Noisy but silent talking parrots fill the classrooms begging for more "duckling stuffing" (Lea 2003a, 2003b). Schooling designed by the "pastoral" (Gabbard 2000) "global masters" (Chomsky 2000) through neocolonialists advocates a patriotism of economic development of students, synonymous as resources, for national productivity and global competitiveness. Students and parents demand "the plain sense of things" (Stevens 1964, 502) for the need to fit the profile of international labor as potential job holders in the global economy.

Across the cultures of the West and among the Chinese, the traditional trickster of fables is characteristically small and weak, but smart. The role is usually culturally perceived in the female gender as a "she"; and its opposite pole is male as a "he." This fable is instrumental to provoking problematization of Darwinian social implications and the use of power or strength for domination/bullying or humanization. The reality is not only that women are victims of domination by men, but women also are capable of domination to inflict oppression. In this instance, the oppressed identify themselves with the oppressor. The oppressed, with the existential duality of identity, if they come to power, are capable of participating in the politics of oppression "with a spirit more revanchist" (Freire 1970, 108). Such an example can be found in the fairy tale *Rapunzel*, in Rapunzel's relationship with the witch, who internalizes the oppression. bell hooks gives insights into the Darwinian model of the use of power, which has

been institutionalized. "The parent-child relationship with its very real imposed survival structure of dependency, of strong and weak, of powerful
and powerless, was a site for the construction of a paradigm of domination
. . . wherein domination could easily occur as a means of exercising and
maintaining control" (hooks 1989, 20). Rapunzel and the sorceress, the
stepdaughter and stepmother, are based on the master and the slave relationship in the name of protection and to sanction control.

A critique of these "mini-oppressors" sheds light on the obscurity of the
clearly defined line between the oppressor and the oppressed. It shows that
liberation happens without, but more as a consequence of the inner freedom already achieved. "The decolonization of mentality is much more difficult to achieve than the physical expulsion of colonialist. Sometimes the
colonizers are thrown-out, but they remain culturally, because they have
been assimilated into the minds of the people they leave behind. There is
the contradictory coexistence of a tiger and a sheep confined within a physical body or educational, political institutions, represented metaphorically
by Rapunzel's tower. The society of the tiger and the sheep or the high tower
is profoundly a site of interrogation for transformation. Denouncing and
announcing mutually complete one another with "nondifferentiation,"
which is the Taoist "ground of being" (Chuang Tzu), or love. Criticity of education affirms, in Freire's words,

> To be a good liberating educator, you need above all to have in faith in human
> beings. You need to love. You must be convinced that the fundamental effort
> of education is to help with the liberation of people, never their domestication.
> You must be convinced when people reflect on their domination they begin a
> first step in changing their relationship to the world. (1971, 61)

Critical discourse, critical pedagogy, feminism, and indigenous epistemologies are underrepresented and suppressed from the vitality of recov-
ering, healing, and transformation. The historical question falls on the
shoulders of those who are lambs. The pedagogues of the oppressed, Lao
Tzu, Chuang Tzu, Gandhi, and H. Arendt, D. T. Suzuki, Merton, Lorde, and
Freire, from the last century, become contemporary. Their prophetic voices
cannot be ignored in the postmodern world and in the moral enterprise of
education. The never-ending stories, however, come to a temporary moral
setback. In the final analysis, a Chinese philosopher, Mencius, in the
fourth century BC of the Western calendar, decoded in a code of parable on
the quandary of time in relation to moral humans on greed. As moral
agents, tiger or sheep, we are urged to ponder our power to deplete and to
dominate or to humanize and to sustain the mountain while taking the
firewood. Our central concern is a question of time in time posed in Chinese poetic imagery that has the power to awaken consciousness: "under
the eternal moonlight, is it found in our city a moral ruin of a civilization
or consciousness illuminated?"

CONCLUSION

The recommended pedagogy has been implemented various times in my classrooms of philosophy of education, cultural diversity in school, and TESOL methodology in the United States. It invites critical perceptions from the participants and provokes political identity in pre- and in-service teachers. Vicariously, the tiger and sheep are experienced in the realities of the participants. The fable engages personal reflection on the micro/personal level. Pedagogically, it initiates the global connection of the individual experiences with the society and the world's making.

The recommended critical Freirean pedagogy is congruent with the view of Peter McLaren: it is "a pedagogy, that brushes against the grain of textual foundationalism, ocular fetishism, and the monumentalist abstraction of theory that characterizes most critical practice within multicultural classrooms . . . and in which multicultural ethics is performed rather than simply reduced to the practice of reading texts" (1999, 351).

Multiculturalism and diversity have been serving as more a politics of representation than a representation of politics. While Black History Month and Cinco de Mayo are celebrated for a month or a day, what about the rest of the year? The exoticized cultural artifact or tokenism implicates that multiculturalism is an interpretation of tolerance of inclusion, turning it into social welfare for the elite minority to secure established privileges and for the purpose of cultural reproduction for domestication rather than production for social transformation. Diversity is racialized rather than ideologized in representation in classrooms and in faculty ratios of colleges of education. The inclusion of ideological racial differences has been mostly exterminated. Diversity is only skin deep and profiled linguistically when the tools of a racist Eurocentrism are used to construct diversity, and the dichotomy of multiculturalism institutionalizes the multiplicity of differences.

> A word is dead
> When it is said,
> Some say.
> I say it just
> Begins to live
> That day.
>
> —Emily Dickinson, "A Word"

The more critical the reading of the fable can become, the deeper the participants engage in rereading their realities. The reading of the fable becomes critical and pedagogical when participants are able to "understand their indigence differently from the fatalistic way they sometimes view injustice" (Freire and Macedo 1987, 36). Folktales by themselves, without a teacher, are left to limited and shallow interpretations. Two requirements are necessary to promote critical literacy: teachers who have experienced critical approaches to folk tales during their teacher preparation, accompanied by a metacognitive discussion about how and why critical educators do the work to promote conscientization through folk literature and cultural circles. Can folk wisdom be counterhegemonic and transformative in quality when folk wisdom helps to rethink modern science and technological implementations, implications, and ramifications? Folk wisdom then ceases to be ancient and archaic and begins to be active in the cultural practices and production of the postmodern world.

Aboriginal warrior dance is reduced to pleasing the seekers of exoticity in indigenous cultures. Multiculturalism and critical pedagogy become mute if absent in the reorganization and mobilization of the cultural reconfiguration of multiple representations of power. Critical pedagogy is power. Cultural workers are to the power of social relations what artists are to the power of creation.

REFERENCES

Arendt, H. 1958. *The human condition.* Chicago: University of Chicago Press.
——. 2004. Critical literacy vs. reading programs: Schooling as a form of control. Eleventh International Literacy and Education Research Network Conference on Learning, Centro De Convenciones Pedagogicas De Cojimar [Cojimar Pedagogical Convention Centre], Common Ground Publishing, Havana, Cuba, June 20.
Bahruth, R. 2004. *Critical literacy vs. Reading programs: Schooling as a form of control.* The Eleventh International Literacy and Education Research Network Conference on Learning Centro De Convenciones Pedagogicas De Cojimar (Cojimar Pedagogical Convention Centre), Havana, Cuba: Common Ground Publishing.
Barsamian, D., ed., *Prosperous few and restless many.* Tucson, AZ: Odonian Press, available at www.zmag.org/chomsky/pfrm/pfrm-07.html (accessed May 22, 2005).
Berthoud, G. 1992. Market. In *The development dictionary: A guide to knowledge as power,* ed. W. Sachs. Atlantic Highlands, NJ: Zed Books.
Chang, C. Y. 1963. *Creativity and Taoism; a study of Chinese philosophy, art, and poetry.* New York: Julian Press.
Chomsky, N. 1994. Gandhi, nonviolence and India [electronic version]. In *Prosperous few and restless many,* ed. D. Barsamian. Tucson, AZ: Odonian Press, available at www.zmag.org/chomsky/pfrm/pfrm-08.html.
——. 2000. Global economy. In *Knowledge and power in the global economy,* ed. D. Gabbard. Mahwah, NJ: Lawrence Erlbaum Associates.
Delbanco, A. 1995. *The death of Satan: How Americans have lost the sense of evil.* New York: Farrar, Strauss, and Giroux.
Freire, P. 1970. *Pedagogy of the oppressed.* New York: Continuum.
——. 1971. To the coordinator of a Cultural Circle. *Convergence* 4 (1): 61–2.
——. 1997. *Pedagogy of the heart.* New York: Continuum.

———. 1998. *Teachers as cultural workers: Letter to those who dare teach.* Boulder, CO: Westview.

Freire, P., and D. Macedo. 1987. *Literacy: Reading the word and the world.* Westport, CT: Bergin and Garvey.

Gabbard, D. 2000. Introduction. In *Knowledge and power in the global economy,* ed. D. Gabbard. Mahwah, NJ: Lawrence Erlbaum Associates.

Gramsci, A. 1971. *Selections from the prison notebooks,* ed. and trans. Q. Hoare and G. N. Smith. New York: International Publishers.

Greene, M. 1995. *Releasing the imagination: Essays on education, the arts, and social change.* San Francisco: Jossey-Bass.

Hines, R. 1999. *World civilization: Opium wars,* available at www.wsu.edu:8080/~dee/ching/opium.htm.

hooks, b. 1989. *Talking back.* Boston: South End Press.

Illich, I. 1992. *In the mirror of the past.* New York: Marion Boyers.

———. 1999. Needs. In *The development dictionary: A guide to knowledge as power,* ed. W. Sachs, 87–101. London: Witwatersrand University Press.

Lea. Y. 2003a. *Cultural work in language and literacy: Reflection of a researcher as a cultural worker.* Unpublished doctoral dissertation, Boise State University, ID.

———. 2003b. Teaching for social justice: Cultural work with teachers on Taiwan. In *Social justice in these times,* ed. J. O'Donnell, M. Pruyn, and R. Chávez Chávez. Greenwich, CT: Information Age Publishing.

Lorde, A. 1984. *Sister outsider.* Trumansburg, NY: Crossing Press.

Macedo, D. and A. M. R. Freire. 1998. Foreword. In *Teachers as cultural workers: Letters to those who dare teach,* ed. P. Freire, ix–xix. Boulder, CO: Westview.

McLaren, P. 1999. Critical pedagogy. In *Knowledge and power in the global economy,* ed. D. Gabbard. Mahwah, NJ: Lawrence Erlbaum Associates.

Merton, T. 1964. *Gandhi on non-violence.* New York: New Directions.

Phizacklea, A. 2001. Women, migration and the state. In *Oxford readings in Feminism: Feminism and race,* ed. K. Bhavnani. New York: Oxford.

Purpel, D. 1999. *Moral outrage in education.* New York: Peter Lang.

Rinpoche, S. 2002. *The Tibetan book of living and dying: Revised and updated.* New York: HarperCollins.

Schutz, A. 1964. Making music together: A study in social relationship. In *Studies in social theory,* 159–78. The Hague: Martinus Nijhoff.

Stevens, W. 1964. *The collected poems of Wallace Stevens.* New York: Alfred Knopf.

Smith, F. 1988. *Joining the literacy club.* Portsmouth, NH: Heinemann Educational Books.

Suzuki, D. T. 1959. *The training of the Zen Buddhist monk.* New York: Cosimo Books.

15

Generating Hope, Creating Change, Searching for Community: Stories of Resistance against Globalization at the U.S.-Mexico Border

Michelle Téllez

Using the community of Maclovio Rojas located east of the city of Tijuana, Baja California, as an example, this chapter outlines the ways in which the global monopoly of "empire," as coined by M. Hardt and A. Negri (2000), is being contested and deconstructed by local communities seeking to re-generate and dignify their everyday lives. The case of the *poblado* Maclovio Rojas stands out as a powerful example of resistance to global capitalism. Rather than see the processes of globalization as totalizing, it is important to recognize that the will and agency of the people can challenge the forces that oppress them. Residents of the community articulate a right of be-longing, a right to land, and a right to a dignified future.

The community of Maclovio Rojas came together in 1988 when twenty-five families, all members of an independent union of agricultural workers called the Central Independiente de Obreros Agricolas y Campesinos (CIOAC), took over the land on kilometer twenty-nine between Tecate and Tijuana with hopes of establishing a new *ejido* (communal land). At the time, the 197 hectares (486 acres) that now make up the community were vacant. Although the area on which Maclovio Rojas was settled was offi-cially declared national lands in 1984 by an edict of the federal Agrarian Re-form Department, and their solicitation for an ejido grant should have been a simple open-and-shut case, their land struggle has been anything but that.

Their movement is rooted in the complicated history of agrarian reform and land-tenure issues of Mexico (Mancillas 2002). When Lázaro Cárde-nas came into power as president of Mexico in 1934, he set in place the in-stitutional mechanisms necessary to redistribute land, a goal established by the Mexican Revolution and the Agrarian Reform Law of 1917. The Mex-ican poor were encouraged to solicit idle national lands for ejidos for the purpose of living and farming. Until the 1980s, most Mexicans believed that the Agrarian Reform made by Cárdenas was "irreversible and final." But in 1991, President Carlos Salinas de Gortari announced his proposal to amend Article 27 to permit the privatization of ejido land. The constitutional obligation to distribute land to qualified petitioners was immediately ended. Communal land would now be available for sale or rent to either Mexican or foreign companies (Adler-Hellman 1994). This move cleared the path for the North American Free Trade Agreement (passed in 1994), which gave multinational corporations the right to own Mexican land for profit at the expense of landless and poor Mexicans, particularly indigenous communities.

While these sorts of changes were taking place at the federal level, in 1989 (a year into the Maclovio Rojas land struggle), Ernesto Ruffo-Appel, a neo-conservative from the PAN party became governor of the state of Baja California. His first edict as governor was to endorse the *No Invasiones* campaign by warning people that he would no longer tolerate land occupations. Under his regime, the state, not the federal government, would regulate land tenure. Ruffo-Appel's approach was to criminalize and discredit the leaders of these settlements by inventing the Crime of Instigating Forced Removal.[1] This made being a leader of irregular settlements a crime (Lara 2003). The legal mechanisms to control and displace families seeking lands were thus set in place, feeding into the goals and pockets of the corporate and political elite.

Globalization scholars A. Appadurai (2001), D. Barkin (2001), W. Bello (2001) and S. Sassen (1998) all have made it clear that the current global market is creating increased inequalities both within and across societies, disrupting traditional ways of life, and wreaking havoc on ecological systems. In the context of the U.S.-Mexico border region, the forces of economic globalization are making not only the political boundary all the more necessary but the demarcation between rich and poor all the starker. Some state that the U.S.-Mexico border, within the North American free trade zone, may be the closest thing to South Africa under apartheid, given the internal wage inequalities within a common region (Staudt and Coronado 2002).

While the situation is bleak, my hope lies in the fact that globalization from above—the collaboration between leading states and the main agents of capital formation—is being challenged by globalization from below—globalization that is both reactive to these developments and responsive to different impulses and influences. Globalization from below "consists of an array of transnational social forces animated by environmental concerns, human rights, hostility to patriarchy, and a vision of community based action on the unity of diverse cultures seeking an end to poverty, oppression, humiliation, and collective violence" (Falk 1993, 49).

Similarly, scholar Dirlik (1996) argues that by the early 1990s local movements, or movements to save and reconstruct local societies, had emerged as the primary expressions of resistance to domination. He states that the "local" has emerged as a site of promise in the relationship between the emergence of a global capitalism and the emergence of concern with the local as a site of resistance and liberation. Stated simply, the global affects the local, but the local also affects the global.

Many examples of this have emerged in Mexico, such as the powerful debtors' movement, El Barzon, which is made up of a group of indebted small farmers and entrepreneurs who have made waves in the political and economic spectrum of Mexico. Also, in the Eastern Sierra Madre, a school called Center for Rural Training (CESDER), aims to keep *campesinos* on their land through the teaching of land-management techniques and small-scale craft production and marketing. This goal—rebuilding an independent campesino economy and community—runs directly counter to the policies of the International Monetary Fund, World Bank, and Mexican government, which call for the development of larger, more profitable enterprises on the land. Local governments, which see the modest efforts of CESDER graduates as threatening, have tried to shut the center down (Barkin, Ortiz, and Rosen 1997).

In Cuernavaca, Morelos, the Frente Cívico Pro-Defensa del Casino de la Selva is against the building of a COSTCO in the Casino de la Selva. Their slogan, *por el derecho que tenemos a decidir la ciudad, el país y el mundo que queremos* (for the right that we have to decide the city, the country and world that we want), is a powerful testament to the will of the people. In San Salvador de Atenco, in the state of Mexico, campesinos were able to halt the construction of an airport, among other projects, that would have invaded their communal land holdings. Finally, the communities of San Juan de Guadalupe y Tierra Blanca in the state of San Luis Potosi are in a struggle to defend their communal land, which the state government wants to take over to build a shopping center that would include the symbol of the McDonalds transnational monopoly.

One example of globalization from below is the project of autonomy. G. Esteva and M. S. Prakash (1998) argue that the struggle for autonomy seems to be but the new name of an old notion of power: people's power, exercising unprecedented impetus in its contemporary forms at the grassroots level. Maclovio Rojas is a path-breaking example of this type of movement. With the following narrative given by Hortensia, the community president, who has been involved with the struggle since its inception, one can see the community's evolution.

> With time Maclovio Rojas has grown, and as a community, we decided that we couldn't wait until the lands were "officially" granted to us because the kids

growing in the community need schooling, the adults need places to grow. Our first objective was the land, to harvest it, to raise animals and since that didn't happen and we had the land, we had to do something. We decided to distribute the land and create an economic, cultural and educational infrastructure. This is when the ideas for all of our projects emerged, and in 1992 we built our first elementary school because we couldn't let the kids be without schooling. In all of these years, we have looked for ways to create better living situations for the residents of Maclovio Rojas.

Hortensia's statement attests to the transformative vision of the Maclovianos and the clarity with which they are claiming rights to the land to live and survive. Furthermore, the creation of a community-run infrastructure is apparent in the various projects that have been completed: they have constructed schools, a women's center, and a two-story cultural center called the Aguascalientes.[2] None of these projects received the support of the state or the federal government; thus, residents actively took matters into their own hands and created these autonomous structures. In fact, the construction of the cultural center creates a link to the Zapatista movement, and Maclovianos recognize that their struggle for land is similar. Hortensia describes the influence:

In 1994 the Chiapas movement emerged, and in 1995 Marcos invited the Mexican people to open up other Aguascalientes. We feel identified with that struggle because it's the same thing, the land struggle is the same, and we are being persecuted by the government too. So, we decided that we were going to create an Aguascalientes. It was built in 1995 soon after Subcomandante Marcos had announced it, and we invited many national and international organizations to show that this was going to be a place for all of these organizations to meet, that the space was for everybody. A representative from the FZLN of Chiapas came, and it was huge, a lot of media was here, and I was even named the Subcomandante Hortensia, so you can imagine the government's reaction. The army came into the community, invading people's homes, and made a huge mess. I was arrested soon after all of this happened. But the Aguascalientes is a symbol of struggle because, although we don't have everything we wanted, it's a symbol because that's where we have our meetings, and from there, all of our ideas for our projects emerge. I don't know if subcomandante Marcos knows or not, but we have fulfilled our commitment to building the space. By being connected to that movement, we have created more problems for ourselves for two reasons. One is that we are playing with the interests of the transnational economy; and two, we have being attacked for being luchadores who accomplish things with actions not just words. We are showing the government that the people are intelligent, that we are dignified and that we have rights.

This powerful testament brings to light the visionary skills of the leadership, and the links that Hortensia makes between the Zapatista movement in Chiapas with Maclovio Rojas demonstrate the ways in which communities across Mexico are actively responding to the conditions created by global capital. In Maclovio Rojas, the idea of autonomy emanated as a response to the denial of basic human services imposed by the state government. Continuously in my conversations with the women and other community residents, I saw that the people had come together because the government didn't provide for them; it was out of necessity, not out of an ideological political conviction that happened before they settled on the land. The idea of communes (in the United States) for example, emerged because groups of people were seeking alternative ways of life. Here, residents simply want what has been denied to them: housing, education, and health care. Their solution: doing it themselves.

For example, community resident Sylvia says,

I think it's created here out of necessity. One comes here needing land, but once you're here, you start seeing . . . it's like when you enter a kitchen, and maybe you have an idea about what you're going to cook, but once you start, you see something else, and you see another idea about what you want to make. I didn't use to have so many ideas, and now that I've been here, I've woken up. If you've never struggled in this way or lived in this way, then you are confronted with something new, but it stems from one's need, which makes one strong to face whatever may come. This is what has kept me here.

Elizabeth adds,

Because of the need that we have for somewhere to live, to be able to leave something to our children, something for the future. That's my feeling; we are in need of a place to live. That's why we have stayed so long, because we need it.

Hortensia also argues,

Necessity has made the community autonomous because, although we have the same rights as all Mexicans because we pay taxes, we are denied everything. If the government doesn't give us what we need, then they obligate us to organize ourselves. So, we built our schools, we created a sports field, and we did it all working together. This is why we are autonomous; we haven't been given absolutely anything but problems. The government treats us like delinquents, even if we are better off than other communities.

In creating this space, Maclovio Rojas has become autonomous and a model for change. However, this indignation has come with a cost. Because Maclovio Rojas sits on prime industrial real estate, the government and transnational corporations have a keen interest in gaining access to their land. Subsequently, the prolonged sixteen-year struggle has been intense. As the residents have struggled to create their community and attempted to move their projects forward, the reality of repression has been talked about repeatedly. This has been especially felt by the leading organizers, where two leaders are currently in hiding, and two are in jail. The government has threatened to evict the community physically on a number of occasions. Luz explains why:

> There are a lot of interests that the government has here. The lands have a lot of value, so we have more problems with them because they want to build state housing or factories here.

Hortensia adds,

> There are millions of dollars at stake. We are in a strategic point where the boulevard 2000 is going to pass, and the interests of the transnational companies are there. Since we are an organized community, we serve as a bad example because we might wake the consciousness of the people. We can have it all if we organize ourselves, and the government doesn't want that, and that's why Nicolasa is in jail and we [the leaders] are forced to be outside of the community so that the organization can fall and the government can meet their goal of bringing us down.

Dora shares,

> The government doesn't like [Maclovio Rojas] because it is an example for other communities. The governor gets paid to build schools, and here our payment has been made by the sacrifice of the people. The government doesn't want other communities to know, from our example, that they too can organize themselves. Why would we need governors or presidents then if the people came together to organize? It's all a business for the government. The governor travels from place to place using our money, and they don't do anything for us.

The reality of the repressive pressure placed by the government is reflected in the various stories shared by the residents. On one occasion, local police forcefully tried to take over the homes of several residents, and they defended their homes with their bodies. Others in the community began dragging furniture onto the highway, blocking the passageway and causing severe disruption. Teresa remembers that

> the police were beating people up. I saw that. The police would grab the people's belongings and throw them into a pile of mud that had gathered from the rain. They were mad because we had blocked the highway.

Eventually, the local police were called off, but instances such as these have been common for residents. In essence, the community is the ultimate symbol of resistance, and the local and state officials are scrambling to get control of their lands to appease the interests of outside corporations vying for a place to build their maquiladoras.

What I would like to highlight in the case of Maclovio Rojas is the role of women in the struggle. Women were the ones who were *al frente*, or in front, leading the movement and actions. Various women commented on this topic. Dora says,

> Women are the ones who work the most here. They are the ones who support the most. If there is a march or something, the majority are always women that attend; if there's some sort of confrontation with the government, the women are the toughest. You see more women and children out in support because they're more courageous. The majority of women who come here are courageous and daring; the men are more reserved.

Juana agrees,

> There are many single moms here who work in the maquilas, and when we have sit-ins or actions, you will see that the majority are women, and I think the women here are very willing to enter (*entronas*) the struggle.

Maria offers her own thoughts:

> Since I've lived in [Maclovio Rojas], I've always seen the participation of women. Women are the ones who come out to defend, especially since most of the problems emerge during the day-time, and the housewives are at home, and the men are working outside of the community. The fact that women are participating more, well, women have always been involved in the *lucha* (struggle) because it's their home that they are defending. It's not a game, and they won't allow their roof to be taken from them. Men are more involved in the construction part of the projects, the heavier work, the physical work, and women support by making food and sometimes help build too, but more than anything, women are the ones who attend the demonstrations and protests. It has always been said that la lucha of [Maclovio Rojas] has always belonged to the women; they are the ones who are in the forefront.

This articulation of women's leadership within the community is particularly important when one recognizes that the stories of women leading social movements often remain untold. The fact that the *casa de la mujer*, or the women's center, has been created and offers support and classes for and by women of the community is an important tribute to the womanist vision of Maclovio Rojas. Yet, as is admitted by leaders of the community, the struggle for land and the constant battle it creates often usurp the need to further engage in issues that affect women, particularly domestic violence, double workloads, and the culture of patriarchy that afflict both men and women in the community. Furthermore, while women don't necessarily name themselves as feminists, I believe that the ways in which they articulated what they had gained by living in Maclovio Rojas gives voice to their evolution as feminist political subjects. For example, Paula states,

> I've learned to defend myself so that they [the government] don't take what is ours. These lands are mine, and just because the government wants them doesn't mean they can take them away from me. I will defend them because I value everything that I have here.

Sylvia shares,

> I've learned to defend myself in a certain way to vocalize myself a bit more, if I don't know something now, well, I used to know less, so I've learned a lot. I will defend my property and my children because this is something for my children.

Juana shares what she values most in Maclovio Rojas:

> Well, the most important is having your land and a place to live. I see people who rent, and its terrible because I have lived it, and here I have a place to live where no one tells me how to be. Before I was like a ball jumping from place to place, and my mother-in-law always had something to say, and that's a super gain to have your own land, and you can say it's yours. I've gained a lot of confidence being here, a lot of self-confidence. *Yo sola valerme por mi misma* (I alone have to make a living for myself), with my children, and I have learned that by myself, I can get ahead. If I would have lived in another community, I wouldn't have been involved in sit-ins and marches, and so forth. In another place this wouldn't happen.

Teresa says that she's learned

> to be more courageous. I'm not scared of the government anymore. I can defend myself, because in the beginning, you do get scared, but as time passes, you learn more, you have more love towards what you have, and you even start getting more angry. I feel good helping my community.

In summary, when long-time resident Teresa, who was involved in the original land takeover and endured the harsh conditions of settlement, tells me, "Thanks to God, I've been happy, and I will be satisfied with my little piece of land. This is where I am going to die," I can recognize the powerful model that residents have created. The experience of Maclovio Rojas is but one example of people collectively coming together to challenge "empire" to put an end to their repressive conditions and to courageously create an alternative for themselves. They simply want to have a piece of land to safely raise their families.

In August of 2003, the Zapatistas announced new plans for the structure of their own autonomous communities in connection with other movements working from the ground up. Their plan, Realidad-Tijuana (REALti), is described by Subcomandante Marcos:

> Confronting the Plan Puebla-Panama in particular and in general against all global plans that fragment the Mexican nation, the EZLN launches the Plan Realidad-Tijuana. The plan consists of bringing together all of the resistances of our country and, with them, recreating, from below, the Mexican nation. (EZLN 2003)

Similarly, at the World Social Forum held in Mumbai, India, in January 2006, author Arundhati Roy called upon all of the intellectuals, activists, and political leaders present to create a "globalization of resistance." I believe this theme of globalizing resistance is extremely important during a time when the accelerated rate of globalization has to be met with an accelerated movement of resistance, and Maclovio Rojas is an important part of this dialogue.

NOTES

1. Fraccion III del articulo 226 del Codigo Penal del Estado. Maclovio Rojas Fact sheet, prepared by Globalifobic@s, 2001.
2. In August 1994, the Zapatistas convened a national democratic convention to open a national dialogue with "civil society." To host the six thousand people, the Zapatistas built an "auditorium," which they called an *Aguascalientes*, evoking the convention held in that city of central Mexico during the revolution of 1910. Several more appeared throughout the communities in resistance in Chiapas. In August 2003, the EZLN announced the closure of the *Aguascalientes* and the opening of the *Caracoles*, which will be the '*Casas' de la Junta de Buen Gobierno* (literally translated, this means "homes of the good government").

REFERENCES

Adler-Hellman, J. 1994. *Mexican lives.* New York: New Press.
Appadurai, A. 2001. Grassroots globalization and the research imagination. In *Globalization*, ed. A. Appadurai. Durham, NC: Duke University Press.
Barkin, D., I. Ortiz, and F. Rosen. 1997. Globalization and resistance: The remaking of Mexico. NACLA report on the Americas.
Barkin, D. 2001. Neoliberalism and sustainable popular development. In *Transcending neoliberalism: Community-based development in Latin America*, ed. H. Veltmeyer and A. O'Malley. Bloomfield, CT: Kumarian Press.

Bello, W. 2001. *The future in the balance: Essays on globalization and resistance.* Oakland: Food First Books.

Dirlick, A. 1996. The global in the local. In *Global/local: Cultural reproduction and the transnational imaginary,* ed. R. Wilson and W. Dissanayake. Durham, NC: Duke University Press.

EZLN. 2003. *Los pasos a la autonomia: Chiapas, la treceava estela.* Chiapas, Mexico: Ediciones del Frente Zapatista de Liberación Nacional.

Esteva, G., and M. S. Prakash. 1998. Grassroots post-modernism: Remaking the soil of cultures. London: Zed Books.

Falk, R. 1993. In *Global visions: Beyond the new world order,* ed. J. Brecher, J. B. Child, and J. Cutler. Montreal, Canada: Black Rose.

Hardt, M., and A. Negri. 2000. *Empire.* Cambridge, MA: Harvard University Press.

Lara, O. 2003. Arte, tierra y dignidad: An intervention in a subaltern community context. Unpublished honors thesis, Stanford University, Palo Alto, California.

Mancillas, M. R. 2002. Transborder collaboration: The dynamics of grassroots globalization. In *Globalization on the line: Culture, capital, and citizenship at U.S. borders,* ed. C. Sadowski-Smith. New York: Palgrave.

Sassen, S. 1998. *Globalization and its discontents: Essays on the new mobility of people and money.* New York: The New York Press.

Staudt, K., and I. Coronado. 2002. *Fronteras no mas: Toward social justice at the U.S.-Mexico border.* New York: Palgrave Macmillan.

Index

Abbas, Mahmoud, 82
Aboriginals, Australian, 114
abstract liberalism, 23–24
Abu Ghraib, 192
Aceves, C., 168
Adorno, T., 101, 131
affluent neighborhoods: microborders and, 37–38
Africanist perspectives and whiteness, 43
Africanness, concerted, 40–41
Afro-Brazilian religions, 114
Agamben, G., 63, 65, 66, 67, 68, 71
agency, 195; critical pedagogy, subject and, 128–29, 137
agrarian reform: Cárdenas and, 225; de Gortari and, 226; irreversibility of, 226; Mexico and, 225–26
Agrarian Reform Department, 225
Aguascalientes, 233n2; Maclovio Rojas and, 228
AIDS, 85
algebra and social justice, 162, 163
alienation, 150, 154; everyday life reproduction and, 151; Freire's analysis of, 101–5; labor, reproduction and, 148; labor, survival and, 149; subject-object

relationship and, 101. *See also* youth alienation
Allman, Paula, 86
Allport, Gordon, 31
Althusser, Louis, 32n3, 73, 102, 126, 129
Ambrosio, T., 71
Americans for Legal Immigration, 38
ancient relicts, 179
Anderson, S. E., 159, 160
Anglos, Chicana/os, and Mexicana/os, 56
animal liberation activists, 183
anthropocentrically induced extinctions, 178, 180
anthropocentric bias, in environmental science textbooks, 182
antiessentialism: ludic postmodernism, relativism and, 131–32
anti-intellectualism, essentialized voice discourse and, 131
Anzaldúa, Gloria, 35, 37, 52, 60, 192; on internalized borderland conflict, 55
Apple, Michael, 128, 136
Arendt, H., 218, 220
Arteaga, A. on Other, 55
Asante, M. K., 41

atrocities/abuses, in religion's history, 115–16
average species lifetime, and extinction, 179

background extinction rate: anthropocentric impacts on, 179–80; current rate vs., 180
Baker, L., 69
Baldwin, James
Baudrillard, Jean, 105
Bible, patriarchal language in, 121
biculturalism, Latina/o youth and, 52
Biesta, G., 137
Bill of Rights, and presumption of guilt, 80
biodiversity, 177, 184n1; decline of, 180; directional selection and, 178
bioremediation, 186n9
biotic rights, 182
Black(s): capitalism, prisons, and labor power of, 68–69; critical pedagogy and, 4; critical pedagogy community and collective, 5, 17n2; teachers in whiteface, 43–45; violence against young, 35–45
Black students: criminal justice system and, 66; punishment/disciplinary referrals and, 65–66; social justice, public education and, 145–46; white gaze and, 44
Blair, Tony, 81
Blitzkrieg, 82
body: commodification of, 204; critical pedagogy and, 129
body measurement and math teaching, 162
Boff, Leonardo, 113
Bonilla-Silva, Eduardo, 5, 21, 31
Books not Bars, 72–73
Boole, Mary Everest, 159
border discourse, 60–61
border identity, 54; Anzaldúa on, 55; critical epistemologies on, 49–63; difference and, 58–59
Border Interface, 122
Borderlands/la frontera (Anzaldúa), 35

border pedagogy: educators and, 57–59; understanding difference and, 58
borders: gaze and, 38; microborders and, 35–38; panopticon and, 38
border studies, 35; microborders and, 35–36; theoretical disconnection of, 35; whiteness and, 35
border theory: border identity critical theories and, 49–63; dialogue and, 60; Mexicanness and, 60
Bourne, J., 128
Brennan, Paul, 80
British empire, 213
Burét, Eugene, 159
Bush, George W., 66, 84; domestic changes under, 80; hawks, Strauss and, 83; inquisition period and, 117; military aggression and Christianity of, 81–82; religion and reelection of, 112, 116; War on Terror, Iraq invasion and Christianity of, 117
Butler, Judith, 129, 195

Calhoun, Craig, 59
California: prison system, 72; Proposition 187, 144; Youth Authority (CYA), 72–73
Camera, Don Helder, 115
capitalism, x, 64, 68, 193; alienation and postmodern, 101; black labor power, prisons and, 68–69; destroyed cultural practices and market, 217; developing nations, poverty and, 85; difference, capital-labor relation and global, 90–91; dominant globalized, 83; educational failures and, 86; everyday life reproduction of, 148; fetish worship and, 149; gendered identities, Hooters and, 193; gender in late, 191–205; gender, working women and late, 193; Hooters, gender construction and, 196; identity politics, privilege and global, 132–33; Iraq and, 80; liberal

leaders of, 115; Bush reelection and, 112, 116; catering to money, 119; critical pedagogy reinvention and consequences of, 114–18; hegemonic dominance and, 115; liberation theology, social transformation and, 111–23; as opiate of people, 111–23; as opium of people vs. spirituality, 113–14; as political weapon, 111; public opinion influence of, 120; shaping politics, 112–13; social responsibility of, 115; -spirituality in different cultures, 113–14; teachers and, 120, 121; white supremacy and, 119, 120; white supremacy justifications by, 120

religious indoctrination and liberation theology, 119

Religious Right, 112, 116, 134

reproduction: of capitalism in everyday life, 148; education and social, 150; of everyday life, 147–51; labor, alienation and, 148

The Reproduction of Everyday Life (Perlman), 147

reproduction theories, critical pedagogy vs., 125

resegregation, 145

resistance: critical pedagogy and everyday modes of, 129; cultural field as site for political, 128; discourse and Event, 41; Event and Eurocentric, 42–43

respeciation events, 177

revolutionary critical pedagogy: class-struggle, socialist anticapitalism and, 86; exploitation, anti-imperialist struggle and, 91–92; historical contribution of, 95; as oppressed people's pedagogy of hope, 92–93; position of, 94–95; postmodernized cultural studies approach vs., 86; questions raised by, 92

The Revolution of Everyday Life (Vaneigem), 151, 154

revolution of everyday life, social justice and, 143–54

rhetorical incoherence, as color-blindness stylistic component, 27–28

Rockefeller, David, 83

Rolston, Holmes, III, 176

Rosaldo, Renato, 60

Ross, E. Wayne, 145, 155n6

Rove, Karl: Strauss, Machiavelli and, 83

Ruffo-Appel, Ernesto, 226; *No Invasiones* campaign and, 226

Rutherford, R., 71

Sachs, Jeff, 84

Sagoff, Mark, 176, 181, 186n9

San Juan, E. Jr., 86, 88, 89, 90

Sankofa, 39–40, 45, 45n2

SARS, 85

Scatamburlo-D'Annabile, V., 128, 136

scatterplots, and mathematics teaching, 166

Schiraldi, V., 71

school, as concentration camp: paradoxes of, 67; school-to-prison pipeline and, 67

schooling, 154; class and, 150; of everyday life, 147; in global capitalism context, 149–50; as shaped by global economy, 219

School of the Americas, 86

school-to-prison pipeline, 63–76; capitalism and, 64; economic argument against, 71; political disenfranchisement and, 70–71; repercussions of, 68–71; school as concentration camp and, 67

Schweitzer, Albert, 183, 187n11

Scott, Joan, 131

Second International Conference on Education, Labor, and Emancipation (SICELE), ix, x

security state, 80, 81; struggle for socialism and, 95

self depreciation, and mathematics, 160

About the Contributors

Ricky Lee Allen is assistant professor of Educational Thought & Sociocultural Studies at the University of New Mexico (UNM). He received his Ph.D. in Education from UCLA, where he specialized in Urban Schooling. His areas of scholarly interest are sociology of education, critical studies of whiteness, critical race theory, and critical pedagogy. His scholarship focuses on the theoretical aspects of these areas, most specifically on the racial politics of critical educational and social thought. His most recent articles are "Whiteness and Critical Pedagogy" and "The Globalization of White Supremacy." At UNM, he teaches Critical Race Theory; Paulo Freire Seminar; Whiteness Seminar; Globalization and Education; Race, Ethnicity, and Education; and Sociology of Education. Before becoming a professor, Dr. Allen was a secondary science teacher in suburban Cincinnati, rural Indiana, and urban Los Angeles.

Cynthia L. Bejarano, a native of Southern New Mexico and the El-Paso/ Juárez border, is an assistant professor of Criminal Justice at New Mexico State University. Her publications and research interests focus on border violence; race, class, and gender issues; and Latino youths' border identities in the Southwest. Bejarano is the author of *"Qué Onda?" Urban Youth Cultures and Border Identity*, published by the University of Arizona Press. Bejarano is also the principal administrator for the NMSU College Assistance Migrant Program, which assists migrant and seasonal farmworker children from primarily the Southern New Mexico and West Texas region in attending NMSU. She is also cofounder of Amigos de las Mujeres de Juarez, a nonprofit organization working to end the violence against women in Chihuahua, Mexico and the borderlands.

Sally Blake has a Ph.D. in Curriculum and Instruction from the University of Mississippi. She is currently working at the University of Memphis in the College of Education. She has worked with NSF, NASA, and the Eisenhower programs while researching how young children learn mathematics and science. She taught in public schools for seventeen years before acquiring her terminal degree.

Eduardo Bonilla-Silva is a research professor of sociology at Duke University. Professor Bonilla-Silva's 1997 article in the *American Sociological Review*, entitled "Rethinking Racism: Toward a Structural Interpretation," challenged sociologists to analyze racial matters from a structural perspective rather than from the typical prejudice problematic. His research has appeared in journals such as the *American Sociological Review, Sociological Inquiry, Racial and Ethnic Studies, Race and Society, Discourse and Society, Journal of Latin American Studies,* and *Research in Politics and Society,* among others. To date he has published three books, *White Supremacy and Racism in the Post-Civil Rights Era* (cowinner of the 2002 Oliver Cox Award given by the American Sociological Association), *Racism Without Racists: Color-Blind Racism and the Persistence of Racial Inequality in the United States,* and *White Out: The Continuing Significance of Racism* (with Ashley Doane). He is currently working on two books: *Anything but Racism: How Social Scientists Minimize the Significance of Racism* (Routledge) and *White Logic, White Methods: Racism and Methodology.* He is also working on a project examining the characteristics of the emerging racial order entitled, "We are all Americans: The Latin Americanization of Race Relations in the USA."

Seehwa Cho is associate professor and director of the Critical Pedagogy doctoral program at the Department of Curriculum and Instruction at the University of St. Thomas. She works in the areas of critical theory, critical pedagogy, sociology of education, and philosophy of education. Her research projects include globalization and its impacts on education in South Korea, and the relationships between labor, gender, and schooling. Her recent research focus is the political economic analysis of critical theories and critical pedagogy.

David G. Embrick is an assistant professor at Loyola University Chicago and a former Fellow of the American Sociological Association Minority Fellowship Program (MFP). David's current research is on the discrepancies between corporations' public views and statements on diversity and their implementation of diversity as a policy. His argument is that corporate managers are using diversity as a mantra while they maintain highly racially inequitable environments. He has published in a number of journals including the *Journal of Intergroup Relations, Race and Society, Research in Politi-*

cal Sociology, Sociological Forum, and is an active member of several organizations, to include: Association of Black Sociologists, Sociologists Without Borders (where he was awarded the Beatrice and Sidney Webb Award), Society for Women in Society, as well as the American Sociological Association. He is currently working on a book (with Angela Hattery and Earl Smith, both at Wake Forest University) titled, *Human Rights: Social, Political, and Economic Inequalities in a Globalizing World.*

Benjamin Frymer is assistant professor of Sociology at the Hutchins School of Liberal Studies, Sonoma State University. He works in the areas of critical theory, alienation, media, cultural studies, aesthetic education, ideology, youth, and the sociology of education, religion, and culture. Recent research projects include a study of the Columbine High School shootings and historical work on hegemonic representations of urban youth.

David K. Goodin is a Ph.D. candidate in Religious Studies and a faculty lecturer at McGill University. He also possesses an M.S. in Environmental Science from Florida International University. His professional background includes over thirteen years in the applied environmental science fields, such as federal, state, and local environmental compliance coordination, contamination assessment and site remediation planning, and agricultural science research. At McGill, he teaches environmental philosophy and science and religion courses, while his doctoral research is in the philosophy of religion (e.g., Albert Schweitzer's work) and Eastern Orthodox Christianity. Publications include articles on topics such as just war theory and biblical hermeneutics.

Nathalia Jaramillo is a doctoral candidate in the division of Urban Schooling, Graduate school of Education and Information Studies at UCLA. She is author and coauthor of numerous articles and texts on critical pedagogy, politics of education and Marxist Feminism.

Violet Jones has been an assistant professor in Literacy Education at the University of Texas at El Paso since 2004. She has also taught high school language arts, social studies, speech, and debate. She received the National Writing Award from the National Black Graduate Student Association in 2003. Her research interests include African-Americans and immigration issues, teacher discourse, and issues related to both physical and theoretical borders.

YiShan Lea grew up in Taiwan and pursued her graduate studies in the United States. She works for both teachers in the United States and in Taiwan. She employs a communicative approach to teach Mandarin, which is a major vehicle to demonstrate and link second language learning theory and practice. YiShan holds an M.A. in Applied Linguistics from Ohio University and an Ed.D. in Teaching English as a Second Language and Literacy from Boise State University. Her doctoral dissertation has been nominated for the Phi Delta Kappan 2004 Outstanding Dissertation.

Lawrence M. Lesser is associate professor of Mathematics Education at the University of Texas at El Paso. His teaching experience also includes two recent years as a high school math department chair. His interest in motivating students with meaningful applications has led him to connect mathematics with areas such as music, lotteries, ethics, social justice, and culture (ethnomathematics).

Tyson Lewis is an assistant professor of educational philosophy at Montclair State University. His interests include biopolitics, utopianism, and critical theories of education.

Peter McLaren is a professor in the Division of Urban Schooling, Graduate School of Education and Information Studies, University of California, Los Angeles. He is the editor and author of over forty books. His writings have been published in seventeen languages. A social activist, McLaren lectures worldwide, and is a member of the Industrial Workers of the World. His most recent books are *Rage and Hope* (Peter Lang) and *Capitalists and Conquerors* (Rowman & Littlefield).

Marc Pruyn works at New México State University as an associate professor of social studies education and as the Director of Elementary Education. Marc's areas of specialty and interest include social justice, multiculturalism, Marxism, anarchism, critical pedagogical theory and the social studies. He is a member of the Rouge Forum (www.rougeforum.org) and the Borderlands Collective for Social Justice. Marc spends his free time watching zombie movies, practicing TaeKwonDo and playing the drums. His most recent book (edited with Luis Huerta-Charles), *Teaching Peter McLaren* (2005), is available through Peter Lang. Feel free to contact him at profefronterizo@yahoo.com.

E. Wayne Ross is a professor in the Department of Curriculum Studies at the University of British Columbia in Vancouver, Canada. He is a former secondary social studies and day care teacher in North Carolina and Georgia and has held faculty appointments at the University of Louisville and the State University of New York campuses at Albany and Binghamton. Ross is the author of numerous articles and reviews on issues of curriculum theory and practice, teacher education, and the politics of education. His books include *Race, Ethnicity and Education, Neoliberalism and Educational*

Reform (with Rich Gibson), *Defending Public Schools, Image and Education* (with Kevin D. Vinson), *The Social Studies Curriculum,* and *Democratic Social Education* (with David W. Hursh). He is the cofounder of The Rouge Forum, a group of educators, parents, and students working for more democratic schools and society and coeditor of the journals *Cultural Logic* and *Workplace: A Journal for Academic Labor.*

César Augusto Rossatto is associate professor and director of the Sociocultural Foundations Division in the Department of Teacher Education at the University of Texas at El Paso. He is author of numerous publications including: *Engaging Paulo Freire's Pedagogy of Possibility: From Blind to Transformative Optimism* (Rowman & Littlefield). He is founder of Paulo Freire SIG (Special Interest Group) at AERA (American Education Research Association). He is founder and chair of the First, Second, and Third International Conference on Education, Labor and Emancipation (http://academics.utep.edu/confele). He teaches courses in critical pedagogy, multiculturalism, education for social justice, and sociology of education. He is committed to dialectic and dialogical education and praxis for the liberation of disenfranchised groups. He is also well versed on organizational politics, international and urban education in the U.S. and Latin America. His main research interests are: globalization and neoliberalism in the U.S.-Mexican border region; Brazilian identity formation and social relations in United States, and their implications for schooling; the phenomena of fatalism and optimism in relation to social classes' differences; the application of critical pedagogy; and the origins and effects of whiteness in Brazil and in the United States.

Elizabeth Vázquez Solórzano is a Ph.D. student in urban schooling at UCLA. Her area of research focuses on the school to prison pipeline.

Michelle Téllez is an assistant professor in the Women's Studies Department at ASU's West Campus where she teaches transnational feminist courses such as "Gender and International Development" and "Women, Cultures and Societies." She specializes in women of color feminist theory, globalization studies, Chicana/o Studies, social movements and border studies. She believes that the academy is an important space for bringing in the voices and life experiences of members of our global community who largely go unnoticed. Her most recent publication is the article "Doing Research at the Borderlands: Notes from a Chicana Feminist Ethnographer," published in *Chicana/Latina Studies: the Journal of Mujeres Activas en Letras y Cambio Social* in Spring 2005.

Kevin D. Vinson is associate professor of Teaching and Teacher Education at the University of Arizona. He received his Ph.D. in Curriculum and Instruction, with a specialization in Social Studies Education, from the University of Maryland. Currently, his work focuses on the philosophical and theoretical contexts of social studies, especially with respect to questions of power, image, culture, standardization, diversity, and social justice, as well as on the meaning and relevance of the philosophies of Michel Foucault and Guy Debord vis-à-vis the potential social and pedagogical relationships among surveillance, spectacle, image, and disciplinarity. His work has appeared in *Theory and Research in Social Education, The Social Studies,* and *Social Education.* He is the coauthor of *Image and Education: Teaching in the Face of the New Disciplinarity* (Peter Lang Publishers) and coeditor of *Defending Public Schools: Curriculum Continuity and Change in the 21st Century* (Praeger Publishers).